P9-DCD-937

The Myth of the Birth of the Hero

and Other Writings

The Myth *of the* Birth *of the* Hero

and Other Writings

by Otto Rank

edited by Philip Freund

Vintage Books

A DIVISION OF RANDOM HOUSE

NEW YORK

THE MYTH OF THE BIRTH OF THE HERO, translated from the German by F. Robbins and Smith Ely Jelliffe, was first published in 1914 by the *Journal of Nervous and Mental Disease.* Of the "Other Writings," sections I through VII inclusive are taken from ART AND ARTIST, translated from the German by Charles Francis Atkinson, copyright 1932 by Alfred A. Knopf, Inc.; sections VIII and XI from MODERN EDUCATION, translated from the German by Mabel E. Moxon, copyright 1932 by Alfred A. Knopf, Inc.; and sections IX and X from, respectively, WILL THERAPY and TRUTH AND REALITY, both translated from the German by Jessie Taft and copyright 1936 by Alfred A. Knopf, Inc.

VINTAGE BOOKS
are published by ALFRED A. KNOPF, INC.
and RANDOM HOUSE, INC.

Reprinted by arrangement with Alfred A. Knopf, Inc.

Editor's Introduction

HAVELOCK ELLIS has spoken of Otto Rank as "perhaps the most brilliant and clairvoyant of Freud's many pupils and associates."

Because Rank later struck off for himself and offered independent theories that at times are even strongly anti-Freudian, he has aroused much enmity and been far less well known than he deserves. In very recent days, however, he is being discovered as one of those explorers who best understood the problems and needs of psychology, its great task, and the direction in which it has yet to go.

In this book I have chosen excerpts from Rank's aesthetic and cultural essays, rather than his technical studies, which are of concern chiefly to professional psychologists. Included here are some writings of his which should have popular appeal as an introduction to Rank's thought on a characteristically wide variety of subjects.

On the whole, Rank writes very well and engagingly; yet he does not have Freud's vividly easy style. Occasionally a passage—let it be said as disarmingly as possible—is difficult reading. Doubtless his language loses some clarity in any translation from his native German, however deft the rendering. One comes across polysyllabic compound words of the sort inherent in German thinking, technical terms peculiar to Freudian psychology and Rank's own glossary, and digressions referring to authorities whom Rank himself has read, but with whom the less learned reader may be unacquainted. His transitions are now and then abrupt, for his mind leaps. But one is still rewarded with a remarkable treasure of insight. I can assure the reader that there is hardly a page in Rank which will not enrich him greatly; something new and provocative is suggested there. It is in this spirit that I myself have read Rank, appreciated him, and proposed that this sampling of his work be offered.

To appraise Rank best it is helpful to know something of his biography. He was born in Vienna in 1884, the second of two sons. His family was middle-class, precariously fixed, and he began his career as an engineering student. His temperament was artistic, and he was unhappy in a polytechnic school. After he had read a few of Freud's early papers, he was drawn to this fellow Viennese, who was then just announcing his pioneer iconoclastic theories. On his own, Rank attempted an ambitious psychoanalytic study, *The Artist,* and finally took it to Freud himself. He was then just twenty-one years old. He was small, dark, and—as the Master described him—"ugly." Freud and his associates were immediately impressed by the young man's unusual gifts. He was allowed to join their small group and was named its secretary. Between Freud and the youthful Rank a father-and-son relationship developed. Freud persuaded him to complete his education and eventually earn a doctorate at the University of Vienna. Young Rank was at that time the only one in the "inner circle" of the founders of psychoanalysis who had no knowledge of medicine. His studies, apart from his dip into engineering, had been in social and cultural fields. Freud recognized the value of this, for the range of psychoanalysis needed to be broadened. At the university, Rank read widely in philosophy, philology and history, literature, pedagogy, art, ethics, cultural history, ethnology, and folklore. His encyclopedic command of these subjects, which is evidenced in all his writing, did much to challenge and stimulate the outlook of Freud and his noted associates in the group's regular discussions. Furthermore, Rank's precocious intelligence was so strong that many of the older men later attested to feeling most complimented when Rank, the youngest among them, approved of their ideas. In this way he influenced both Jung and Adler.

Rank continued to be one of Freud's closest co-workers for two decades—lecturing, editing journals, writing, practicing lay analysis—until a bitter separation that took place during the years from 1922 to 1924. His relationship to Freud had been too personal and dependent. He stayed with Freud during the schisms that occurred when Jung and Adler left the fold, but he was growing restless and dissatisfied with what seemed to him to be the increasing rigidity of Freudian doctrine, especially as it was set up by the Master's perfervid disciples. With the publication of *The Trauma of Birth,* Rank and Freud reached a final division. Rank had not expected this, for he believed *The Trauma of Birth* to be another contribution to the general body of psychoanalysis, not a sharp rejection of it. Although at first Freud himself was not very hostile to this new book, merely characterizing Rank's deductions as "extreme," his faithful followers were enraged; they attacked Rank himself mercilessly. He was accused of being unstable, treacherous, mercenary, and of having changed his name from a Jewish one (Rosenfeld) for ignoble reasons. At one time, when he believed himself fatally ill, Freud had considered naming Rank as guardian of the education of his children. But now he was moved to declare: "I have forgiven him for the last time." To judge the merits of this quarrel, one must recall the strange and autocratic personality of Freud himself and the eccentric nature of the circle around him.

Hurt by this wordy storm, Rank finally left Vienna for Paris, intending only a temporary visit. But he found the atmosphere of Paris to his liking. The rest of his life he spent in Paris and New York. He lived a number of years in both places, practicing and lecturing.

In this new environment, Rank progressed ever farther from Freudian dogma. He came to look upon it as essentially a "philosophy of despair" and a negative approach to human problems. He was convinced that Freud had generalized too much on the basis of clinical observations of the sick and abnormal. Freudianism was also in spirit a Central European psychology; in France and the United States, Rank found a more vigorous social climate in which people were far nearer to mental health. To him this was a challenge not met by the nihilism, the biological determinism, permeating orthodox psychoanalysis. He sought to explore a new psychology that stressed positive social and cultural values.

Rank now emphasized the rôle of the conscious will. He argued that every man makes a deliberate attempt to form an effective and integrated personality for himself. He held that in most men there is a creative impulse dedicated to this goal of character-formation. He developed new therapeutic techniques which, by making use of the conscious will and the added force of the creative impulse, allow the overlong term of analytic treatment to be shortened. His innovations proved of great help in social work, where Rank soon won his most devoted followers. His stress on the social aspect of psychotherapy, a name he now used instead of psychoanalysis, is a salient feature of his approach.

Rank also put much less weight on the importance of the sexual drive. He stated that an equally strong constituent in the make-up of people is their antisexual feeling, their fear and resentment of anything that reduces them to the biological. He also thought that Freudianism belittled too much the rôle and character of women. The cult of Freud was colored too much by the personality of Freud himself, a patriarchal figure who in youth had been the victim of an Oedipus complex (wherefore he greatly exaggerated its importance in others); for Freud had been the adoring child of a young mother nearer in age to her son than to her husband—Sigmund Freud's father had been old enough to be his grandfather instead. In Rank's hands, then, the Oedipus complex was discounted and given a different reading—actually, as we shall see, several readings. Rank was also impressed by the effect of mankind's urge for immortality. Every man's conscious thinking and unconscious doing are influenced by his concept of the soul, the mystical agent in him through which he hopes to achieve eternal life. In successive historical epochs, man has been dominated by different ideas about the nature of the soul and even about its actual place—primitive man endlessly asked himself where the soul resides in the body. To understand man's behavior, and particularly his art, one must grasp that he is controlled by his overpowering wish to put death to rout. He seeks to perpetuate himself, physically or spiritually.

For the full scope of Rank's tireless probing, the reader must go through many books. His output of ideas is prodigious. Even now, a goodly number of his studies have not been translated into English. But let me comment briefly on the essays that have been selected here. They are representative, as I have said, of only one side of Rank's work. I was first drawn to *The Myth of the Birth of the Hero* because I came across so many references to it in my reading that I decided I must look it up for myself. It is one of those germinal works which have had incalculable influence. In very original and bold fashion, Rank applies psychoanalytic techniques to an examination of myths about great culture heroes and savior gods and seeks to explain why such heroes and demigods are popularly held to be immaculately conceived changelings. The obvious parallels to the story of Jesus are highlighted. This famous essay, though far shorter, ranks in importance with Frazer's *The Golden Bough* in its elucidation of certain vital aspects of world-wide religious beliefs. A classic, it is referred to in many branches of modern education, not only depth psychology, religion, and anthropology, but even the theater —for the myth of the changeling, a humanization of the story of the Year-God, has been a constant theme of the drama in both tragedy and comedy throughout the ages. The essay, therefore, is or ought to be required reading for all students of comparative culture, and deserves above all others to be reprinted. At the time Rank published it, of course, he was still a devout Freudian. What it amazes me to learn is that he was only twenty-five years old when he wrote it.

I have already alluded to the occasional difficulty and obscurity of Rank's prose. A particular instance of this is the first short chapter of *The Myth of the Birth of the Hero,* simply because Rank assumes that the reader is familiar with the literature of the subject. To alleviate this brief difficulty, I have added here and elsewhere a few footnotes for clarification, and occasionally have made some minor emendations of the text. The rest of the text is lucid in style, and generally permits very quick reading.

Art and Artist is one of Rank's major works. The subject was his lifelong preoccupation, and we have already seen that his first effort at psychologizing was an essay entitled *The Artist.* Almost twenty-five years later, he returned to it and set down his more mature reflections. The result is an astonishing book indeed. How did Rank, who began his adult life as an engineering student, gain so much insight into art and the creative spirit? His erudition is daunting—the footnotes and allusions in *Art and Artist* are mountainous, especially in some passages not quoted here—but even this cannot account for his remarkable intuition and seemingly firsthand perception. In the Author's Preface to *Art and Artist,* Rank himself says: "Not that this book came into being through dissatisfaction with other art theories and a desire to replace them by a better one: rather is it an organic growth rising out of an intensive struggle of many years' standing over a personal problem—a lived experience that ultimately took shape in the present work." What is this "intensive struggle of many years' standing over a personal problem" to which Rank refers? Ira Progoff, in a recent discussion of Rank, suggests that Rank, feeling himself destined to be an artist, had been diverted into the realm of psychology instead, and that as a result he had guilt feelings and a sense of inner conflict all his life. He attempted, therefore, to make of psychology a new art-form, and we do find Rank—elsewhere in this volume—referring to the psychoanalyst as a new kind of artist. However that may be, Rank's accomplishment in *Art and Artist* is quite incredible. It is an outstanding instance of his clairvoyance.

What Rank gives us here is a startling psychological profile of a man of the "artist-type": his fear of death, his abnormal striving for immortality, his probable bisexuality (suggestively portrayed by an analysis of the sonnets of Michelangelo and Shakespeare), and his profound conflict with society and the epoch's dominant "soul-concept." There is also a brilliant exposition of the psychological differences between the Classical and Romantic artist, and an explanation of why so many twentieth-century artists have been drawn to a "modern art" expressed in a host of egoistic and anarchic and, as in Dada, even antisocial cults. Still another point made by Rank with great force and clarity is that art does not arise from a sublimation of the sexual instinct, as Freud has claimed; instead, it is much infused with a compulsive antisexual feeling that is typical of the artist. Especially valuable is Rank's delineation of the *artiste-manqué* and the fundamental ways in which the neurotic personality is unlike the truly creative one.

Rank consistently saw art as a social phenomenon as well as a personal one. Elsewhere in the Author's Preface, he declares: "In this book also, as in all my works on the psychology of art, I propose to follow the line of reaching out beyond what is individual in the artist-personality and to show, or at least suggest, the collective aspect, whether as material, inspiration, or ultimate aim. My intention is to point out the relation between these two tendencies, inherent in art and creativity: the individual and the collective, the personal and the social, in their interaction, and correspondingly in their counteraction. For now, more than ever before, my feeling is insistent that artistic creativity, and indeed the human creative impulse generally, originate solely in the constructive harmonizing of this fundamental dualism of all life." As Rank sees it, the creative personality is one that successfully overcomes this dualism, and the neurotic personality is one that fails to do so. The *artiste-manqué* is the neurotic.

In a Preface to the original English edition of *Art and Artist,* Ludwig Lewisohn recorded his impression of it: "Anyone who has the creative experience will, like myself, read and ponder with a kind of awe the revelations concerning the character of that experience, especially in the opening and closing chapters of the work before us. . . . All these explanations and revelations made by Dr. Rank I cannot conscientiously call otherwise than literally epoch-making. They should and will open a new period in the study of the soul of the artist. They have, it is almost needless to say, this mark of all truths of the first order, that, once grasped, one can no longer imagine the landscape of the mind without them."

One can only agree with Lewisohn's appraisal. It is the three opening and the three closing chapters of *Art and Artist* which have been selected for this present volume. No one can peruse them without having exposed to him much of the mystery of the artistic process, even though another part—as Rank honestly admits—remains irreducible. I believe that to a practicing artist who wishes to understand himself better—to understand his strange and sometimes irrational behavior, as he struggles with his daemon—a careful study and restudy of Rank's *Art and Artist* is indispensable.

The other excerpts here are much shorter. They are from scattered chapters and lectures. "Sexual Enlightenment and the Sexual Impulse" is a surprising repudiation of the psychoanalytic contention that the way to prevent our young from growing up as neurotics is to replace harsh religious taboos with frank teaching on the subject of sex to them in early childhood. Rank holds that this is not so. He sees our attitude toward sex as more complex than most psychoanalysts believe it to be, and he seeks to depict its nature. This is a chapter that will cause many parents, educators, and "liberal" moralists to pause and think again about a possibly too facile application of teaching about sex to the young.

"Life Fear and Death Fear" is an arresting summary of many of Rank's leading ideas: the birth trauma; his disparagement of Freud's belief in the prevalence of the death wish; a description of the analyst as an artist—of which I have made mention before—almost godlike in his potentiality to create new human beings; and a tracing of the relationship of life fear and death fear and masochism and criminality. It also includes a brief but illuminating comment on sexual promiscuity and its opposition to the monogamous impulse that may accompany spiritual love. This chapter, indeed, is typical of how Rank often ranges widely, if impressionistically, digressing interestingly and stirring us to think with him quickly and penetratingly on many subjects.

"Self and Ideal" describes the psychological process by which a man, on his way to maturity, provides himself with a code of sexual ethics. It is, in a sense, a complement to Rank's discussion of the problem of the child's sexual education. It presents three categories of men who move toward their goal of a sexual ethics by somewhat different routes—or rather, who stop short, fail, or excel, in accord with their very different types of personality.

To the vast literature that has by now accumulated on how to interpret Sophocles' great play *Oedipus Rex,* Rank adds a chapter of his own, "Forms of Kinship and the Individual's Rôle in the Family." It is above all an attack on the popular Freudian description of the Oedipus complex, which Rank considers mislabeled; it is also an attempt to derive quite novel meanings from Sophocles' tragic drama. I am not sure that the reader will always be persuaded by the subtle involutions of Rank's analysis—which is also somewhat ambiguous out of the context of Rank's whole psychology—but any student of the Greek theme should find the essay highly stimulating. Rank's insistence here is that Oedipus is not hostile to his father (whom, as Bachofen has pointed out, Oedipus did not actually know) or abnormally in love with his mother (who he is not yet aware *is* his mother). Oedipus, therefore, must have quite different motivations. This essay does not contain all that Rank has to say about the Oedipus myth; he finds still other significances in it in other works, including *The Trauma of Birth* and later in his lecture "Likeness and Difference," reprinted in his volume *Will Therapy.* In this latter, he sees Oedipus' fault—as intended by the Greeks—to have been that of too much intellectual pride, a will-to-know, which in the end is self-destructive; because Oedipus, the self-vaunting riddle-solver, fails to take full account of his own fundamental emotional impulses. If nothing else, Rank succeeds in making us realize that the overfacile Freudian description of the meaning of the Oedipus legend is hardly the whole one, or even a completely valid one. Rank's lead in this has been quite challengingly followed by Erich Fromm, who has subsequently dissected the Oedipus story.

We are told by those who knew Rank that he was very unhappy over his split from Freud, who in earlier years had been so kind and perhaps financially generous to him, and certainly an overpowering influence on him. This inner disturbance in Rank, who was torn between feelings of gratitude and loss and feelings of anger and rebellion, is described as profound. He was much inclined to melancholy and experienced this break as a lasting personal tragedy. But in this essay in particular, as in a lesser degree elsewhere, we find such strong criticism of Freudianism—overtly and by implication—that we can discern how far Rank had actually cast off most, though not all, of his allegiance to Freudian doctrine. He had founded his own psychology.

Rank died in 1939 in his mid-fifties, with his major work far from complete. At the time of his death, he left an unfinished book—posthumously and privately published—*Beyond Psychology,* which some of his admirers believe expresses his most significant views, though others find it chaotic and infused with a bitter disillusion perhaps occasioned by his last illness and his witnessing of the unhappy spectacle of a Europe apparently doomed by the imminent onslaught of Hitlerism.

By no means a systematic thinker or a "system-maker," Rank himself frequently changed his opinions. He had a remarkably candid mind. He did not hesitate to reject his own earlier guesses. The reader has an extra license, then, to accept or be critical of much that is offered to him here. He can choose among Rank's profusion of ideas those which strike him as of value. Rank did not think that he had come upon the whole truth about man. He wrote often that psychology is still in a very early stage, that it is limited in what it can hope to accomplish, and that it is merely a transitional discipline to the discovery of something that must lie beyond psychology, a faith that vouchsafes us a glimpse of salvation.

PHILIP FREUND

New York

Contents

The Myth *of the* Birth *of the* Hero

A Psychological Interpretation of Mythology

I *Introduction*

THE prominent civilized nations—the Babylonians and Egyptians, the Hebrews and Hindus, the Persians, the Greeks and the Romans, as well as the Teutons and others—all began at an early stage to glorify their national heroes—mythical princes and kings, founders of religions, dynasties, empires, or cities—in a number of poetic tales and legends. The history of the birth and of the early life of these personalities came to be especially invested with fantastic features, which in different nations—even though widely separated by space and entirely independent of each other—present a baffling similarity or, in part, a literal correspondence. Many investigators have long been impressed with this fact, and one of the chief problems of mythological research still consists in the elucidation of the reason for the extensive analogies in the fundamental outlines of mythical tales, which are rendered still more puzzling by the unanimity in certain details and their reappearance in most of the mythical groupings.[1]

The mythological theories, aiming at the explanation of these remarkable phenomena, are, in a general way, as follows:[2]

[1] EDITOR'S NOTE: There are, indeed, widespread correspondences in the myths of early and primitive peoples—very often the same stories, with only slight variations, are told by the Eskimos and the aborigines of South Africa, by the Carib Indians and the natives of Polynesia, and around the globe. Among the stories are those describing the creation of the world and its first inhabitants—or, at least, the ancestors of the tribe—and later a great deluge, a vast and destructive conflagration, and the coming of the tribe's culture hero. It is to the stories of this typical culture hero that Rank addresses himself in his present essay. The legends he compiles and discusses, however, are those that have already become more refined and sophisticated.

[2] A short and fairly complete review of the general theories of mythology, and of the principal advocates of each, is to be found in Wilhelm Wundt: *Völkerpsychologie* (Leipzig, 1905–9), Vol. II, Part I, p. 527.

1. The "Idea of the People," propounded by Adolf Bastian.[3] This theory assumes the existence of *elemental ideas*, so that the unanimity of the myths is a necessary sequence of the uniform disposition of the human mind and the manner of its manifestation, which within certain limits is identical at all times and in all places. This interpretation was urgently advocated by Adolf Bauer as accounting for the wide distribution of the hero myths.[4]

2. The explanation by *original community*, first applied by Theodor Benfey to the widely distributed parallel forms of folklore and fairy tales.[5] Originating in a favorable locality (India), these tales were first accepted by the primarily related (Indo-Germanic) peoples, then continued to grow while retaining the common primary traits, and ultimately radiated over the entire earth. This mode of explanation was first adapted to the wide distribution of the hero myths by Rudolf Schubert.[6]

3. The modern theory of *migration*, or *borrowing*, according to which individual myths originate from definite peoples (especially the Babylonians) and are accepted by other peoples through oral tradition (commerce and traffic) or through literary influences.[7]

The modern theory of migration and borrowing can be readily shown to be merely a modification of Benfey's theory, necessitated by newly discovered and irreconcilable material. This profound and extensive research of modern investigations has shown that India, rather than Babylonia, may be regarded as the first home of the myths. Moreover, the tales presumably did not radiate from a single point, but traveled over and across the entire inhabited globe. This brings into prominence the idea of the interdependence of mythological structures, an idea which was generalized by Braun as the basic law of the nature of the human

[3] *Das Beständige in den Menschenrassen und die Spielweise ihrer Veränderlichkeit* (Berlin, 1868).

[4] "*Die Kyros Sage und Verwandtes,*" *Sitzungsberichte der Wiener Akademie*, No. 100 (1882), p. 495.

[5] *Pantschatantra* (1859).

[6] *Herodots Darstellung der Cyrussage* (Breslau, 1890).

[7] Compare E. Stucken: *Astral Mythen* (Leipzig, 1896–1907), especially Part V, "Moses"; and H. Lessmann: "*Die Kyrossage in Europe,*" *Wissen. beit. z. Jahresbericht d. städt. Realschule zu Charlottenburg* (1906).

mind: Nothing new is ever discovered as long as it is possible to copy.[8] The theory of elemental ideas, so strenuously advocated by Bauer over a quarter of a century ago, is unconditionally declined by the most recent investigators (Winckler,[9] Stucken), who maintain the migration theory.

There is really no such sharp contrast between the various theories or their advocates, for the concept of elemental ideas does not interfere with the claims of primary common possession or of migration. Furthermore, the ultimate problem is not whence and how the material reached a certain people; the question is: Where did it come from to begin with? All these theories would explain only the variability and distribution of the myths, but not their origin. Even Schubert, the most inveterate opponent of Bauer's view, acknowledges this truth, by stating that all these manifold sagas date back to a single very ancient prototype. But he is unable to tell us anything of the origin of this prototype. Bauer likewise inclines to this mediating view; he points out repeatedly that in spite of the multiple origin of independent tales, it is necessary to concede a most extensive and ramified borrowing, as well as an original community of the concepts in related peoples.[1] The same conciliatory attitude is maintained by Lessmann in a recent publication (1908), in which he rejects the assumption of elemental ideas, but admits that primary relationship and borrowing do not exclude each other.[2] As pointed out by Wundt, however, it must be kept in mind that the appropriation of mythological contents always represents at the same time an independent mythological construction; because only that can be retained permanently which corresponds to the borrower's stage of mythological ideation. The faint recollections of preceding narratives would hardly suffice for the refiguration of the same material, without

[8] *Naturgeschichte der Sage,* 2 vols. (Munich, 1864–5), tracing all religious ideas, legends, and systems back to their common family tree and primary root.

[9] Some of the important writings by Winckler will be mentioned in the course of this article.

[1] *Zeitschrift für der Oesterr. Gymnasium* (1891), pp. 161 ff. Schubert's reply is also found here, pp. 594 ff.

[2] "Object and Aim of Mythological Research," *Mytholog. Bibliot.* (Leipzig), Vol. I, No. 4.

the persistent presence of the underlying motifs; but precisely for this reason, such motifs may produce new contents that agree in their fundamental themes, even in the absence of similar associations.[3]

Leaving aside for the present the inquiry as to the mode of distribution of these myths, the origin of the hero myth in general is now to be investigated, fully anticipating that migration (or borrowing) will prove to be directly and fairly positively demonstrable in a number of the cases. When this is not feasible, other viewpoints will have to be conceded, at least for the present, rather than bar the way to further progress by the somewhat unscientific attitude of Hugo Winckler, who says: When human beings and products, exactly corresponding to each other, are found at remote parts of the earth, we must conclude that they have wandered thither; whether we have knowledge of the how or when makes no difference in the assumption of the fact itself.[4] Even granting the migration of all myths, the origin of the first myth would still have to be explained.[5]

Investigations along these lines will necessarily help to provide a deeper insight into the contents of the tales. Nearly all authors who have hitherto been engaged in the interpretation of the birth myths of heroes find in them a personification of the processes of nature, following the dominant mode of natural mythological interpretation.[6]

[3] Wundt, op. cit., Part III.

[4] "*Die babylonische Geisteskultur in ihren Beziehungen zur Kulturentwicklung der Menschheit,*" *Wissenschaft und Bildung,* Vol. XV (1907), p. 47.

[5] Of course no time will be wasted here on the futile question as to what the first legend may have been; in all probability this never existed, any more than "the first human couple."

[6] EDITOR'S NOTE: At the time Rank wrote this essay, there was a well-established school of German and American mythologists and anthropologists, among whom Leo Frobenius was particularly prominent, who held that all myths had an original allegorical reference to the sun: its rising, setting, and supernatural influence. The figures who appeared as actors in the myths could be interpreted as disguises of the sun in its various aspects. A rival school soon claimed that all myths were lunar—referring allegorically to the moon, instead. Thus the culture hero would really be a representation of the sun, or of the moon. The two schools, and others with a similar trend of thought, lumped together, are referred to by Rank in the course of this essay as the "astral school." Because of its popularity and the authority of many of its proponents, he was constrained to speak of it with some respect. But this "naturalistic" approach to mythology

The newborn hero is the young sun rising from the waters, first confronted by lowering clouds, but finally triumphing over all obstacles.[7] The taking into consideration of all natural (chiefly atmospheric) phenomena—as was done by the first representatives of this method of myth interpretation[8] —and the regarding of the legends, in a more restricted sense, as astral myths (Stucken, Winckler, and others) are approaches not so essentially distinct as the followers of each individual direction believe to be the case. Nor does it seem a basic improvement when the purely solar interpretation, as advocated especially by Frobenius,[9] was no longer accepted and the view was advanced that all myths were originally lunar. Hüsing holds this theory in his discussion of the myth of Cyrus the Great; Siecke also claims this view as the only legitimate, obvious interpretation of the birth myths of the heroes; and it is a concept that is beginning to gain popularity.[1]

The interpretation of the myths themselves will be taken up in detail later on, and we shall refrain here from all detailed critical comments on the above mode of explanation. Although significant, and undoubtedly in part correct, the astral theory is not altogether satisfactory and fails to afford an insight into the motives of myth formation. The objection may be raised that the tracing to astronomical processes does not fully represent the content of these myths, and that much clearer and simpler relations might be established through another mode of interpretation. The much abused theory of elemental ideas indicates a prac-

---

has since sharply declined, and in his later writings Rank pays it scant attention.

[7] Brodbeck: *Zoroaster* (Leipzig, 1893), p. 138.

[8] As an especially discouraging example of this mode of procedure may be mentioned a contribution by the well-known natural mythologist Schwartz, which touches on this circle of myths, and is entitled: *Der Ursprung der Stamm und Gründungssage Roms unter dem Reflex indogermanischer Mythen* (Jena, 1898).

[9] Leo Frobenius: *Das Zeitalter des Sonnengotten* (Berlin, 1904).

[1] G. Hüsing: *Contributions to the Kyros Myth* (Berlin, 1906). Siecke, *"Hermes als Mondgott," Mytholog. Bibliot.*, Vol. II, No. 1 (1908), p. 48. Compare, for example, Paul Koch: *Sagen der Bibel und ihre Ubereinstimmung mit der Mythologie der Indogermanen* (Berlin, 1907). Compare also the partly lunar, partly solar, but at any rate entirely one-sided conception of the hero myth in Gustav Friedrich: *Grundlage, Entstehung und genaue Einzeldeutung der bekanntesten germanischen Märchen, Mythen und Sagen* (Leipzig, 1909), p. 118.

tically neglected aspect of mythological research. At the beginning, as well as at the end of his contribution, Bauer points out how much more natural and probable it would be to seek the reason for the general unanimity of these myths in the very general traits of the human psyche, rather than in primary community or migration. This assumption appears to be more justifiable, since such general movements of the human mind are also expressed in still other forms and in other domains, where they can be demonstrated as universal.[2]

Concerning the character of these general movements of the human mind, the psychological study of the essence of these myths might help to reveal the source from which has flowed uniformly, at all times and in all places, an identical mythological content. Such a derivation of an essential constituent, from a common human source, has already been successfully attempted with one of these legendary motifs. Freud, in his *Interpretation of Dreams,* reveals the connection of the Oedipus fable—where Oedipus is told by the oracle that he will kill his father and marry his mother, as he unwittingly does later—with two typical dreams experienced by many now living: the dream of the father's death, and the dream of sexual intercourse with the mother. Of King Oedipus he says:[3]

> His fate moves us only because it might have been our own, because the oracle laid upon us before our birth the very curse which rested upon him. It may be that we were all destined to direct our first sexual impulses toward our mothers, and our first impulses of hatred and resistance toward our fathers; our dreams convince us that we were. King Oedipus, who slew his father Laius and wedded his mother Jocasta, is

[2] EDITOR'S NOTE: The problem of "elemental ideas" (and their continuing influence in modern life) is one which has much concerned Carl Jung and his disciples; it has led to their famous if controversial theories of the "archetype" and the "collective unconscious." It has been pointed out that it is not fully appreciated how close Rank came to Jung's theory of the "archetype," though of course Rank's emphasis is rather different. If anything, it is less mystical.

[3] EDITOR'S NOTE: First published in 1900. The translation used here is that of Dr. A. A. Brill in his Modern Library edition: *The Basic Writings of Sigmund Freud* (New York, 1938), p. 308.

nothing more or less than a wish-fulfillment—the fulfillment of the wish of our childhood.[4]

The manifestation of the intimate relationship between dream and myth—not only in regard to the content but also as to the form and motor forces of this and many other, more particularly pathological, psyche structures—entirely justifies the interpretation of the myth as a dream of the masses of the people, which I have recently shown elsewhere.[5] At the same time, the transference of the method, and in part also of the results, of Freud's technique of dream interpretation to the myths would seem to be justifiable, as was defended by Abraham, and illustrated in an example, in his paper on "Dreams and Myths." [6] In the circle of myths that follow, the intimate relations between dream and myth find further confirmation, with frequent opportunity for reasoning from analogy.

The hostile attitude of the most modern mythological tendency (chiefly represented by the Society for Comparative Mythological Research) against all attempts at establishing a relation between dream and myth is for the most part the outcome of the restriction of the parallelization to the so-called nightmares (*Alpträume*), as attempted in Laistner's notable book, and also of ignorance of the relevant teachings of Freud.[7] The latter not only help us to understand the dreams themselves but also show their symbolism and close relationship with all psychic phenomena in general, especially with daydreams or fantasies, with artistic creativeness, and with certain disturbances of the normal psychic function. A common share in all

[4] The fable of Shakespeare's Hamlet also permits of a similar interpretation, according to Freud. It will be seen later on how mythological investigators bring the Hamlet legend from entirely different viewpoints into the correlation of the circle of myths.

[5] EDITOR'S NOTE: The reference here is to *Der Kunstler* ("The Artist"), Rank's first published work (1907).

[6] EDITOR'S NOTE: Karl Abraham's contribution was published in German in the same year as this essay (1909). English translation by W. A. White in Nervous and Mental Diseases Monograph Series, No. 15 (New York, 1913).

[7] Laistner: *The Riddle of the Sphinx* (1889). Compare Lessmann, "Object and Aim . . . ," loc. cit. Ehrenreich alone (*General Psychology*, p. 149) admits the extraordinary significance of dream-life for the myth-fiction of all times. Wundt does so likewise, for individual mythological motifs.

these productions belongs to a single psychic function: the human imagination. It is to this imaginative faculty—of humanity at large rather than of the individual—that the modern myth theory is obliged to concede a high rank, perhaps the first, as the ultimate source of all myths. The interpretation of the myths in the astral sense—or more accurately speaking, as "almanac tales"—gives rise to the query: In view of a creative imagination in humanity, should we seek (with Lessmann) for the first germ of the origin of such tales precisely in the processes of the heavens, or on the contrary, should we conclude that ready-made tales of an entirely different (but presumably psychic) origin were only subsequently transferred to the heavenly bodies?[8] Ehrenreich makes a more positive admission: The mythologic evolution certainly begins on terrestrial soil, in so far as experiences must first be gathered in the immediate surroundings before they can be projected into the heavenly universe.[9] And Wundt tells us that the theory of the evolution of mythology according to which it first originates in the heavens, whence at a later date it descends to earth, is contradictory both to the history of the myth (which is unaware of such a migration) and to the psychology of myth formation (which must repudiate such a translocation as internally impossible).[1] We are also convinced that the myths,[2] originally at least, are structures of the human faculty of imagination, which were at some time projected for certain reasons upon the heavens, and may be secondarily transferred to the heavenly bodies, with their baffling phenomena. The significance

[8] Stucken (op. cit., p. 432) says in this sense: The myth transmitted by the ancestors was transferred to natural processes and interpreted in a naturalistic way, not vice versa. "Interpretation of nature is a motive in itself" (p. 636 *n.*). In a very similar way, Eduard Meyer (*Geschichte des Altertums*, 1884–1902, Vol. V. p. 48) has written: "In many cases, the natural symbolism, sought in the myths, is only apparently present or has been secondarily introduced, as often in the Vedas and in the Egyptian myths; it is a primary attempt at interpretation, like the myth-interpretations that arose among the Greeks as early as the fifth century."

[9] Op. cit., p. 104.

[1] Op. cit., p. 282.

[2] For fairy tales, in this as well as in other essential features, Thimme advocates the same point of view as is here claimed for the myths. Compare Adolf Thimme: *Das Märchen*, Vol. II of *Handbücher zur Volkskunde* (Leipzig, 1909).

of the unmistakable traces—the fixed figures, and so forth—that have been imprinted upon the myth by this transference must by no means be underrated, although the origin of these figures was possibly psychic in character; they were subsequently made the basis of the almanac and firmament calculations precisely on account of this significance.

In a general way, it would seem as if the investigators who apply an exclusively "natural" scheme of interpretation have been unable, in any sense—in their endeavor to discover the original sense of the myths—to get away entirely from a psychological process such as must be assumed similarly for the creators of the myths.[3] The motive is identical, and led to the same course for myth-creators and for myth-interpreters. It is most naïvely uttered by one of the founders and champions of comparative myth investigation and of the natural mythological mode of interpretation; Max Müller points out in his *Essays* that this procedure not only invests meaningless legends with a significance and beauty of their own but also helps to remove some of the most revolting features of classical mythology, as well as to elucidate their true meaning.[4] This readily understandable revulsion naturally prevents the mythologist from assuming that such motifs—incest with mother, sister, or daughter; murder of father, grandfather, or brother—could be based on universal fantasies, which according to Freud's teachings have their source in the infantile psyche, with its peculiar interpretation of the external world and its denizens. This revulsion is, therefore, only the reaction of the dimly sensed painful recognition of the actuality of these relations; and this reaction impels the myth interpreters, for their own subconscious rehabilitation, and that of all mankind, to credit these motifs with an entirely different meaning from their original significance. The same internal repudiation prevents the myth-creating people from believing in the possibility of such revolting thoughts, and this defense probably was

[3] Of this myth interpretation, Wundt (op. cit., p. 352) has well said that it really should have accompanied the original myth formation.

[4] Vol. II, p. 143, in the German translation (Leipzig, 1869).

the first reason for projecting these relations onto the firmament. The psychological pacifying through such a rehabilitation, by projection upon external and remote objects, can still be realized—to a certain degree, at least—by a glance at one of these interpretations, for instance that of the objectionable Oedipus fable, as given by Goldhizer, a representative of the natural school of myth interpreters: Oedipus (who kills his father, marries his mother, and dies old and blind) is the solar hero who murders his procreator, the darkness; he shares *his* couch with his mother, the gloaming, from whose lap, the dawn, he has been born; he dies, blinded, as the setting sun.[5]

It is understandable that some such interpretation is more soothing to the mind than the revelation of the fact that incest and murder impulses against their nearest relatives are found in the fantasies of most people, as remnants of infantile ideation. But this is not a scientific argument, and revulsion of this kind—although it may not always be equally conscious—is altogether out of place in view of existing facts. One must either become reconciled to these indecencies, provided they are felt to be such, or one must abandon the study of psychological phenomena. It is evident that human beings, even in the earliest times, and with a most naïve imagination, never saw incest and parricide in the firmament on high,[6] but it is far more probable that these ideas are derived from another source, presumably human. In what way they came to reach the sky, and what modifications or additions they received in the process, are questions of a secondary character that can-

[5] See Ignaz Goldhizer: *Der Mythus bei den Hebräern und seine geschichtliche Entwickelung* (Leipzig, 1876), p. 125. According to the writings of Siecke (loc. cit., p. 39), the incest myths lose all unusual features through being referred to the moon and its relation to the sun. His explanation is quite simple: the daughter (the new moon) is the repetition of the mother (the old moon); with her the father (the sun) (also the brother, the son) becomes reunited.

[6] Is it to be believed? In an article entitled "*Urreligion der Indogermanen*" (Berlin, 1897), where Siecke points out that the incest myths are descriptive narrations of the seen but inconceivable process of nature, he objects to the assumption by Oldenburg (*Religion der Veda*, p. 5) of a primeval tendency of myths to the incest motif, with the remark that in the days of yore the theme was thrust upon the narrator, without an inclination of his own, through the forcefulness of the witnessed facts.

not be settled until the psychic origin of the myths in general has been established.

At any rate, besides the astral conception, the claims of the part played by the psychic life must be credited with the same rights for myth formation, and this argument will be amply vindicated by the results of our method of interpretation. With this object in view, we shall first take up in the following pages the legendary material on which such a psychological interpretation is to be attempted on a large scale for the first time.

II *The Circle of Myths*

FROM the mass of chiefly biographic hero myths, we have selected those that are best known and some that are especially characteristic.[1] These myths will be given in abbreviated form, as far as relevant for this investigation, with statements concerning the sources. Attention will be called to the most important and constantly recurring motifs by the use of italic type.

SARGON

Probably the oldest transmitted hero myth in our possession is derived from the period of the foundation of Babylonia (about 2800 B.C.)[2] and concerns the birth history of its founder, Sargon the First.[3] The literal translation

[1] Attention has been drawn to the great variability and wide distribution of the birth myths of the hero by the writings of Bauer, Schubert, and others referred to in the preceding pages. The comprehensive contents of the myths and their fine ramifications have been especially discussed by Hüsing, Lessmann, and other representatives of the modern trend.

[2] EDITOR'S NOTE: More recent archaeological and other studies have cast some doubt on the traditional dating of the establishment of the Babylonian kingdom. Ceram places Sargon's reign as 2360–2305 B.C., and says, "The legend of his birth brings to mind Cyrus, Romulus, Krishna, Moses, and Perseus. . . . For a long time it was believed that Sharrukên ("legitimate king," Sargon) had never really existed. Today the fact has been established that Sargon did live and wield a memorable historical influence." C. W. Ceram: *Gods, Graves, and Scholars* (New York: Alfred A. Knopf; 1951), pp. 303–4.

[3] Innumerable fairy tales, stories, and poems of all times, up to the most recent dramatic and novelistic literature, show very distinct individual main motifs of this myth. The exposure-romance appears in the late Greek pastorals—Heliodorus' *Aethiopica,* Eustathius' *Ismenias and Ismene,* and Longus' story of the two exposed children, Daphnis and Chloe. The more recent Italian pastorals are likewise very frequently based upon the exposure of children, who are raised as shepherds by

of the report—according to the mode of rendering, it appears to be an original inscription by King Sargon himself—is as follows:

> Sargon, the mighty king, King of Agade, am I. *My mother was a vestal, my father I knew not*, while my father's brother dwelt in the mountains. In my city Azuripani, which is situated on the bank of the Euphrates, my mother, the vestal, bore me. *In a hidden place she brought me forth. She laid me in a vessel made of reeds,* closed my door with pitch, *and dropped me down into the river,* which did not drown me. The river carried me to Akki, the water carrier. Akki the water carrier lifted me up in the kindness of his heart, Akki the water carrier raised me as his own son, Akki the water carrier made of me his gardener. In my work as a gardener I was beloved by Ishtar, I became the king, and for forty-five years I held kingly sway.[4]

MOSES

The biblical birth history of Moses, which is told in the second chapter of Exodus, presents the greatest similarity to the Sargon legend, even an almost literal correspondence of individual traits.[5] Already the first chapter (22) relates that Pharaoh commanded his people to throw into

---

their foster parents, but are later recognized by the true parents, through identifying marks received at the time of their exposure. To the same set belong the family history in Grimmelshausen's *Limplizissimus* (1665), in Jean Paul's *Titan* (1800), as well as certain forms of the Robinson stories and Cavalier romances (compare Würzbach's Introduction to Hesse's edition of *Don Quixote*).

[4] The various translations of the partly mutilated text differ only in unessential details. Compare Hommel: *History of Babylonia and Assyria* (Berlin, 1885), p. 302, where the sources of the tradition are likewise found; and A. Jeremias: *The Old Testament in the Light of the Ancient Orient,* 2d ed. (Leipzig, 1906), p. 410.

[5] On account of these resemblances, a dependence of the Exodus tale from the Sargon legend has often been assumed, but apparently not enough attention has been paid to certain fundamental distinctions, which will be taken up in detail in the interpretation.

the river all sons that were born to Hebrews, while the daughters were permitted to live; the reason for this order is given as fear of the overfertility of the Israelites. The second chapter continues as follows:

> And there went a man of the house of Levi, and took to wife a daughter of Levi.[6] And the woman conceived, and bare a son: and when she saw him that he was a goodly child, she hid him three months. And when she could not longer hide him, she took for him an ark of bulrushes, and daubed it with slime and with pitch, and put the child therein; and she laid it in the flags by the river's brink. And his sister stood afar off, to wit what would be done to him. And the daughter of Pharaoh came down to wash herself at the river; and her maidens walked along by the river's side; and when she saw the ark among the flags, she sent her maid to fetch it. And when she had opened it, she saw the child and, behold, the babe wept. And she had compassion on him and said, this is one of the Hebrews' children. Then said his sister to Pharaoh's daughter, Shall I go and call to thee a nurse of the Hebrew women, that she may nurse the child for thee? And Pharaoh's daughter said to her, Go. And the maid went and called the child's mother. And Pharaoh's daughter said unto her, Take this child away, and nurse it for me, and I will give thee thy wages. And the woman took the child, and nursed it. And the child grew, and she brought him unto Pharaoh's daughter, and he became her son. And she called his name Moses:[7] and she said, Because I drew him out of the water.

[6] The parents of Moses were originally nameless, as were all persons in this, the oldest account. Their names were only conferred upon them by the priesthood. Chapter 6.20, says: "And Amram took him Jochebed his father's sister to wife; and she bare him Aaron and Moses"; Numbers 26.59 adds: ". . . and Miriam their sister." Also compare Winckler: *History of Israel*, Vol. II; and Jeremias, op. cit., p. 408.

[7] The name, according to Winckler ("*Die babylonische Geisteskultur . . .*" loc. cit., p. 119), means "The Water-Drawer" (see also Winckler: *Ancient Oriental Studies*, Vol. III, pp. 468 ff.)—which would still further approach the Moses legend to the Sargon legend, for the name Akki signifies "I have drawn water."

This account is ornamented by rabbinical mythology with an account of the events preceding Moses' birth. In the sixtieth year after Joseph's death, the reigning Pharaoh saw in a dream an old man who held a pair of scales; all the inhabitants of Egypt lay on one side, with only a suckling lamb on the other, but nevertheless this outweighed all the Egyptians. The startled king at once consulted the wise men and astrologers, who declared the dream to mean that a son would be born to the Israelites who would destroy all Egypt. The king was frightened, and at once ordered the death of all newborn children of the Israelites in the entire country. On account of this tyrannical order, the Levite Amram, who lived in Goshen, decided to separate from his wife Jochebed, so as not to foredoom to certain death the children conceived through him. But this resolution was opposed later on by his daughter Miriam, who foretold with prophetic assurance that precisely the child suggested in the king's dream would come forth from her mother's womb, and would become the liberator of his people.[8]

Amram therefore rejoined his wife, from whom he had been separated for three years. At the end of three months, she conceived, and later on bore a boy at whose birth the entire house was illuminated by an extraordinary luminous radiance, suggesting the truth of the prophecy.[9]

Similar accounts are given of the birth of the ancestor of the Hebrew nation, Abraham. He was a son of Terah—Nimrod's captain—and Amtelai. Prior to his birth, it was revealed to King Nimrod from the stars that the coming child would overthrow the thrones of powerful princes and take possession of their lands. King Nimrod planned to have the child killed immediately after its birth. But when the boy was requested from Terah, he said, "Truly a son was born to me, but he has died." He then delivered a strange child, concealing his own son in a cave underneath the ground, where God permitted him to suck milk from a finger of the right hand. In this cave, Abraham is

[8] Schemot Rabba 2.4 says concerning Exodus 1.22 that Pharaoh was told by the astrologers of a woman who was pregnant with the Redeemer of Israel.

[9] After Bergel: *Mythology of the Hebrews* (Leipzig, 1882).

said to have remained until the third (according to others the tenth) year of his life.[1]

In the next generation, in the story of Isaac, the same mythological motifs appear. Prior to his birth, King Abimelech is warned by a *dream* not to touch Sarah, as this would cause woe to betide him. After a long period of barrenness, she finally bears her son, who (in later life, in this report) after having been destined to be *sacrificed by his own father,* Abraham, is ultimately rescued by God. But Abraham casts out his elder son Ishmael, with Hagar, the boy's mother.[2]

KARNA

A close relationship with the Sargon legend is also shown in certain features of the ancient Hindu epic Mahabharata, in its account of the birth of the hero Karna.[3] The contents of the legend are briefly rendered by Lassen.[4]

The princess Pritha, also known as Kunti, bore as a virgin the boy Karna, whose father was the sun-god Surya. The young Karna was born with the golden ear ornaments of his father and with an unbreakable coat of mail. The mother in her distress concealed and exposed the boy. In the adaptation of the myth by A. Holtzmann, verse 1458 reads: "Then my nurse and I made a large basket of rushes, placed a lid thereon, and lined it with wax; into this basket I laid the boy and carried him down to the river Acva." Floating on the waves, the basket reaches the river

[1] Compare Beer: *The Life of Abraham* (Leipzig, 1859), according to the interpretation of Jewish traditions; also August Wünsche: *From Israel's Temples of Learning* (Leipzig, 1907).

[2] See chapters 20 and 21 of Genesis, and also Bergel, op. cit.

[3] The Hindu birth legend of the mythical king Vikramaditya must also be mentioned in this connection. Here again occur the barren marriage of the parents, the miraculous conception, ill-omened warnings, the exposure of the boy in the forest, his nourishment with honey, finally the acknowledgment by the father. See Jülg: *Mongolische Märche* (Innsbruck, 1868), pp. 73 ff.

[4] *Indische Alterumskunde* (Karlsruhe, 1846).

Ganges and travels as far as the city of Campa. "There was passing along the bank of the river, the charioteer, the noble friend of Dhritarashtra, and with him was Radha, his beautiful and pious spouse. She was wrapt in deep sorrow, because no son had been given to her. On the river she saw the basket, which the waves carried close to her on the shore; she showed it to Azirath, who went and drew it forth from the waves." The two take care of the boy and raise him as their own child.

Kunti later on marries King Pandu, who is forced to refrain from conjugal intercourse by the curse that he is to die in the arms of his spouse. But Kunti bears three sons, again through divine conception, one of the children being born in the cave of a wolf. One day Pandu dies in the embrace of his second wife. The sons grow up, and at a tournament which they arrange, Karna appears to measure his strength against the best fighter, Arjuna, the son of Kunti. Arjuna scoffingly refuses to fight the charioteer's son. In order to make him a worthy opponent, one of those present anoints him as king. Meanwhile Kunti has recognized Karna as her son, by the divine mark, and prays him to desist from the contest with his brother, revealing to him the secret of his birth. But he considers her revelation as a fantastic tale, and insists implacably upon satisfaction. He falls in the combat, struck by Arjuna's arrow.[5]

A striking resemblance to the entire structure of the Karna legend is presented by the birth history of Ion, the ancestor of the Ionians. The following account is based on a relatively late tradition.[6]

Apollo, in the grotto of the rock of the Athenian Acropolis, procreated a son with Creusa, the daughter of Erechtheus. In this grotto the boy was also born, and exposed; the mother leaves the child behind in a woven basket, in the hope that Apollo will not leave his son to

[5] Compare the detailed account in Lefmann: *History of Ancient India* (Berlin, 1890), pp. 181 ff.

[6] See Röscher, concerning the *Ion* of Euripides. Where no other source is stated, all Greek and Roman myths are taken from the *Ausführliches Lexikon der griechischen und römischen Mythologie*, edited by W. H. Röscher, which also contains a list of all sources.

perish. At Apollo's request, Hermes carries the child the same night to Delphi, where the priestess finds him on the threshold of the temple in the morning. She brings the boy up, and when he has grown into a youth makes him a servant of the temple. Erechtheus later gave his daughter Creusa in marriage to Xuthus. As the marriage long remained childless, they addressed the Delphian oracle, praying to be blessed with progeny. The god reveals to Xuthus that the first to meet him on leaving the sanctuary is his son. He hastens outside and meets the youth, whom he joyfully greets as his own son, giving him the name Ion, which means "walker." Creusa refuses to accept the youth as her son; her attempt to poison him fails, and the infuriated people turn against her. Ion is about to attack her, but Apollo, who does not wish the son to kill his own mother, enlightens the mind of the priestess so that she understands the connection. By means of the basket in which the newborn child had lain, Creusa recognizes him as her son, and reveals to him the secret of his birth.

OEDIPUS

The parents of Oedipus, King Laius and his queen, Jocasta, lived for a long time in childless wedlock. Laius, who longs for an heir, asks the Delphic Apollo for advice. The oracle answers that he may have a son if he so desires; but fate has ordained that his own son will kill him. Fearing the fulfillment of the oracle, Laius refrains from conjugal relations, but being intoxicated one day he nevertheless procreates a son, whom he causes to be exposed in the river Cithaeron, barely three days after his birth. In order to be quite sure that the child will perish, Laius orders his ankles to be pierced. According to the account of Sophocles, which is not the oldest, however, the shepherd who has been intrusted with the exposure, surrenders the boy to a shepherd of King Polybus, of Corinth, at whose court he is brought up, according to the universal statement. Others say that the boy was exposed in a box on the sea, and was taken from the water by Periböa, the wife of King Polybus, as she was rinsing her clothes by the shore.[7] Polybus brought him up as his own son.

Oedipus, on hearing accidentally that he is a foundling, asks the Delphian oracle about his true parents, but receives only the prophecy that he will kill his father and marry his mother. In the belief that this prophecy refers to his foster parents, he flees from Corinth to Thebes, but on the way unwittingly kills his father Laius. By solving a riddle, he frees the city from the plague of the Sphinx, a man-devouring monster, and in reward is given the hand of Jocasta, his mother, as well as the throne of his father. The revelation of these horrors and the subsequent misfortune of Oedipus were a favorite subject for spectacular display among the Greek tragedians.

An entire series of Christian legends have been elaborated on the pattern of the Oedipus myth, and the summarized contents of the Judas legend may serve as a paradigm of this group.[8] Before his birth, his mother, Cyboread, is warned by a dream that she will bear a wicked son, to the ruin of all his people. The parents expose the boy in a box on the sea. The waves cast the child ashore on the Isle of Scariot, where the childless queen finds him, and brings him up as her son. Later on, the royal couple have a son of their own, and the foundling, who feels himself slighted, kills his foster brother. As a fugitive from the country, he takes service at the court of Pilate, who makes a confidant of him and places him above his entire household. In a fight, Judas kills a neighbor, without knowing that he is his father. The widow of the murdered man—his own mother—then becomes his wife. After the revelation of these horrors, he repents and seeks

[7] According to Bethe (*Thebanische Heldenlieder*), the exposure on the waters was the original rendering. According to other versions, the boy is found and raised by horseherds; according to a later myth, by a countryman, Melibios.

[8] EDITOR'S NOTE: In 1912, three years after the appearance of this essay, Rank published *Das Inzestmotiv in Dichtung und Sage* ("The Incest Theme in Fiction and Legend"). A revised edition appeared in 1926, and a French translation in 1934. The cycle of Christian legends mentioned above has been discussed in detail in Chapter X of the book. Further references to this book will be abbreviated herein as *Inzestmotiv*

the Saviour, who receives him among his apostles. His betrayal of Jesus is known from the Gospels.

The legend of St. Gregory on the Stone—the subject of the narrative of Hartmann von Aue—represents a more complicated type of this mythological cycle. Gregory, the child of the incestuous union of royal lovers, is exposed by his mother in a box on the sea, saved and raised by fishermen, and is then educated in a convent for the church. But he prefers the life of a knight, is victorious in combats, and in reward is given the hand of the princess, his mother. After the discovery of the incest, Gregory does penance for seventeen years on a rock in the midst of the sea, and he is finally made the Pope, at the command of God.[9]

A very similar legend is the Persian epic of King Darab, told by the poet Firdausi.[1] The last Kiranian Behmen nominated as his successor his daughter and simultaneous wife Humâi; his son Sâsân was grieved and withdrew into solitude. A short time after the death of her husband, Humâi gave birth to a son, whom she resolved to expose. He was placed in a box, which was put into the Euphrates and drifted downstream, until it was stopped by a stone that had been placed in the water by a tanner. The box with the child was found by him, and he carried the boy to his wife, who had recently lost her own child. The couple agreed to raise the foundling. As the boy grew up, he soon became so strong that the other children were unable to resist him. He did not care for the work of his foster father, but learned to be a warrior. His foster mother was forced by him to reveal the secret of his origin, and he joined the army that Humâi was then sending out to fight the king of Rûm. Her attention being called to him by his bravery, Humâi readily recognized him as her son, and named him her successor.

[9] Cholevicas: *History of German Poetry According to the Antique Elements.*

[1] Firdausi: *Shah Namah* ("The Book of Kings"), as rendered by F. Spiegel: *Eranische Alterumskunde,* Vol. II, p. 584.

PARIS

The famed Greek legend of the birth of Paris relates that King Priam of Troy had with his wife Hecuba a son, named Hector. When Hecuba was about to bear another child, *she dreamed* that she brought forth a burning log of wood, which set fire to the entire city. Priam asked the advice of Aisakos, who was his son with his first wife, Arisbe, and an expert in the interpretation of dreams. Aisakos declared that the child would bring trouble upon the city, and advised that it be exposed. Priam gave the little boy to a slave, Agelaos, who carried him to the top of Mount Ida. *The child was nursed during five days by a she-bear.* When Agelaos found that he was still alive, he picked him up, and carried him home to raise him. He named the boy Paris; but after the child had grown into a strong and handsome youth, he was called Alexander, because he fought the robbers and protected the flocks. Before long he discovered his parents. How this came about is told by Hyginus, according to whose report the infant is *found by shepherds.* One day messengers, sent by Priam, come to these herders to fetch a bull which is to serve as the prize for the victor in some commemorative games. They selected a bull that Paris valued so highly that he followed the men who led the beast away, assisted in the combats, and won the prize. This aroused the anger of his brother Deiphobus, who threatened him with his sword, but his sister Cassandra recognized him as her brother, and Priam joyfully received him as his son. The misfortune which Paris later brought to his family and his native city, through the abduction of Helen, is well known from Homer's *Iliad*, as well as from countless earlier and later poems.

A certain resemblance with the story of the birth of Paris is presented by the poem of Zal, in Firdausi's Persian hero myths.[2] The first son is born to Sam, king of Sistan, by one of his consorts. Because he had white hair, *his*

[2] Ibid., translated by Schack.

mother concealed the birth.[3] But the nurse reveals the birth of his son to the king. Sam is disappointed, and commands that the child be exposed. The servants carry it to the top of Mount Elburz, where it is raised by the Seemurgh, a powerful bird. The full-grown youth is seen by a traveling caravan, whose members speak of him as "whose nurse a bird is sufficient." King Sam once *sees his son in a dream,* and sallies forth to seek the exposed child. He is unable to reach the summit of the elevated rock where he finally espies the youth. But the Seemurgh bears his son down to him; he receives him joyfully and nominates him as his successor.

TELEPHUS

Aleos, King of Tegea, was informed by the *oracle* that his sons would perish through a descendant of his daughter. He therefore made his daughter Auge a priestess of the goddess Athena, and threatened her with death should she mate with a man. But when Hercules dwelt as a guest in the sanctuary of Athena, on his expedition against Augeas, he saw the maiden, and while intoxicated, he raped her. When Aleos became aware of her pregnancy, he delivered her to Nauplius, a rough sailor, with the command to throw her into the sea. But on the way she gave birth to Telephus on Mount Parthenios, and Nauplius, unmindful of the orders he had received, carried both her and the child to Mysia, where he delivered them to King Teuthras.

According to another version, Auge secretly brought forth as a priestess, but kept the child hidden in the temple. When Aleos discovered the sacrilege, he caused the child to be exposed in the Parthenian mountains. Nauplius was instructed to sell the mother in foreign lands, or to

[3] EDITOR'S NOTE: Zal, a semi-divinity of Persian mythology, was the father of Rustam (the Hercules of Persia). A child born with white hair was then assumed to be the offspring of a deer.

kill her. She was delivered by him into the hands of Teuthras.[4]

According to the current tradition, *Auge exposes the newborn child* and escapes to Mysia, where the childless King Teuthras adopts her as his daughter. The boy, however, is nursed by a doe, and is found by shepherds who take him to King Corythos. The king brings him up as his son. When Telephus has grown into a youth, he betakes himself to Mysia, on the advice of the oracle, to seek his mother. He frees Teuthras, who is in danger from his enemies, and in reward receives the hand of the supposed daughter of the king, namely his own mother Auge. But she refuses to submit to Telephus, and when he in his ire is about to pierce the disobedient one with his sword, she calls on her lover Hercules in her distress, and Telephus thus recognizes his mother. After the death of Teuthras he becomes King of Mysia.

PERSEUS

Acrisius, the king of Argos, had already reached an advanced age without having male progeny. As he desired a son, he consulted the Delphian oracle, but this warned him against male descendants, and informed him that his daughter Danaë would bear a son through whose hand he would perish. In order to prevent this, he had his daughter locked up in an iron tower, which he caused to be carefully guarded. But Zeus penetrated through the roof, in the guise of a golden shower, and Danaë became the mother of a boy.[5] One day Acrisius heard the voice of young Perseus in his daughter's room, and in this way learned that she had given birth to a child. *He killed the nurse,* but carried his daughter with her son to the domes-

[4] In the version of Euripides, *Aleos caused the mother and the child to be thrown into the sea in a box,* but through the protection of Athena this box was carried to the end of the Mysian river Kaikos. There it was found by Teuthras who made Auge his wife and took her child into his house as his foster son.

[5] Later authors, including Pindar, state that Danaë was impregnated, not by Zeus, but by the brother of her father.

tic altar of Zeus, to have an oath taken on the true father's name. But he refuses to believe his daughter's statement that Zeus is the father, and *he encloses her with the child in a box, which is cast into the sea.*[6] The box is carried by the waves to the coast of Seriphos, where *Dictys, a fisherman,* usually called a brother of King Polydectes, *saves mother and child by drawing them out of the sea with his nets.* Dictys leads the two into his house and keeps them as his relations. Polydectes, however, becomes enamored of the beautiful mother, and *as Perseus was in his way, he tried to remove him* by sending him forth to fetch the head of the Gorgon Medusa. But against the king's anticipations Perseus accomplishes this difficult task, and a number of heroic deeds besides. Later, in throwing the discs during a contest, he accidentally kills his grandfather, as foretold by the oracle. He becomes the king of Argos, then of Tiryns, and the builder of Mycenae.[7]

GILGAMESH

Aelian, who lived about 200 A.D., relates in his "Animal Stories" the history of *a boy who was saved by an eagle:*

> Animals have a characteristic fondness for man. An eagle is known to have nourished a child. I shall tell the entire story, in proof of my assertion. When Senechoros reigned over the Babylonians, the Chaldean fortunetellers foretold that the son of the king's daughter would take the kingdom from his grandfather; this verdict was a prophecy of the Chaldeans. The king was afraid of this prophecy, and humorously speaking, he became a second Acrisius for his daughter, over whom he watched with the greatest severity. But his daughter, fate being wiser than the Baby-

[6] Simonides of Ceos speaks of a casement strong as ore, in which Danaë is said to have been exposed. Geibel: *Klassisches Liederbuch,* p. 52.

[7] According to Hüsing, the Perseus myth in several versions is also demonstrable in Japan. Compare also Sydney Hartland: *Legend of Perseus,* 3 vols. (London, 1894–6).

lonian, conceived secretly from an inconspicuous man. For fear of the king, the guardians threw the child down from the acropolis, where the royal daughter was imprisoned. The eagle, with his keen eyes, saw the boy's fall, and before the child struck the earth, he caught it on his back, bore it into a garden, and set it down with great care. When the overseer of the place saw the beautiful boy, he was pleased with him and raised him. The boy received the name Gilgamesh, and became the king of Babylonia. If anyone regards this as a fable, I have nothing to say, although I have investigated the matter to the best of my ability. Also of Achaemenes, the Persian, from whom the nobility of the Persians is derived, I learn that he was the pupil of an eagle.[8]

CYRUS

The myth of Cyrus the Great, which the majority of investigators place in the center of this entire mythical circle—without entirely sufficient grounds, it would appear—has been transmitted to us in several versions. According to the report of Herodotus (about 450 B.C.), who states that among four renderings known to him, he selected the least "glorifying" version,[9] the story of the birth and youth of Cyrus is as follows:

Royal sway over the Medes was held, after Cyaxares, by his son Astyages, who had a daughter named Mandane. Once he saw, in a dream, so much water passing from her as to fill an entire city and inundate all Asia. He related his dream to the dream interpreters among the magicians, and was in great

[8] Claudius Aelianus: *Historia Animalium,* translated by F. Jacobs (Stuttgart, 1841), Vol. XII, p. 21. The same book tells of Ptolemy I, the son of Lagus and Arsinoë, that an eagle protected the exposed boy with his wings against the sunshine, the rain, and birds of prey.

[9] F. E. Lange: *Herodots Geschichten* (Reclam edition), Vol. I, pp. 95, 107 ff. Compare also Duncker: *History of Antiquity* (Leipzig, 1880), p. 256, *n.* 5.

fear after they had explained it all to him. When Mandane had grown up, he gave her in marriage, not to a Mede, his equal in birth, but to a Persian, by name of Cambyses. This man came of a good family and led a quiet life. The king considered him of lower rank than a middle-class Mede. After Mandane had become the wife of Cambyses, Astyages saw another dream-vision in the first year. He dreamed that a vine grew from his daughter's lap, and this vine overshadowed all Asia. After he had again related this vision to the dream interpreters, he sent for his daughter, who was with child, and after her arrival from Persia, he watched her, because he meant to kill her offspring. For the dream interpreters among the magicians had prophesied to him that his daughter's son would become king in his place. In order to avert this fate, he waited until Cyrus was born, and then sent for Harpagos, who was his relative and his greatest confidant among the Medes, and whom he had placed over all his affairs. Him he addressed as follows: "My dear Harpagos, I shall charge thee with an errand which thou must conscientiously perform. But do not deceive me, and let no other man attend to it, for all might not go well with thee. Take this boy, whom Mandane has brought forth, carry him home, and kill him. Afterwards thou canst bury him, how and in whatsoever manner thou desirest." But Harpagos made answer: "Great King, never hast thou found thy servant disobedient, and also in future I shall beware not to sin before thee. If such is thy will, it behooves me to carry it out faithfully." When Harpagos had thus spoken, and the little boy with all his ornaments had been delivered into his hands, for death, he went home weeping. On his arrival he told his wife all that Astyages had said to him. But she inquired, "What art thou about to do?" He made reply: "I shall not obey Astyages, even if he raved and stormed ten times worse than he is doing. I shall not do as he wills, and consent to such a murder. I have a number of reasons: in the first place, the boy is my blood relative; then, Astyages is old, and he has no male heir. Should he die, and the kingdom go to his daughter, whose son he bids me kill at present, would I not run the greatest danger? But the boy must die, for the sake of my safety. However, one of Astyages' men is to be his murderer, not one of mine."

Having thus spoken, he at once despatched a messenger to one of the king's cattle herders, by name Mithradates, who, as he happened to know, was keeping his herd in a very suitable mountain pasturage, full of wild animals. The herder's wife was also a slave of Astyages', by name Cyno in Greek, or Spako ("a bitch") in the Median language. When the herder hurriedly arrived, on the command of Harpagos, the latter said to him: "Astyages bids thee take this boy and expose him in the wildest mountains, that he may perish as promptly as may be, and the King has ordered me to say to thee: If thou doest not kill the boy, but let him live, in whatever way, thou art to die a most disgraceful death. And I am charged to see to it that the boy is really exposed." When the herder had listened to this, he took the boy, went home, and arrived in his cottage. His wife was with child, and was in labor the entire day, and it happened that she was just bringing forth, when the herder had gone to the city. They were greatly worried about each other. But when he had returned and the woman saw him again so unexpectedly, she asked in the first place why Harpagos had sent for him so hurriedly. But he said: "My dear wife, would that I had never seen what I have seen and heard in the city, and what has happened to our masters. The house of Harpagos was full of cries and laments. This startled me, but I entered, and soon after I had entered, I saw a small boy lying before me, who struggled and cried and was dressed in fine garments and gold. When Harpagos saw me, he bid me quickly take the boy, and expose him in the wildest spot of the mountains. He said Astyages had ordered this, and added awful threats if I failed to do so. I took the child and went away with it, thinking that it belonged to one of the servants, for it did not occur to me whence it had come. But on the way, I learned the entire story from the servant who led me from the city, and placed the boy in my hands. He is the son of Mandane, daughter of Astyages, and Cambyses, the son of Cyrus; and Astyages has ordered his death. Behold, here is the boy."

Having thus spoken, the herder uncovered the child and showed it to her, and when the woman saw that he was a fine strong child, she wept, and fell at her husband's feet, and implored him not to expose it. But he said he could not do otherwise, for Harpagos would send servants to see if this had been done; he would have to die a disgraceful death unless he did so. Then she said again: "If I have failed to move thee, do as follows, so that they may see an exposed child: I have brought forth a dead child; take it and expose it, but the son of the daughter of Astyages we will raise as our own child. In this way, thou wilt not be found a disobedient servant, nor will we fare ill ourselves. Our stillborn child will be given a kingly burial, and the living child's life will be preserved." The herder did as his wife had begged and advised him to do. He placed his own dead boy in a basket, dressed him in all the finery of the other, and exposed him on the most desert mountain. Three days later he announced to Harpagos that he was now enabled to show the boy's cadaver. Harpagos sent his most faithful body guardians, and ordered the burial of the cattle herder's son. The other boy, however, who was known later on as Cyrus, was brought up by the herder's wife. They did not call him Cyrus, but gave him another name.

When the boy was twelve years old the truth was revealed, through the following accident. He was playing on the road, with other boys of his own age, in the village where the cattle were kept. The boys played "King," and elected the supposed son of the cattle herder.[1] But he commanded some to build

[1] The same "playing king" is found in the Hindu myth of Chandra-

houses, others to carry lances; one he made the king's watchman, the other was charged with the bearing of messages; briefly, each received his appointed task. One of the boy's playmates, however, was the son of Artembares, a respected man among the Medes, and when he did not do as Cyrus ordained, the latter made the other boys seize him. The boys obeyed, and Cyrus chastised him with severe blows. After they let him go, he became furiously angry, as if he had been treated improperly. He ran into the city and complained to his father of what Cyrus had done to him. He did not mention the name of Cyrus for he was not yet called so, but said the cattle herder's son. Artembares went wrathfully with his son to Astyages, complained of the disgraceful treatment, and spoke thus: "Great king, we suffer such outrageous treatment from thy servant, the herder's son," and he showed him his own son's shoulders. When Astyages heard and saw this, he wished to vindicate the boy for the sake of Artembares, and he sent for the cattle herder with his son. When both were present, Astyages looked at Cyrus and said: "Thou, a lowly man's son, hast had the effrontery to treat so disgracefully the son of a man whom I greatly honor!" But he made answer: "Lord, he has only received his due. For the boys in the village, he being among them, were at play, and made me their king, believing me to be the best adapted thereto. And the other boys did as they were told, but he was disobedient, and did not mind me at all. For this he has received his reward. If I have deserved punishment, here I am at your service."

When the boy spoke in this way, Astyages knew

---

gupta, the founder of the Maurya dynasty, whom his mother exposed after his birth, in a vessel at the gate of a cowshed, where a herder found him and raised him. Later on he came to a hunter, where he as cowherd played "king" with the other boys, and as king ordered that the hands and feet of the great criminals be chopped off. (The mutilation motif occurs also in the Cyrus saga, and is generally widely distributed.) At his command, the separated limbs returned to their proper position. Kanakja, who once looked on as they were at play, admired the boy, and bought him from the hunter for one thousand kârshâpana; at home he discovered that the boy was a Maurya. (After Lassen, op. cit., Vol. II, p. 196, *n.* 1.)

him at once. For the features of the face appeared to him as his own, and the answer was that of a high-born youth; furthermore, it seemed to him that the time of the exposure agreed with the boy's age. This smote his heart, and he remained speechless for a while. Hardly had he regained control over himself, when he spoke to get rid of Artembares, so as to be able to question the cattle herder without witnesses. "My dear Artembares," he said, "I shall take care that neither thou nor thy son shall have cause for complaint." Thus he dismissed Artembares. Cyrus, however, was led into the palace by the servants, on the command of Astyages, and the cattle herder had to stay behind. When he was all alone with him, Astyages questioned him whence he had obtained the boy, and who had given the child into his hands. But the herder said that he was his own son, and that the woman who had borne him was living with him. Astyages remarked that he was very unwise, to look out for most cruel tortures, and he beckoned the sword-bearers to take hold of him. As he was being led to torture, the herder confessed the whole story, from beginning to end, the entire truth, finally beginning to beg and implore forgiveness and pardon. Meanwhile Astyages was not so incensed against the herder, who had revealed to him the truth, as against Harpagos; he ordered the sword-bearers to summon him, and when Harpagos stood before him, Astyages asked him as follows: "My dear Harpagos, in what fashion hast thou taken the life of my daughter's son, whom I once delivered over to thee?" Seeing the cattle herder standing near, Harpagos did not resort to untruthfulness, for fear that he would be refuted at once, and so he proceeded to tell the truth. Astyages concealed the anger which he had aroused in him, and first told him what he had learned from the herder; then he mentioned that the boy was still living, and that everything had turned out all right. He said that he had greatly regretted what he had done to the child, and that his daughter's reproaches had pierced his soul. "But as everything has ended so well, send thy son to greet the newcomer, and then come to eat with me, for I am ready to prepare a feast in honor of the Gods who have brought all this about."

When Harpagos heard this, he prostrated himself on the ground before the king, and praised himself for his error having turned out well, and for being invited to the king's table, in commemoration of a happy event. So he went home, and when he arrived there, he at once sent off his only son, a boy of about thirteen years, telling him to go to Astyages, and to do as he was bid. Then Harpagos joyfully told his wife what had befallen him. But Astyages butchered the son of Harpagos when he came, cut him to pieces, and roasted the flesh in part; another portion of the flesh was cooked, and when everything was prepared he kept it in readiness. When the hour of the meal had come, Harpagos and the other guests arrived. A table with sheep's meat was arranged in front of Astyages and the others, but Harpagos was served with his own son's flesh, without the head, and without the choppings of hands and feet, but with everything else. These parts were kept hidden in a basket. When Harpagos seemed to have taken his fill, Astyages asked him if the meat had tasted good to him, and when Harpagos answered that he had enjoyed it, the servants, who had been ordered to do so, brought in his own son's covered head, with the hands and feet, stepped up to Harpagos, and told him to uncover and take what he desired. Harpagos did so, uncovered the basket, and saw the remnants of his son. When he saw this, he did not give way to his horror, but controlled himself. Astyages then asked him if he knew of what game he had eaten; and he replied that he knew it very well, and that whatever the king did was well done. Thus he spoke, took the flesh that remained, and went home with it, where he probably meant to bury it together.

This was the revenge of Astyages upon Harpagos. Concerning Cyrus, he took counsel, and summoned the same magicians who had explained his dream, then he asked them how they had at one time interpreted his vision in a dream. But they said that the boy must become a king, if he remained alive, and did not die prematurely. Astyages made reply: "The boy is alive, and is here, and as he was staying in the country, the boys of the village elected him for their king. But he did everything like the real kings, for he ordained to himself as the master, sword-bearers, gatekeepers, messengers, and everything. How do you mean to interpret this?" The magicians made reply: "If the boy is alive, and has been made king without the help of anyone, thou canst be at ease so far as he is concerned, and be of good cheer, for he will not again be made a king. Already several prophecies of ours have applied to insignificant trifles, and what rests upon dreams is apt to be vain." Astyages made reply: "Ye sorcerers, I am entirely of your opinion that the dream has been fulfilled when the boy was king in name, and that I have nothing more to fear from him. Yet counsel me carefully as to what is safest for my house and for yourselves." Then the magicians said: "Send the boy away, that he may get out of thy sight, send him to the land of the Persians, to his parents." When Astyages had heard this, he was greatly pleased. He sent for Cyrus, and said to him: "My son, I have wronged thee greatly, misled by a deceitful dream, but thy good fortune has saved thee. Now go cheerfully to the land of the Persians; I shall give thee safe conduct. There wilt thou find a very different father, and a very different mother than the herders, Mithradates and his wife." Thus spake Astyages, and Cyrus was sent away. When he arrived in the house of Cambyses, his parents received him with great joy when they learned who he was, for they believed him to have perished at that time, and they desired to know how he had been preserved. He told them that he had believed himself to be the son of the cattle herder, but had learned everything on the way from the companions whom Astyages had sent with him. He related that the cattle herder's wife had saved him, and praised her throughout. The "bitch" (Spako) played the principal part in his conversation. The parents took hold of this name, so that the preservation of the child might appear still more wonderful, and thus was laid the foundation of the myth that the exposed Cyrus was nursed by a bitch.

Later on, Cyrus, on the instigation of Harpagos, stirred up the Persians against the Medes. War was declared, and Cyrus, at the head of the Persians, conquered the Medes in battle. Astyages was taken prisoner alive, but Cyrus did not harm him, and kept him with him until his end. Herodotus' report concludes with the words: "But from that time on the Persians and Cyrus reigned over Asia. Thus was Cyrus born and raised, and made a king."

The report of Pompeius Trogus is preserved only in the extract by Justin, according to whom Astyages had a daughter but no male heir.[2] This version continues:

> In his dream he saw a vine grow forth from her lap, the sprouts of which overshadowed all Asia. The dream interpreters declared that the vision signified the magnitude of his grandson, whom his daughter was to bear; but also his own loss of his dominions. In order to banish this dread, Astyages gave his daughter in marriage neither to a prominent man nor to a Mede, so that his grandson's mind might not be uplifted by the paternal estate besides the maternal; but he married her to Cambyses, a middle-class man from the then unknown people of the Persians. But this was not enough to banish the fears of Astyages, and he summoned his pregnant daughter, in order to have her infant destroyed before his eyes. When a boy had been born, he gave him to Harpagos, his friend and confidant, to kill him. For fear that the daughter of Astyages would take revenge upon him for the death of her boy, when she came to reign

[2] Justin (Marcus Junianus Justinus): *Extract from Pompeius Trogus' Philippian History*, Vol. I, pp. 4–7. Deinon's Persian tales (written in the first half of the fourth century before Christ) are presumably the sources of Trogus' narrative.

after her father's death, he delivered the boy to the king's herder for exposure. At the same time that Cyrus was born, a son happened to be born also to the herder. When his wife learned that the king's child had been exposed, she urgently prayed for it to be brought to her, that she might look at it. Moved by her entreaties, the herder returned to the woods. There he found a bitch standing beside the child, giving it her teats, and keeping the beasts and birds away from it. At this aspect he was filled with the same compassion as the bitch; so that he picked up the boy and carried him home, the bitch following him in great distress. When his wife took the boy in her arms, he smiled at her as if he already knew her; and as he was very strong, and ingratiated himself with her by his pleasant smile, she voluntarily begged the herder to [expose her own child instead and] [3] permit her to raise the boy; be it that she was interested in his welfare, or that she placed her hopes on him.

Thus the two boys had to exchange fates; one was raised in place of the herder's child, while the other was exposed instead of the grandson of the king. The remainder of this apparently more primitive report agrees essentially with the account of Herodotus.

An altogether different version of the Cyrus myth is extant in the report of Ctesias, a contemporary of Herodotus. The original of his narrative, which comprised more than an entire book in his Persian history, has been lost; but a surviving fragment of Nicholas of Damascus summarizes the Ctesian account.[4] Astyages is said to have been the worthiest king of the Medes, after Abakes. Under his rule occurred the great transmutation through which the rulership passed from the Medes to the Persians, in the following manner:

The Medes had a law that a poor man who went to a

[3] The words in parentheses are said to be lacking in certain manuscripts.

[4] Nicol. Damasc. Frag. 66, Ctes.; Frag. Pers., II, 5.

rich man for his support, and surrendered himself to him, had to be fed and clothed and kept like a slave by the rich man, or in case the latter refused to do so, the poor man was at liberty to go elsewhere. In this way a boy by name of Cyrus, a Mard by birth, came to the king's servant who was at the head of the palace sweepers. Cyrus was the son of Atradates, whose poverty made him live as a robber, and whose wife, Argoste, Cyrus' mother, made her living by tending the goats. Cyrus surrendered himself for the sake of his daily bread, and helped to clean the palace. As he was diligent, the foreman gave him better clothing and advanced him from the outside sweepers to those who cleaned the interior of the king's palace, placing him under their superintendent. This man was severe, however, and often whipped Cyrus. The boy left him and went to the lamplighter, who liked Cyrus and moved him closer to the king, by placing him among the royal torchbearers. As Cyrus distinguished himself also in his new position, he came to Artembares, who was at the head of the cupbearers and himself presented the cup to the king. Artembares gladly accepted Cyrus, and bade him pour the wine for the guests at the king's table. Not long afterwards, Astyages noticed the dexterity and nimbleness of Cyrus' service, and his graceful presentation of the wine cup, so that he asked of Artembares whence this youth had come who was so skillful a cupbearer.

> "O Lord," spake he, "this boy is thy slave, of Persian parentage, from the tribe of the Mards, who has surrendered himself to me to make a living." Artembares was old, and once on being attacked by a fever, he prayed the king to let him stay at home until he had recovered. "In my stead, the youth whom thou hast praised will pour the wine, and if he should please thee, the king, as a cupbearer, *I who am a eunuch, will adopt him as my son.*" Astyages consented, but the other confided in many ways in Cyrus *as in a son.* Cyrus thus stood at the king's side, and poured his wine by day and by night, showing great ability and cleverness. Astyages conferred upon him

the income of Artembares, as if he had been his son, adding many presents, and Cyrus became a great man whose name was heard everywhere.

Astyages had a very noble and beautiful daughter,[5] whom he gave to the Mede Spitamas, adding all Media as her dowry. Then Cyrus sent for his father and mother, in the land of the Medes, and they rejoiced in the good fortune of their son, and *his mother told him the dream which she had at the time that she was bearing him,* while asleep in the sanctuary as she was tending the goats. *So much water passed away from her that it became as a large stream, inundating all Asia, and flowing as far as the sea.* When the father heard this, he ordered the dream to be placed before the Chaldeans in Babylon. Cyrus summoned the wisest among them, and communicated the dream to him. He declared that the dream foretold great good fortune to Cyrus, and *the highest dignity in Asia;* but Astyages must not learn of it, "for else he would disgracefully kill thee, as well as myself the interpreter," said the Babylonian. They swore to each other to tell no one of this great and incomparable vision. *Cyrus later on rose to still higher dignities, created his father a Satrap of Persia, and raised his mother to the highest rank and possessions among the Persian women.* But when the Babylonian was killed soon afterwards by Oebares, the confidant of Cyrus, his wife betrayed the fateful dream to the king, when she learned of Cyrus' expedition to Persia, which he had undertaken in preparation of the revolt. The king sent his horsemen after Cyrus, with the command to deliver him dead or alive. But Cyrus escaped them by a ruse. Finally a combat took place, terminating in the defeat of the Medes. Cyrus also conquered Egbatana, and here the daughter of Astyages and her husband Spitamas, with their two sons, were taken prisoners. But Astyages himself could not be found,

[5] This daughter's name is Amatyis (not Mandane) in the version of Ctesias.

for Amytis and Spitamas had concealed him in the palace, under the rafters of the roof. Cyrus then ordered that Amytis, her husband, and the children should be tortured until they revealed the hiding place of Astyages, but he came out voluntarily, that his relatives might not be tortured on his account. *Cyrus commanded the execution of Spitamas,* because he had lied in affirming to be in ignorance of Astyages' hiding place; *but Amytis became the wife of Cyrus. He removed the fetters of Astyages,* with which Oebares had bound him, *honored him as a father,* and made him a Satrap of the Barkanians.

A great similarity to Herodotus' version of the Cyrus myth is found in the early history of the Persian royal hero, Kaikhosrav, as related by Firdausi in the *Shah Namah.* This myth is most extensively rendered by Spiegel.[6] During the warfare of King Kaikâus, of Bactria and Iran, against King Afrâsiâb, of Turan, *Kaikâus fell out with his son, Siâvaksh,* who applied to Afrâsiâb for protection and assistance. He was kindly received by Afrâsiâb, who gave him his daughter Feringis to wife, on the persuasion of his vizier, Pirân, *although he had received the prophecy that the son to be born of this union would bring great misfortune upon him.* Garsevaz, the king's brother, and a near relative of Siâvaksh, calumniates the son-in-law, and Afrâsiâb leads an army against him. *Before the birth of his son, Siâvaksh is warned by a dream, which foretold destruction and death to himself, but royalty to his offspring.* He therefore flies from Afrâsiâb, but is taken prisoner and killed, on the command of the Shah. His wife, who is pregnant, is saved by Pirân from the hands of the murderers. On condition of announcing at once the delivery of Feringis to the king, Pirân is granted permission to keep her in his house. The shade of the murdered Siâvaksh once comes to him in a dream and tells him that an avenger has been born; Pirân actually finds in the room of Feringis a newborn boy, whom he names Kaikhosrav. Afrâsiâb no longer insisted upon the killing of the boy, but he or-

[6] Op. cit., Vol. I, pp. 581 ff.

dered Pirân *to surrender the child with a nurse to the herders, who were to raise him in ignorance of his origin.* But his royal descent is promptly revealed in his courage and his demeanor; and as Pirân takes the boy back into his home, Afrâsiâb becomes distrustful, and orders the boy to be led before him. Instructed by Pirân, Kaikhosrav plays the fool,[7] and reassured as to his harmlessness, the Shah dismisses him to his mother, Feringis. Finally, Kaikhosrav is crowned as king by his grandfather, Kaikâus. After prolonged, complicated, and tedious combats, Afrâsiâb is at last taken prisoner, with divine assistance. Kaikhosrav strikes his head off, and also causes Garsevaz to be decapitated.

A certain resemblance to the preceding saga, although more remote, is presented by the myth of Feridun, as told by Firdausi.[8] *Zohâk, the king of Iran, once sees in a dream three men of royal tribe.* Two of them are bent with age, but between them is a *younger man* who holds a club,

[7] On the basis of this motif of simulated dementia and certain other corresponding features, Jiriczek ("Hamlet in Iran," in the *Zeitschrift des Vereins für Volkskunde,* Vol. X [1900], p. 353) has represented the Hamlet saga as a variation of the Persian myth of Kaikhosrav. This idea was followed up by H. Lessmann (*"Die Kyrossage . . . ,"* loc. cit.), who shows that the Hamlet saga strikingly agrees in certain items—for example, in the simulated folly—with the sagas of Brutus and of Tell. (Compare also the protestations of Moses.) In another connection, the deeper roots of these relations have been more extensively discussed, especially with reference to the Tell saga. (See *Inzestmotiv,* Chapter vii.)

Attention is also directed to the story of David, as it is told in the books of Samuel. Here again, the royal scion, David, is made a shepherd, who gradually rises in the social scale up to the royal throne. He likewise is given the king's (Saul's) daughter in marriage, and the king seeks his life, but David is always saved by miraculous means from the greatest perils. He also evades persecution by simulating dementia and playing the fool. The relationship between the Hamlet saga and the David saga has already been pointed out by Jiriczek and Lessmann. The biblical character of this entire mythological cycle is also emphasized by Jiriczek, who finds in the tale of Siâvaksh's death certain features from the Passion of the Saviour.

[8] Translated by Schack (op. cit.). The name Zohâk here is a mutilation of the original Zend Avesta expression *Ashi-dahaka* (*Azis-dahaka*), meaning "pernicious serpent." (See "The Myth of Feridun in India and Iran," by Dr. R. Roth, in the *Zeitschrift der Deutschen Morgenländischen Gesellschaft,* Vol. II., p. 216.) To the Persian Feridun corresponds the Hindu Trita, whose Avestian double is Thraetaona. The last-named form is the most predominantly authenticated; from it was formed, by transition of the aspirated sounds, first Phrenduna, then Frêdûn or Afrêdun; Feridun is a more recent corruption. Compare Spiegel, op. cit., Vol. I, pp. 537 ff.

with a bull's head, in his right hand; this man steps up to him, and *fells him with his club to the ground.* The dream interpreters declared to the king that the young hero who will dethrone him is Feridun, a scion of the tribe of Dschemschid. Zohâk at once sets out to look for the tracks of his dreaded enemy. Feridun is the son of Abtin, a grandson of Dschemschid. His father hides from the pursuit of the tyrant, but he is seized and killed. Feridun himself, a boy of tender age, *is saved by his mother, Firânek, who escapes with him and entrusts him to the care of the guardian of a distant forest. Here he is suckled by a cow.* For three years he remains hidden in this place, but then his mother no longer believes him safe, and she carries him to a hermit on Mount Elburz. Soon afterwards Zohâk comes to the forest and kills the guardian as well as the cow.

When Feridun was sixteen years old, he came down from Mount Elburz, learned of his origin through his mother, and swore to avenge the death of his father and of his nurse. On the expedition against Zohâk he is accompanied by his two older brothers, Purmâje and Kayânuseh. He orders a club to be forged for his use, and ornaments it with the bull's head, in memory of his foster mother, the cow. With this club he smites Zohâk, as foretold by the dream.

TRISTAN

The theme of the Feridun story is pursued in the Tristan saga, as related in the epic poem by Gottfried von Strassburg. This is especially evident in the prologue of the Tristan saga, which is repeated later on in the adventures of the hero himself (duplication). Riwalin, king in the land of the Parmenians, in an expedition to the court of Mark, king of Cornwall and England, had become acquainted with the latter's beautiful sister, Blancheflure, and his heart was aflame with love for her. While assisting Mark in a compaign, Riwalin was mortally wounded and was carried to Tintajole. Blancheflure, *disguised as a beggar maid,* hastened to his sickbed, and her devoted love saved the king's life. She fled with her lover to his native land (obstacles) and was there proclaimed as his consort. But Morgan attacked Riwalin's country, for the sake of Blancheflure, whom the king entrusted to his *faithful retainer* Rual, because she was carrying a child. Rual placed the queen for safekeeping in the castle of Kaneel. Here *she gave birth to a son and died, while her husband fell in the battle against Morgan. In order to protect the king's offspring from Morgan's pursuits,* Rual spread the rumor that the infant had been born dead. The boy was named Tristan, because he had been conceived and born in sorrow. Under the care of his *foster parents,* Tristan grew up, equally straight in body and mind, until his fourteenth year, when he was kidnapped by Norwegian merchants, who then put him ashore in Cornwall because they feared the wrath of the gods. Here *the boy was found by the soldiers of King Mark,* who was so well pleased with the brave and handsome youth that he promptly made him his master of the chase (career), and held him in great affection. Meanwhile, faithful Rual had set forth to seek his abducted foster son, whom he found at last in Cornwall, where Rual had come begging his way. Rual *revealed Tristan's descent* to the king, who was delighted to see in him the son of his beloved sister, and raised him to the rank of knight. In order *to avenge his father,* Tristan proceeded with Rual to Parmenia, vanquished Morgan, the usurper, and gave the country to Rual as liege, while he himself returned to his uncle Mark.[9]

The actual Tristan saga goes on with a repetition of the principal themes. In the service of Mark, Tristan kills Morald, the bridegroom of Isolde, and being wounded unto death, he is saved by Isolde. He asks her hand in marriage on behalf of his uncle Mark. When he fulfills the condition of killing a dragon, she accompanies him reluctantly to Cornwall, to which they travel by ship. On the journey they partake unwittingly of the disastrous love potion

[9] After Chop: *Erläuterungen zu Wagner's Tristan* (Reclam edition).

which binds them together in frenzied passion; they betray King Mark. On the wedding night, Isolde's faithful maid, Brangäne, represents the queen, and sacrifices her virginity to the king. Next follows the banishment of Tristan, his several attempts to regain his beloved, although he had meanwhile married another Isolde—"Isolde the White Hand," of Brittany, who resembled his love, "Isolde the Fair." At last he is again wounded unto death, and Isolde arrives too late to save him.[1]

A plainer version of the Tristan saga—in the sense of the characteristic features of the myth of the birth of the hero—is found in the fairy tale "The True Bride," quoted by Riklin from Rittershaus.[2] A royal pair have no children. The king having threatened to kill his wife unless she bears a child by the time of his return from his sea voyage, she is brought to him during his journey, by his zealous maid-servant, as the fairest of three promenading ladies, and he takes her into his tent without recognizing her.[3] She returns home without having been discovered, gives birth to a daughter, Isol, and dies. Isol later on finds, in a box by the seaside, a most beautiful little boy, whose name is Tristram, and she raises him to become engaged to him. The subsequent story, which contains the motif of the true bride, is noteworthy for present purposes only in so far as here again occurs the draught of oblivion, and two Isoldes. The king's second wife gives a potion to Tristram, which causes him to forget the fair Isol entirely, so that he wishes to marry the black Isota. Ultimately he discovers the deception, however, and becomes united with Isol.

[1] Compare Immermann: *Tristan und Isolde, Ein Gedicht in Romanzen* (Düsseldorf, 1841). Like the epic of Gottfried von Strassburg, his version begins with the preliminary history of the loves of Tristan's parents, King Riwalin Kannlengres of Parmenia and Mark's beautiful sister Blancheflur. The maiden never reveals her love, which is not sanctioned by her brother, but she visits the king, who is wounded unto death, in his chamber, and dying he procreates Tristan, "the son of the most daring and doleful love." Grown up as a foundling in the care of Rual and his wife, Florete, the winsome youth Tristan introduces himself to Mark in a stag hunt, as an expert huntsman, is recognized as his nephew by a ring, the king's gift to his beloved sister, and becomes his favorite.

[2] *Wunscherfüllung und Symbolik im Märchen*, p. 56; from the Rittershaus collection of fairy tales (XXVII, p. 113). See translation by W. A. White, M.D., *Psychoanalytic Review*, Vol. I, No. 1.

[3] Compare the substitution of the bride, through Brangäne.

ROMULUS

The original version of the story of Romulus and Remus —as told by the most ancient Roman annalist Quintus Fabius Pictor—is rendered as follows by Mommsen:[4]

> *The twins* borne by Ilia, the daughter of the preceding king Numitor, *from the embrace of the war-god Mars were condemned by King Amulius, the present ruler of Alba, to be cast into the river.* The king's servants took the children and carried them from Alba as far as the Tiber on the Palatine Hill; but when they tried to descend the hill to the river, to carry out the command, they found that the river had risen, and they were unable to reach its bed. The tub with the children was therefore thrust by them into the shallow water at the shore. *It floated* for a while; *but the water promptly receded,* and *knocking against a stone, the tub capsized,* and the screaming infants were upset into the river mud. *They were heard by a she-wolf who had just brought forth and had her udders full of milk; she came and gave her teats to the boys, to nurse them,* and as they were drinking she licked them clean with her tongue. Above them flew a woodpecker, which guarded the children, and also carried food to them. The father was providing for his sons: for the wolf and the woodpecker are animals consecrated to father Mars. This was seen by one of the royal herdsmen, who was driving his pigs back to the pasture from which the water had receded. Startled by the spectacle, he summoned his mates, who found the she-wolf attending like a mother to the children, and the children treated her as their mother. The men made a loud noise to scare the animal away; but the

[4] Theodor Mommsen: "*Die echte und die falsche Acca Larentia*"; in *Festgaben für G. Homeyer* (Berlin, 1891), pp. 93 ff; and *Römische Forschungen* (Berlin, 1879), Vol. II, pp. 1 ff. Mommsen reconstructs the lost narrative of Fabius from the preserved reports of Dionysius (I, 79–831) and of Plutarch (*Romulus*).

wolf was not afraid; she left the children, but not from fear; slowly, without heeding the herdsmen, she disappeared into the wilderness of the forest, at the holy site of Faunus, where the water gushes from a gully of the mountain. Meanwhile the men picked up the boys and carried them to the chief swineherd of the king, Faustulus, for they believed that the gods did not wish the children to perish. *But the wife of Faustulus had just given birth to a dead child, and was full of sorrow. Her husband gave her the twins, and she nursed them; the couple raised the children, and named them Romulus and Remus.*

After Rome had been founded, later on, King Romulus built himself a house not far from the place where his tub had stood. The gully in which the she-wolf had disappeared has been known since that time as the Wolf's Gully, the Lupercal. The image in ore of the she-wolf with the twins was subsequently erected at this spot,[5] and the she-wolf herself, the Lupa, was worshipped by the Romans as a divinity.

The Romulus saga later on underwent manifold transmutations, mutilations, additions, and interpretations.[6] It is best known in the form transmitted by Livy (I, 3 ff.), where we learn something about the antecedents and subsequent fate of the twins:

King Proca bequeaths the royal dignity to his firstborn son, Numitor. But his *younger brother, Amulius, pushes him from the throne,* and becomes king himself. So that no scion from Numitor's family may arise, as the avenger, he kills the male descendants of his brother. *Rhea Silvia, the daughter, he elects as a vestal, and thus deprives her of the hope of progeny, through perpetual virginity* as enjoined upon her under the semblance of a most honorable distinction. But the vestal maiden was overcome by violence, and

[5] The Capitoline She-Wolf is considered the work of very ancient Etruscan artists; it was erected at the Lupercal in the year 296 B.C., according to Livy (X, 231).

[6] All these renderings were compiled by Schwegler, in his *Roman History,* Vol. I, pp. 384 ff.

having *brought forth twins,* she named *Mars* as the *father of her illegitimate offspring,* be it from conviction, or because a god appeared more creditable to her as the perpetrator of the crime.

The narrative of the exposure in the Tiber goes on to relate that the floating tub, in which the boys had been exposed, was left on dry land by the receding waters, and that a thirsty wolf, attracted from the neighboring mountains by the children's cries, offered them her teats. The boys are said to have been found by the chief royal herder, supposedly named Faustulus, who took them to the homestead of his wife, Larentia, where they were raised. Some believe that Larentia was called Lupa ("she-wolf") by the herders because she offered her body, and that this was the origin of the wonderful saga.

Grown to manhood, the youths Romulus and Remus protect the herds against the attacks of wild animals and robbers. One day Remus is taken prisoner by the robbers, who accuse him of having stolen Numitor's flocks. But Numitor, to whom he is surrendered for punishment, was touched by his tender age, and when he learned of the twin brothers, he suspected that they might be his exposed grandsons. While he was anxiously pondering the resemblance with the features of his daughter, and the boy's age as corresponding to the time of the exposure, Faustulus arrived with Romulus, and a conspiracy was hatched when the descent of the boys had been learned from the herders. The youths armed themselves for vengeance, while Numitor took up weapons to defend his claim to the throne he had usurped. After *Amulius had been assassinated,* Numitor was reinstituted as the ruler, and the youths resolved to found a city in the region where they had been exposed and brought up. A furious dispute arose upon the question of which brother was to be the ruler of the newly erected city, for neither twin was favored by the right of primogeniture, and the outcome of the bird oracle was equally doubtful. The saga relates that Remus jumped over the new wall, to deride his twin, and *Romulus became so much enraged that he slew his brother.* Romulus then usurped the sole mastery, and the city was named Rome after him.

The Roman tale of Romulus and Remus has a close counterpart in the Greek myth of a city foundation by the twin brothers Amphion and Zethus, who were the first to found the site of Thebes of the Seven Gates. The enormous rocks which Zethus brought from the mountains were joined by the music drawn from Amphion's lyre strings to form the walls which became so famous later on. Amphion and Zethus passed as *the children of Zeus and Antiope,* daughter of King Nykteus. She escaped by flight from the punishment of her father, who died of grief; on his deathbed he implored *his brother and successor on the throne, Lycus,* to punish the wrongdoing of Antiope. Meantime she had married Epopeus, the king of Sicyon, who was killed by Lycus. Antiope was led away by him in fetters. She gave birth to twin sons in the Cithaeron, where she left them. A shepherd raised the boys and called them Amphion and Zethus. Later on, Antiope succeeded in escaping from the torments of Lycus and his wife, Dirce. She accidentally sought shelter in the Cithaeron, with the twin brothers, now grown up. The shepherd reveals to the youths the fact that Antiope is their mother. Thereupon they cruelly kill Dirce, and deprive Lycus of the rulership.

The remaining twin sagas,[7] which are extremely numerous, cannot be discussed in detail in this connection. Possibly they represent a complication of the birth myth by another very ancient and widely distributed myth complex, that of the hostile brothers, the detailed discussion of which belongs elsewhere. The apparently late and secondary character of the twin type in the birth myths justifies the separation of this part of mythology from the present theme. As regards the Romulus saga, Mommsen considers it highly probable that it originally told only of Romulus, while the figure of Remus was added subsequently, and somewhat disjointedly, when it became de-

[7] Some Greek twin sagas are quoted by Schubert (op. cit. pp. 13 ff.) in their essential content. Concerning the extensive distribution of this legendary form, compare the somewhat confused book of J. H. Becker: *The Twin Saga as the Key to the Interpretation of Ancient Tradition* (Leipzig, 1891).

sirable to invest the consulate with a solemnity founded on old tradition.[8]

HERCULES[9]

After the loss of his numerous sons, Electryon betroths his daughter, Alcmene, to Amphitryon, the son of his brother, Alcaeus. However, Amphitryon, through an unfortunate accident, causes the death of Electryon, and escapes to Thebes with his affianced bride. He has not enjoyed her love, for she has solemnly pledged him not to touch her until he has avenged her brothers on the Thebans. An expedition is therefore started by him, from Thebes, and he conquers the king of the hostile people, Pterelaos, with all the islands. As he is returning to Thebes, Zeus in the form of Amphitryon betakes himself to Alcmene, to whom he presents a golden goblet as evidence of victory.[1] He rests with the beauteous maiden during three nights, according to the later poets, holding back the sun one day. In the same night, Amphitryon arrives, exultant in his victory and aflame with love. In the fullness of time, the fruit of the divine and the human embrace is brought forth, and Zeus announces to the gods his son, as the most powerful ruler of the future.[2] But his jealous spouse, Hera, knows how to obtain from him the pernicious oath that the first-born grandson of Perseus is to be the ruler of all the other descendants of Perseus. Hera hurries to Mycenae,

[8] Mommsen: *Die Remus Legende* (Berlin, 1881).

[9] After Preller: *Greek Mythology* (Leipzig, 1854), Vol. II, pp. 120 ff.

[1] The same transformation of the divine procreator into the form of the human father is found in the birth history of the Egyptian queen, Hatshepsut (about 1500 B.C.), who believed that the god Amen, in the form of her father, Thothmes I, cohabited with her mother, Aahames. (See Budge: *A History of Egypt.*) Later on she married her brother, Thothmes II, after whose dishonorable death she endeavored to eradicate his memory, and herself assumed the rulership, in masculine fashion. (See *The Deuteronium,* edited by Schrader.)

[2] A similar mingling of the divine and human posterity is related in the myth of Theseus, whose mother, Aethra, the beloved of Poseidon, was visited in one night by this god and by the childless King Aegeus of Athens, who had been brought under the influence of wine. The boy was raised in secret and in ignorance of his father. (See Röscher, op. cit., article "Aegeus.")

to deliver the wife of Perseus' third son, Sthenelos, of the seven-months child, Eurystheus. At the same time she hinders and endangers the confinement of Alcmene, through all sorts of wicked sorcery, precisely as at the birth of the god of light, Apollo. Alcmene finally gives birth to Hercules and Iphicles, the latter in no way the former's equal in courage or in strength, but destined to become the father of his faithful friend, Iolaos.[3] In this way Eurystheus became the king in Mycenae, in the land of the Argolians, in conformity with the oath of Zeus, and the laterborn Hercules was his subject.

The old legend related the raising of Hercules on the strength-giving waters of the Fountain of Dirce, the nourishment of all Theban children. Later on, however, another version arose. Fearing the jealousy of Hera, Alcmene *exposed the child she had borne* in a place that for a long time after was known as the Field of Hercules. About this time, Athena arrived, in company with Hera. She marveled at the beautiful form of the child, and persuaded Hera to put him to her breast. But the boy took the breast with far greater strength than his age seemed to warrant; Hera felt pains and angrily flung the child to the ground. Athena, however, carried him to the neighboring city and *took him to Queen Alcmene, whose maternity was unknown to her, as a poor foundling, whom she begged her to raise for the sake of charity*. This peculiar accident is truly remarkable! The child's own mother allows him to perish, disregarding the duty of maternal love, and the stepmother, who is filled with natural hatred against the child, saves her enemy without knowing it.[4] Hercules had drawn only a few drops from Hera's breast,

[3] Alcmene bore Hercules as the son of Zeus, and Iphicles as the offspring of Amphitryon. According to Apollodorus, they were twin children, born at the same time; according to others, Iphicles was conceived and born one night later than Hercules. (See Röscher, op. cit., articles "Amphitryon" and "Alcmene.") The shadowy character of the twin brother, and his loose connection with the entire myth, is again evident. In a similar way, Telephus, the son of Auge, was exposed together with Parthenopaeus, the son of Atalanta, nursed by a doe, and taken by herders to King Corythos. The external subsequent insertion of the partner is here again quite obvious.

[4] After Diodorus Siculus, Book IV, p. 9 of Wurm's German translation (Stuttgart, 1831).

but the divine milk was sufficient to endow him with immortality. An attempt on Hera's part to kill the boy, asleep in his cradle, by means of two serpents, proved a failure, for the child awakened and crushed the beasts with a single pressure of his hands. As a boy, Hercules one day killed his tutor, Linos, being incensed over an unjust chastisement. Amphitryon, fearing the wildness of the youth, sent him to tend his ox-herds in the mountains, with the herders, among whom he is said by some to have been raised entirely, like Amphion and Zethus, Cyrus, and Romulus. Here he lives from the hunt, in the freedom of nature.[5]

The myth of Hercules suggests in certain features the Hindu saga of the hero Krishna, who like many heroes escapes a general infanticide, and is then brought up by a herder's wife, Iasodha. A wicked she-demon appears, who has been sent by King Kansa to kill the boy. She takes the post of wet nurse in the home, but is recognized by Krishna, who bites her so severely in suckling—like Hera, when nursing Hercules, whom she also means to destroy—that she dies.

JESUS

The Gospel according to Luke (1:26–35) relates the prophecy of the birth of Jesus, as follows:

> And in the sixth month the angel Gabriel sent from God unto a city of Galilee, named Nazareth, *to a virgin espoused to a man whose name was Joseph,* of the house of David; and the virgin's name was Mary. And the angel came in unto her, and said, Hail! thou that art highly favored, the Lord is with thee: blessed art thou among women. And when she saw him, she was troubled at his saying, and cast in her mind what manner of salutation this should be. And the angel said unto her, Fear not, Mary: for thou hast found favour

[5] After Preller, op. cit., Vol. II, p. 123.

with God. And, behold, *thou shalt conceive in thy womb, and bring forth a son, and shalt call his name JESUS. He shall be great and shall be called the* Son *of the Highest:* and the Lord God shalt give unto him the throne of his father David. And he shall reign over the house of Jacob for ever; and of his kingdom there shall be no end. Then said Mary unto the angel, How shall this be, *seeing I know not a man?* And the angel answered and said unto her, The Holy Ghost shall come upon thee, and the power of the Highest shall overshadow thee: therefore also that holy thing which shall be born of thee *shall be called the* Son *of God.*

This report is supplemented by the Gospel according to Matthew (1:18–25), in the narrative of the birth and childhood of Jesus:[6]

Now the birth of Jesus Christ was on this wise: when as his mother Mary was espoused to Joseph, before they came together, *she was found with child of the Holy Ghost.* Then Joseph, her husband, being a just man, and not willing to make her a publick example, was minded to put her away privily. But, while he thought on these things, behold, *the angel of the Lord appeared unto him in a dream,* saying, Joseph, thou son of David, fear not to take unto thee Mary thy wife: for that which is conceived in her is of the Holy Ghost. And she shall bring forth a son, and thou shall call his name JESUS: for he shall save his people from their sins. Now all this was done that it might be fulfilled which was spoken of the Lord by

[6] For the formal demonstration of the entire identity with the other hero myths of the birth story and early history of Jesus, the author has presumed to rearrange the corresponding paragraphs from the different versions in the Gospels, irrespective of the traditional sequence and the originality of the individual parts. The age, origin, and genuineness of these parts are briefly summarized and discussed in W. Soltan: *Birth History of Jesus Christ* (Leipzig, 1902). The transmitted versions of the several Gospels—which according to Usener: "The Birth and Childhood of Christ," in *Lectures and Essays* (Leipzig, 1907), contradict and even exclude each other—have been placed, or left, in juxtaposition, precisely for the reason that the apparently contradictory elements in these birth myths are to be elucidated in the present research, no matter if these contradictions be encountered within a single uniform saga, or in its different versions (as, for example, in the Cyrus myth).

the prophet, saying, Behold, a virgin shall be with child, and shall bring forth a son, and they shall call his name Emmanuel, which being interpreted is, God with us. Then Joseph being raised from sleep did as the angel of the Lord had bidden him and took unto him his wife: *And knew her not till she had brought forth her firstborn son:* and he called his name JESUS.

Here we interpolate the detailed account of the birth of Jesus, from Gospel of Luke (2:4–20):

And Joseph also went up from Galilee, out of the city of Nazareth, into Judæa, unto the city of David, which is called Bethlehem; (because he was of the house and lineage of David:) to be taxed with Mary his espoused wife, being great with child. And so it was, that, while they were there, the days were accomplished that she should be delivered. And *she brought forth her firstborn son, and wrapped him in swaddling clothes, and laid him in a manger;*[7] because there was no room for them in the inn. And there were in the same country shepherds abiding in the field, keeping watch over their flocks by night. And, lo, the angel of the Lord came upon them, and the glory of the Lord shone round about them, and they were sore afraid. And the angel said unto them, Fear not; for, behold, I bring you good tidings of great joy, which shall be to all people. For unto you is born this day in the city of David a Saviour, which is Christ the Lord. And this shall be a sign unto you; Ye shall find the babe wrapped in swaddling clothes, lying in a manger. And suddenly there was with the angel a multitude of the heavenly host praising God, and saying, Glory to God in the Highest, and on earth peace, good will toward men. And it came to pass, as the angels were gone away from them into heaven,

[7] Concerning the birth of Jesus in a cave, and the furnishing of the birthplace with the typical animals (ox and ass), compare Jeremias: *Babylonisches im Neuen Testament* (Leipzig, 1905), p. 56; and Preuschen, "*Jesu Geburt in einer Höhle,*" *Zeitschrift für die Neutest. Wissenschaften*, 1902, p. 359.

the shepherds said one to another, Let us now go even unto Bethlehem, and see this thing which has come to pass, which the Lord has made known unto us. And they came with haste, and found Mary, and Joseph, and the babe lying in a manger. And when they had seen it, they made known abroad the saying which was told them concerning this child. And all they that heard wondered at those things which were told them by the shepherds. But Mary kept all these things, and pondered them in her heart. And the shepherds returned, glorifying and praising God for all the things which they had heard and seen, as it was told unto them.

We now continue the account after Matthew, in the second chapter:

Now when Jesus was born in Bethlehem of Judæa in the days of Herod the king, behold, there came *wise men from the east* to Jerusalem, Saying, *Where is he that is born King of the Jews?* for we have seen his star in the east, and are come to worship him. When *Herod the king* had heard these things, he was troubled, and all Jerusalem with him. And when he had gathered all the chief priests and scribes of the people together, he demanded of them where Christ should be born. And they said unto him, In Bethlehem of Judæa: for thus it is written by the prophet, And thou Bethlehem, in the land of Juda, art not the least among the princes of Juda, for out of thee shall come a Governor, that shall rule my people Israel.

Then Herod, when he had privily called the wise men, enquired of them diligently what time the star appeared. And he sent them to Bethlehem, and said, Go and search diligently for the young child; and when ye have found him, bring me word again, that I may come and worship him also. When they had heard the king, they departed; and, lo, the star, which they saw in the east, went before them, till it came and stood over where the young child was. When they saw the star, they rejoiced with exceeding great joy.

And when they were come into the house, they saw the young child with Mary his mother, and fell down, and worshipped him: and when they had opened their treasures, they presented unto him gifts; gold, and frankincense, and myrrh. And being warned of God in a dream, that they should not return to Herod, they departed into their own country another way. And when they were departed, behold, *the angel of the Lord appeareth to Joseph in a dream, saying, Arise, and take the young child and his mother, and flee into Egypt,* and be thou there until I bring thee word: for Herod will seek the young child to destroy him. When he arose, he took the young child and his mother by night, and departed into Egypt: and was there until the death of Herod: that it might be fulfilled which was spoken of the Lord by the prophet, saying, Out of Egypt have I called my son.

Then Herod, when he saw that he was mocked of the wise men, was exceeding wroth, and sent forth, and *slew all the children that were in Bethlehem, and in all the coasts thereof, from two years old and under,* according to the time which he had diligently enquired of the wise men. . . .

But when Herod was dead, behold, an angel of the Lord appeareth in a dream to Joseph in Egypt, Saying, Arise, and take the young child and his mother, and go into the land of Israel: *for they are dead which sought the young child's life.* And he arose, and took the young child and his mother, and came into the land of Israel. But when he heard Archelaus did reign in Judæa in the room of his father Herod, he was afraid to go thither: notwithstanding, being warned of God in a dream, he turned aside into the parts of Galilee: And he came and dwelt in a city called Nazareth: that it might be fulfilled which was spoken by the prophets, He shall be called a Nazarene.[8]

[8] According to recent investigations, the birth history of Christ is said to have the greatest resemblance with the royal Egyptian myth, over five thousand years old, which relates the birth of Amenophis III. Here again recurs the divine prophecy of the birth of a son, to the waiting queen;

Similar birth legends to those of Jesus have also been transmitted of other founders of religions, such as Zoroaster, who is said to have lived about the year 1000 B.C.[9] His mother, Dughda, dreams, *in the sixth month of her pregnancy,* that the wicked and the good spirits are fighting for the embryonic Zoroaster; a monster tears the future Zoroaster from the mother's womb; but a light god fights the monster with his horn of light, re-encloses the embryo in the mother's womb, blows upon Dughda, and she becomes pregnant again. On awakening, she hurries in her fear to a wise dream-interpreter, who is unable to explain the wonderful dream before the end of three days. He then declares that the child she is carrying is destined to become a man of great importance; the dark cloud and the mountain of light signify that she and her son will at first have to undergo numerous trials, through tyrants and other enemies, but at last they will overcome all perils. Dughda at once returns to her home and informs Pourushacpa, her husband, of everything that has happened. Immediately after his birth, the boy was seen to laugh; this was the first miracle through which he drew attention to himself. *The magicians announce the birth of the child as a portent of disaster to the prince of the realm,* Durânsarûn, who betakes himself without delay to the dwelling of Pourushacpa, in order to stab the child. But his hand falls paralyzed, and he must leave with his errand undone; this was the second miracle. Soon after, the wicked demons steal the child from his mother and carry him into the desert, in order to kill him; but Dughda finds the unharmed child, calmly sleeping. This is the third miracle. Later on, Zoroaster was to be trampled upon, in a narrow passage-

---

her fertilization by the breath of heavenly fire; the divine cows, which nurse the newborn child; the homage of the kings; and so forth. In this connection, compare A. Malvert: *Wissenschaft und Religion* (Frankfort, 1904), pp. 49 ff.; also the suggestion of Professor Idleib of Bonn (*Feuilleton* of *Frankfurter Zeitung,* November 8, 1908).

[9] EDITOR'S NOTE: More recent studies have resulted in new dates for many of the ancient heroes. Thus Zoroaster is now generally placed at one or another of several periods between 660 B.C. and 500 B.C., and Amenophis (Amenhotep) III, referred to in the preceding footnote, is now thought to have reigned about 1400 B.C.

way, by a herd of oxen, by command of the king.[1] But the largest of the cattle took the child between his feet and preserved it from harm. This was the fourth miracle. The fifth is merely a repetition of the preceding: what the cattle had refused to do, was to be accomplished by horses. But again the child was protected by a horse from the hoofs of the other horses. Durânsurûn thereupon had the cubs in a wolf's den killed during the absence of the old wolves, and Zoroaster was laid down in their place. But a god closed the jaws of the furious wolves, so that they could not harm the child. Two divine cows arrived instead and presented their udders to the child, giving it to drink. This was the sixth miracle through which Zoroaster's life was preserved.[2]

Related themes are also encountered in the history of Buddha (sixth century before Christ), such as the long sterility of the parents, the dream, the birth of the boy under the open sky, the death of the mother and her substitution by a foster mother, the announcing of the birth to the ruler of the realm, and later on the losing of the boy in the temple.[3]

SIEGFRIED

The old Norse Thidreksaga, as recorded about the year 1250 by an Icelander, according to oral traditions and ancient songs, relates the history of the birth and youth of Siegfried.[4] King Sigmund of Tarlungaland, on his return

[1] Very similar traits are found in the Celtic saga of Habis, as transmitted by Justin. Born as the illegitimate son of a king's daughter, Habis is persecuted in all sorts of ways by his royal grandfather, Gargoris, but is always saved by divine providence, until he is finally recognized by his grandfather and assumes royal sway. As in the Zoroaster legend, there occurs an entire series of the most varied methods of persecution. He is at first exposed, but nursed by wild animals; then he was to be trampled upon by a herd in a narrow path; then he was cast before hungry beasts, but they again nursed him; and finally he is thrown into the sea, but is gently lapped ashore and nursed by a doe, near which he grows up.

[2] Compare Spiegel, op. cit., Vol. I., pp. 688 ff.; also Brodbeck, op. cit.

[3] As in the history of Jesus; compare Luke 2:41–49.

[4] Compare August Rassmann: *Die deutsche Heldensage und ihre Hei-*

from an expedition, banishes his wife Sisibe, the daughter of King Nidung of Hispania, who is *accused* by Count Hartvin, whose advances she has spurned, of having had *illicit relations with a menial.* The king's counselors advise him to mutilate the innocent queen, instead of killing her, and Hartvin is ordered to cut out her tongue in the forest, so as to bring it to the king as a pledge. His companion, Count Hermann, opposes the execution of the cruel command, and proposes to present the tongue of a dog to the king. While the two men are engaged in a violent quarrel, *Sisibe gives birth to a remarkably beautiful boy; she then took a glass vessel, and after having wrapped the boy in linens, she placed him in the glass vessel,* which she carefully closed again and placed beside her. Count Hartvin was conquered in the fight, and in falling kicked the glass vessel, *so that it fell into the river.* When the queen saw this she swooned, and died soon afterwards. Hermann went home, told the king everything, and was banished from the country. *The glass vessel meantime drifted downstream to the sea,* and it was not long before the tide turned. *Then the vessel floated onto a rocky cliff,* and the water ran off so that the place where the vessel was was perfectly dry. The boy inside had grown somewhat, and when the vessel struck the rock, it broke, and the child began to cry. The boy's wailing was heard *by a doe,* which seized him with her lips, and carried him to her litter, *where she nursed him together with her young.* After the child had lived twelve months in the den of the doe, he had grown to the height and strength of other boys four years of age. One day he ran into the forest, where dwelt the wise and skillful *smith Mimir, who had lived for nine years in childless wedlock.* He saw the boy, who was followed by the faithful doe, took him to his home, *and resolved to bring him up as his own son.* He gave him the name of Siegfried. In Mimir's home, Siegfried soon attained an enormous stature and strength, but his wilfulness

---

mat (Hanover, 1857–8), Vol. II, pp. 7; for the sources, see Jiriczek: *Die deutsche Heldensage,* and Piper's introduction to the volume *Die Nibelungen,* in Kürschner's *German National Literature.*

caused Mimir *to get rid of him.* He sent the youth into the forest, where it had been arranged that the dragon Regin, Mimir's brother, was to kill him. But Siegfried conquers the dragon, and kills Mimir. He then proceeds to Brunhild, who names his parents to him.

Similar to the early history of Siegfried is an Austrasian saga that tells of the birth and youth of Wolfdietrich.[5] His mother is likewise accused of *unfaithfulness,* and of intercourse with the devil, by a vassal whom she has repulsed, and who speaks evil of her to the returning king, Hugdietrich of Constantinople.[6]

The king surrenders the child to the faithful Berchtung, who is to kill it, but exposes it instead in the forest, near the water, in the hope that it will fall in of its own accord and thus find its death. But the frolicking child remains unhurt, and even *the wild animals*—lions, bears, and wolves, which come at night to the water—*do not harm it.* The astonished Berchtung resolves to save the boy, and he *surrenders him to a gamekeeper* who, together with his wife, raises him and names him Wolfdietrich.[7]

Three later hero epics may also be quoted in this connection: First, there is the thirteenth-century French saga of Horn, the son of Aluf, who, after having been exposed on the sea, finally reaches the court of King Hunlaf; after numerous adventures, he wins the king's daughter, Rimhilt, for his wife. Secondly, a detail suggestive of Siegfried appears in the saga of the skillful smith Wieland, who, after avenging his foully murdered father, floats down the river Weser, artfully enclosed in the trunk of a tree, and loaded

[5] Compare: *Deutsches Heldenbuch,* Vol. I, Part III (Berlin, 1871), edited by Amelung and Jaenicke, which also contains a second version of the Wolfdietrich saga.

[6] The motive of calumniation of the wife by a rejected suitor, in combination with the exposure and nursing by an animal (doe), forms the nucleus of the story of Genovefa and her son Schmerzenreich, as told, for example, by the Grimm brothers: *Deutsche Sagen* (Berlin, 1818), Vol. II, pp. 280 ff. Here again the faithless calumniator proposes *to drown the countess and her child.* For literary and historical orientation, compare L. Zacher: *Die Historie von der Pfalzgräfin Genovefa* (Koenigsberg, 1860); and B. Seuffert: *Die Legende von der Pfalzgräfin Genovefa* (Wurzburg, 1877). Similar legends of wives suspected of infidelity and punished by exposure are discussed in Chapter xi of my *Inzestmotiv.*

[7] The same accentuation of the animal motif is found in the saga of Schalû, the Hindu wolf-child. Compare Julg, op. cit.

with the tools and treasures of his teachers.[8] Finally, the King Arthur legend contains the commingling of divine and human paternity, the exposure, and the early life with a lowly man.

LOHENGRIN

The widely distributed group of sagas that have been woven around the mythical Knight with the Swan (the old French *Chevalier au cigne*) can be traced back to very ancient Celtic traditions. The following is the version which has been made familiar by Wagner's dramatization of this theme—the story of Lohengrin, the Knight with the Swan, as transmitted by the medieval German epic (modernized by Junghaus) and briefly rendered by the Grimm brothers under the title "Lohengrin in Brabant." [9]

> The Duke of Brabant and Limburg died, without leaving other heirs than a young daughter, Els, or Elsa by name; her he recommended on his deathbed to one of his retainers, Friedrich von Telramund. Friedrich, the intrepid warrior, became emboldened to demand the youthful duchess' hand and lands, under the false claim that she had promised to marry him. She steadfastly refused to do so. Friedrich complained to Emperor Henry I ("the Fowler"), and the verdict was that she must defend herself against him, through some hero, in a so-called divine judgment, in which God would accord the victory to the innocent, and defeat the guilty. As none were ready to take her part, the young duchess prayed ardently to God to save her; and far away in distant Montsalvatsch, in the Council of the Grail, the sound of the bell was heard, showing that there was someone in

[8] EDITOR'S NOTE: Wieland, wonderful blacksmith of the Teutonic gods, appears in the Siegfried epic and in many Scandinavian, German, and English legends. The name is given variously as Volünd, Volunder, Wayland, and (in Scott's *Kenilworth*) as Wayland Smith.

[9] Junghaus: *Lohengrin* (Reclam edition); Grimm brothers, op. cit., Vol. II, p. 306.

urgent need of help. The Grail therefore resolved to despatch as a rescuer, Lohengrin, the son of Parsifal. Just as he was about to place his foot in the stirrup *a swan came floating down the water drawing a skiff behind him.* As soon as Lohengrin set eyes upon the swan, he exclaimed: "Take the steed back to the manger; I shall follow this bird wherever he may lead me." Having faith in God's omnipotence, he took no food with him in the skiff. After they had been afloat five days, the swan dipped his bill in the water, caught a fish, ate one half of it, and gave the other half to the prince to eat. *Thus the knight was fed by the swan.*

Meanwhile Elsa had summoned her chieftains and retainers to a meeting in Antwerp. Precisely on the day of the assembly, a swan was sighted swimming upstream (river Scheldt) and drawing behind him a skiff, in which Lohengrin lay asleep on his shield. The swan promptly came to land at the shore, and the prince was joyfully welcomed. Hardly had his helmet, shield, and sword been taken from the skiff, when the swan at once swam away again. Lohengrin heard of the wrong which had been done to the duchess and willingly consented to become her champion. Elsa then summoned all her relatives and subjects. A place was prepared in Mainz for Lohengrin and Friedrich to fight in the emperor's presence. The hero of the Grail defeated Friedrich, who confessed having lied to the duchess, and was executed with the axe. Elsa was awarded to Lohengrin, they having long been lovers; but he secretly *insisted upon her avoiding all questions as to his ancestry, or whence he had come,* saying that otherwise he would have to leave her instantaneously and she would never see him again.

For some time, the couple lived in peace and happiness. Lohengrin was a wise and mighty ruler over his land, and also served his emperor well in his expeditions against the Huns and the heathen. But it came to pass that one day in throwing the javelin he unhorsed the Duke of Cleve, so that the latter broke an arm. The Duchess of Cleve was angry, and spoke out amongst the women, saying, "Lohengrin may be brave enough, and he seems to be a good Christian; what a pity that his nobility is not of much account *for no one knows whence he has come floating to this land.*" These words pierced the heart of the Duchess of Brabant, and she changed color with emotion. At night, when her spouse was holding her in his arms, she wept, and he said, "What is the matter, Elsa, my own?" She made answer, "The Duchess of Cleve has caused me sore pain." Lohengrin was silent and asked no more. The second night, the same came to pass. But in the third night, Elsa could no longer retain herself, and she spoke: "Lord, do not chide me! *I wish to know, for our children's sake, whence you were born;* for my heart tells me that you are of high rank." When the day broke, Lohengrin declared in public whence he had come, that Parsifal was his father, and God had sent him from the Grail. He then asked for his two children, which the duchess had borne him, kissed them, told them to take good care of his horn and sword, which he would leave behind, and said: "Now, I must be gone." To the duchess he left a little ring which his mother had given him. Then the swan, his friend, came swimming swiftly, with the skiff behind him; the prince stepped in and crossed the water, back to the service of the Grail. Elsa sank down in a faint. The empress resolved *to keep the younger boy Lohengrin, for his father's sake, and to bring him up as her own child.* But the widow wept and mourned the rest of her life for her beloved spouse, who never came back to her.[1]

On inverting the Lohengrin saga in such a way that the end is placed first—on the basis of the rearrangement, or even transmutation of motifs, not uncommonly found in

[1] The Grimm brothers (op. cit., Vol. II., pp. 306 ff.) quote six further versions of the saga of the Knight with the Swan. Certain fairy tales of the Grimm brothers—such as "The Six Swans" (No. 49), "The Twelve Brothers" (No. 9), and the "Seven Ravens" (No. 25), with their parallels and variations, mentioned in the third volume of *Kinder- und Hausmärchen*—also belong to the same mythological cycle. Further material from this cycle may be found in H. Leo: *Beowulf* (Halle, 1839), and in Görre: *Introduction to Lohengrin* (Heidelberg, 1813).

myths—we find the type of saga with which we have now become familiar: The infant Lohengrin, who is identical with his father of the same name, *floats in a vessel upon the sea and is carried ashore by a swan. The empress adopts him as her son, and he becomes a valorous hero.* Having married a noble maiden of the land, he forbids her to inquire as to his origin. When the command is broken he is obliged to reveal his miraculous descent and divine mission, after which the swan carries him back in his skiff to the Grail.

Other versions of the saga of the Knight with the Swan have retained this original arrangement of the motifs, although they appear commingled with elements of fairy tales. The saga of the Knight with the Swan, as related in the Flemish *People's Book,*[2] contains in the beginning the history of the birth of seven children,[3] borne by Beatrix, the wife of King Oriant of Flanders. Matabruna, the wicked mother of the absent king, orders that the children be killed and the queen be given seven puppy dogs in their stead. But the servant contents himself with the exposure of the children, who are found by a hermit named Helias, and are nourished by a goat until they are grown. Beatrix is thrown into a dungeon. Later on, Matabruna learns that the children have been saved; her repeated command to kill them causes her hunter to bring her as a sign of apparent obedience the silver neck chains which the children already wore at the time of their birth. One of the boys—named Helias, after his foster father—alone keeps his chain, and is thereby saved from the fate of his brothers, who are transformed into swans as soon as their chains are removed. Matabruna volunteers to prove the relations of the queen with the dog, and upon her instigation, Beatrix

[2] Grimm: *Deutsche Sagen,* Vol. I., p. 29.

[3] The ancient Lombard tale of the exposure of King Lamissio, related by Paulus Diaconus (L, 15), gives a similar incident. A public woman had thrown her seven newborn infants into a fishpond. King Agelmund passed by and looked curiously at the children, turning them around with his spear. But when one of the children took hold of the spear, the king considered this as a good augury; he ordered this boy to be taken out of the pond, and to be given to a wet nurse. As he had taken him from the pond, which in his language is called *lama,* he named the boy Lamissio. He grew up into a stalwart champion, and after Agelmund's death, became king of the Lombards.

is to be killed, unless a champion arises to defend her. In her need, she prays to God, who sends her son Helias as a rescuer. The brothers are also saved by means of the other chains, except one, whose chain has already been melted down. King Oriant now transfers the rulership to his son Helias, who causes the wicked Matabruna to be burned. One day, Helias sees his brother, the swan, drawing a skiff on the lake surrounding the castle. This he regards as a heavenly sign; he arms himself and mounts the skiff. The swan takes him through rivers and lakes to the place where God has ordained him to go. Next follows the liberation of an innocently accused duchess, in analogy with the Lohengrin saga; and his marriage to her daughter Clarissa, who is forbidden to ask about her husband's ancestry. In the seventh year of their marriage she disobeys and puts the question, after which Helias returns home in the swan's skiff. Finally, his lost brother swan is likewise released.

The characteristic features of the Lohengrin saga—the disappearance of the divine hero in the same mysterious fashion in which he has arrived; the transference of mythical motifs from the life of the older hero to a younger one bearing the same name (a universal process in myth formation)—are likewise embodied in the Anglo-Lombard saga of Sceaf, who reappears in the Prelude to the Anglo-Saxon *Beowulf*, the oldest Teutonic epic.[4] Here, he is called Scyld the Scefung (meaning "son of Sceaf") and his origin as a foundling is referred to. The older legend tells that he received his name because as a very young boy he was cast ashore, as a stranger, asleep in a boat on a sheaf of grain (Anglo-Saxon: *sceaf*). The waves of the sea carried him to the coast of the country he was destined to defend. The inhabitants welcomed his arrival as a miracle, raised him, and later on made him their king, considering him a divine emissary.[5] What was told of the father now is

[4] EDITOR'S NOTE: In Norse mythology, Sceaf (or Scaf) is a descendant of the great god Odin (Wodin, Wotan), father of Thor. In *Beowulf*, as Scyld the Scefing, he is the founder of the Danish royal house of the Scyldings (Skjoldungar)—his son is called in the poem, variously, Scyld, "son of Scyld," and Beowulf. This Beowulf was in turn the father of Beowulf the Great, hero of the Anglo-Saxon epic.

[5] Compare Grimm: *Deutsche Sagen*, Vol. I, p. 306; Vol. III, p. 391; and Leo, op. cit., p. 24.

transferred in the Beowulf epic to his son, also called Scyld.[6] His body is exposed, as he had ordered before his death, surrounded by kingly splendor, upon a ship without a crew, which is sent out into the sea. Thus he vanished in the same mysterious manner in which his father arrived ashore, this trait being accounted for, in analogy with the Lohengrin saga, by the mythical identity of father and son.

[6] *Scaf* is the High German *Schaffing* ("barrel"), which leads Leo (op cit.) to assume, in connection with Scyld's being called Scefing, that he had no father Sceaf or Schaf at all, but was himself the boy cast ashore by the waves, and was named the "son of the barrel" (*Schaffing*). The name Beowulf itself, explained by Grimm as *Bienen-Wolf* ("bee-wolf"), seems to mean originally, according to H. von Wolzogen (translator into German of the Reclam edition of *Beowulf*), *Bärwelf,* namely *Jungbär* ("bear cub" or "bear whelp"), which is suggestive of the saga of the origin of the Guelphs (Grimm: *Deutsche Sagen,* Vol. II, p. 233), where the boys are to be thrown into the water as "whelps."

III *The Interpretation of the Myths*

A CURSORY review of these variegated hero myths forcibly brings out a series of uniformly common features, with a typical groundwork, from which a standard saga, as it were, may be constructed. This schedule corresponds approximately to the ideal human skeleton that is constantly seen, with minor deviations, on transillumination of figures that outwardly differ from one another. The individual traits of the several myths, and especially the apparently crude variations from the prototype, can be entirely elucidated only by myth interpretation.

The standard saga itself may be formulated according to the following outline: The hero is the child of most distinguished parents, usually the son of a king. His origin is preceded by difficulties, such as continence, or prolonged barrenness, or secret intercourse of the parents due to external prohibition or obstacles. During or before the pregnancy, there is a prophecy, in the form of a dream or oracle, cautioning against his birth, and usually threatening danger to the father (or his representative). As a rule, he is surrendered to the water, in a box. He is then saved by animals, or by lowly people (shepherds), and is suckled by a female animal or by an humble woman. After he has grown up, he finds his distinguished parents, in a highly versatile fashion. He takes his revenge on his father, on the one hand, and is acknowledged, on the other. Finally he achieves rank and honors.[1]

Since the normal relations of the hero toward his father and his mother regularly appear impaired in all these

[1] The possibility of further specification of separate items of this outline will be seen from the compilation given by Lessmann at the conclusion of his "*Die Kyrossage in Europe*" (loc. cit.).

myths, as shown by the outline, there is reason to assume that something in the nature of the hero must account for such a disturbance, and motives of this kind are not very difficult to discover. It is readily understood—and may be noted in the modern imitations of the heroic age—that for the hero, who is exposed to envy, jealousy, and calumny to a much higher degree than all others, the descent from his parents often becomes the source of the greatest distress and embarrassment. The old saying that "A prophet is not without honour, save in his own country and in his father's house," has no other meaning but that he whose parents, brothers and sisters, or playmates, are known to us, is not so readily conceded to be a prophet. There seems to be a certain necessity for the prophet to deny his parents; the well-known Meyerbeer opera is based upon the avowal that the prophetic hero is allowed, in favor of his mission, to abandon and repudiate even his tenderly loving mother.

A number of difficulties arise, however, as we proceed to a deeper inquiry into the motives which oblige the hero to sever his family relations. Numerous investigators have emphasized that the understanding of myth formation requires our going back to their ultimate source, namely the individual faculty of imagination.[2] The fact has also been pointed out that this imaginative faculty is found in its active and unchecked exuberance only in childhood. Therefore, the imaginative life of the child should first be studied, in order to facilitate the understanding of the far more complex and also more handicapped mythological and artistic imagination in general.

Meanwhile, the investigation of the juvenile faculty of imagination has hardly commenced, instead of being sufficiently advanced to permit the utilization of the findings for the explanation of the more complicated psychic activities. The reason for this imperfect understanding of the psychic life of the child is traceable to the lack of a suitable instrument, as well as of a reliable avenue, leading into the intricacies of this very delicate and rather inaccessible domain. These juvenile emotions can by no means be

[2] See also Wundt, who interprets the hero psychologically as a projection of human desires and aspirations (op. cit., p. 48).

studied in the normal human adult, and it may actually be charged, in view of certain psychic disturbances, that the normal psychic integrity of normal subjects consists precisely in their having overcome and forgotten their childish vagaries and imaginations; so that the way has become blocked. In children, on the other hand, empirical observation (which as a rule must remain merely superficial) fails in the investigation of psychic processes because we are not as yet enabled to trace all manifestations correctly to their motive forces; so that we are lacking the instrument. There is a certain class of persons, the so-called psychoneurotics, shown by the teachings of Freud to have remained children, in a sense, although otherwise appearing grown-up. These psychoneurotics may be said not to have given up their juvenile psychic life, which on the contrary, in the course of maturity has become strengthened and fixed, instead of modified. In psychoneurotics, the emotions of the child are preserved and exaggerated, thus becoming capable of pathological effects, in which these humble emotions appear broadened and enormously magnified. The fancies of neurotics are, as it were, the uniformly exaggerated reproductions of the childish imaginings. This would point the way to a solution of the problem. Unfortunately, however, access is still much more difficult to establish in these cases than to the child mind. There is only one known instrument which makes this road practicable, namely the psychoanalytic method, which has been developed through the work of Freud. Constant handling of this instrument will clear the observer's vision to such a degree that he will be enabled to discover the identical motive forces, only in delicately shaded manifestations, also in the psychic life of those who do not become neurotics later on.

Professor Freud had the kindness to place at the author's disposal his valuable experience with the psychology of the neuroses; and on this material are based the following comments on the imaginative faculty of the child as well as of the neurotic.

The detachment of the growing individual from the authority of the parents is one of the most necessary, but also one of the most painful achievements of evolution. It is absolutely necessary for this detachment to take place, and it may be assumed that all normal grown individuals have accomplished it to a certain extent. Social progress is essentially based upon this opposition between the two generations. On the other hand, there exists a class of neurotics whose condition indicates that they have failed to solve this very problem. For the young child, the parents are, in the first place, the sole authority and the source of all faith. To resemble them, i.e., the progenitor of the same sex—to grow up like father or mother—this is the most intense and portentous wish of the child's early years. Progressive intellectual development naturally brings it about that the child gradually becomes acquainted with the category to which the parents belong. Other parents become known to the child, who compares these with his own, and thereby becomes justified in doubting the incomparability and uniqueness with which he had invested them. Trifling occurrences in the life of the child, which induce a mood of dissatisfaction, lead up to a criticism of the parents; and the gathering conviction that other parents are preferable in certain ways is utilized for this attitude of the child toward the parents.

From the psychology of the neurosis, we have learned that very intense emotions of sexual rivalry are also involved in this connection. The causative factor evidently is the feeling of being neglected. Opportunities arise only too frequently when the child is neglected, or at least feels himself neglected, when he misses the entire love of the parents, or at least regrets having to share this with the other children of the family. The feeling that one's own inclinations are not entirely reciprocated seeks its relief in the idea—often consciously remembered from very early years—of being a stepchild, or an adopted child. Many persons who have not become neurotics very frequently remember occasions of this kind, when the hostile behavior of the parents was interpreted and reciprocated by them in this fashion, usually under the influence of storybooks. The influence of sex is already evident, in so far as the boy shows a far greater tendency to harbor hostile feelings against his father than his mother, with a much stronger inclination to emancipate himself from the father than from the mother. The imaginative faculty of girls is possibly much less active in this respect.

These consciously remembered psychic emotions of the years of childhood supply the factor which permits the interpretation of the myth. What is not often consciously remembered, but can almost invariably be demonstrated through psychoanalysis, is the next stage in the development of this incipient alienation from the parents, which may be designated by the term "family romance of neurotics." The essence of neurosis, and of all higher mental qualifications, comprises a special activity of the imagination that is primarily manifested in the play of the child, and which from about the period preceding puberty takes hold of the theme of the family relations. A characteristic example of this special imaginative faculty is represented by the familiar *daydreams,*[3] which are continued until long after puberty. Accurate observation of these daydreams shows that they serve for the fulfillment of wishes, for the righting of life, and that they have two essential objects, one erotic, the other of an ambitious nature (usually with the erotic factor concealed therein). About the time in question, the child's imagination is engaged upon the task of getting rid of the parents, who are now despised and are as a rule to be supplanted by others of a higher social rank. The child utilizes an accidental coincidence of actual happenings (meetings with the lord of the manor or the proprietor of the estate, in the country; with the reigning prince, in the city; in the United States, with some great statesman or millionaire). Accidental occurrences of this kind arouse the child's envy, and this finds its expression in fancy fabrics which replace the two parents by others of a higher rank. The technical elaboration of these two imaginings, which of course by this time have become conscious, depends upon the child's adroitness and also upon the material at his disposal. It is likewise a factor

[3] Compare Freud: "Hysterical Fancies, and their Relation to Bisexuality," with references to the literature on this subject. This contribution is contained in the second series of *Sammlung kleiner Schriften zur Neurosenlehre* (Vienna and Leipzig, 1909).

whether these fancies are elaborated with more or less claim to plausibility. This stage is reached at a time when the child is still lacking all knowledge of the sexual conditions of descent.

With the added knowledge of the manifold sexual relations of father and mother—with the child's realization of the fact that the father is always uncertain, whereas the mother is very certain—the family romance undergoes a peculiar restriction: it is satisfied with ennobling the father, while the descent from the mother is no longer questioned, but accepted as an unalterable fact. This second (or sexual) stage of the family romance is moreover supported by another motive, which did not exist in the first (or asexual) stage. Knowledge of sexual matters gives rise to the tendency to picture erotic situations and relations, impelled by the pleasurable emotion of placing the mother, or the subject of the greatest sexual curiosity, in the situation of secret unfaithfulness and clandestine love affairs. In this way the primary or asexual fantasies are raised to the standard of the improved later understanding.

The motive of revenge and retaliation, which was originally to the front, is again evident. These neurotic children are mostly those who were punished by the parents to break them of bad sexual habits, and they take their revenge upon their parents by their imaginings. The younger children of a family are particularly inclined to deprive their predecessors of their advantage by fables of this kind (exactly as in the intrigues of history). Frequently they do not hesitate in crediting the mother with as many love affairs as there are rivals. An interesting variation of this family romance restores the legitimacy of the plotting hero himself, while the other children are disposed of in this way as illegitimate. The family romance may be governed besides by a special interest, all sorts of inclinations being met by its adaptability and variegated character. The little romancer gets rid in this fashion, for example, of the kinship of a sister who may have attracted him sexually.

Those who turn aside with horror from this corruption of the child mind, or perhaps actually contest the possibility of such matters, should note that all these apparently hostile imaginings have not such a very bad significance after all, and that the original affection of the child for his parents is still preserved under their thin disguise. The faithlessness and ingratitude on the part of the child are only apparent, for on investigating in detail the most common of these romantic fancies—the substitution of both parents, or of the father alone, by more exalted personages—the discovery will be made that these new and highborn parents are invested throughout with the qualities which are derived from real memories of the true lowly parents, so that the child does not actually remove his father but exalts him. *The entire endeavor to replace the real father by a more distinguished one is merely the expression of the child's longing for the vanished happy time, when his father still appeared to be the strongest and greatest man, and the mother seemed the dearest and most beautiful woman.* The child turns away from the father, as he now knows him, to the father in whom he believed in his earlier years, his imagination being in truth only the expression of regret for this happy time having passed away. *Thus the overvaluation of the earliest years of childhood again claims its own in these fancies.*[4] An interesting contribution to this subject is furnished by the study of dreams. Dream-interpretation teaches that even in later years, in the dreams of the emperor or the empress, these princely persons stand for the father and the mother.[5] Thus the infantile overvaluation of the parents is still preserved in the dream of the normal adult.

As we proceed to fit the above features into our scheme, we feel justified in analogizing the ego of the child with the hero of the myth, in view of the unanimous tendency of family romances and hero myths; keeping in mind that the myth throughout reveals an endeavor to get rid of the parents, and that the same wish arises in the fantasies of the individual child at the time when he is trying to

[4] For the idealizing of the parents by the children, compare Maeder's comments (*Jahrbuch für Psychoanalyse*, I (1909), p. 152, and *Zentralblatt für Psychoanalyse*, I, p. 51) on Varendonk's essay, "*Les idéals d'enfant.*"

[5] *Interpretation of Dreams.*

establish his personal independence. The ego of the child behaves in this respect like the hero of the myth, and as a matter of fact, the hero should always be interpreted merely as a collective ego, which is equipped with all the excellences. In a similar manner, the hero in personal poetic fiction usually represents the poet himself, or at least one side of his character.

Summarizing the essentials of the hero myth, we find the descent from noble parents, the exposure in a river, and in a box, and the raising by lowly parents; followed in the further evolution of the story by the hero's return to his first parents, with or without punishment meted out to them. It is very evident that the two parent-couples of the myth correspond to the real and the imaginary parent-couple of the romantic fantasy. Closer inspection reveals the psychological identity of the humble and the noble parents, precisely as in the infantile and neurotic fantasies.

In conformity with the overvaluation of the parents in early childhood, the myth begins with the noble parents, exactly like the romantic fantasy, whereas in reality adults soon adapt themselves to the actual conditions. Thus the fantasy of the family romance is simply realized in the myth, with a bold reversal to the actual conditions. The hostility of the father, and the resulting exposure, accentuate the motive which has caused the ego to indulge in the entire fiction. The fictitious romance is the excuse, as it were, for the hostile feelings which the child harbors against his father, and which in this fiction are projected against the father. The exposure in the myth, therefore, is equivalent to the repudiation or nonrecognition in the romantic fantasy. The child simply gets rid of the father in the neurotic romance, while in the myth the father endeavors to lose the child. Rescue and revenge are the natural terminations, as demanded by the essence of the fantasy.

In order to establish the full value of this parallelization, as just sketched in its general outlines, it must enable us to interpret certain constantly recurring details of the myth which seem to require a special explanation. This demand would seem to acquire special importance in view of the fact that no satisfactory explanation of these details is forthcoming in the writings of even the most enthusiastic astral mythologists or natural philosophers. Such details are represented by the regular occurrence of dreams (or oracles) and by the mode of exposure in a box and in the water. These motifs do not at first glance seem to permit a psychological derivation. Fortunately the study of dream-symbolisms permits the elucidation of these elements of the hero myth. The utilization of the same material in the dreams of healthy persons and neurotics[6] indicates that the exposure in the water signifies no more and no less than the *symbolic expression of birth.* The children come out of the water.[7] The basket, box, or receptacle simply means the container, the womb;[8] so that the exposure directly sig-

[6] Compare the "birth dreams" in Freud's *Interpretation of Dreams,* also the examples quoted by the author in *Die Lohengrin Saga* (Vienna, 1911), pp. 27 ff.

[7] In fairy tales, which are adapted to infantile ideation, and especially to the infantile sexual theories (compare Freud in the December, 1908, number of *Sexuelle Probleme*), the birth of man is frequently represented as a lifting of the child from a well or a lake (Thimme, op. cit. p. 157). The story of "Dame Holle's Pond" (Grimm: *Deutsche Sagen,* Vol. I, p. 7) relates that the newborn children come from her well, whence she brings them forth. The same interpretation is apparently expressed in certain national rites; for example, when a Celt had reason to doubt his paternity, he placed the newborn child on a large shield and put it adrift in the nearest river. If the waves carried it ashore, it was considered as legitimate, but if the child drowned, this was proof of the contrary, and the mother was also put to death (see Franz Helbing: *History of Feminine Infidelity*). Additional ethnological material from folklore has been compiled by the author in *Die Lohengrin Saga,* pp. 20 ff.

[8] The "box" in certain myths is represented by the *cave,* which also distinctly symbolizes the womb; aside from statements in Abraham, Ion, and others, a noteworthy case is that of Zeus, who is born in a cave on Mount Ida and nourished by the goat Amalthea, his mother concealing him for fear of her husband, the Titan Cronus. According to Homer's *Iliad* (XVIII, 396 ff.), Hephaestus is also cast into the water by his mother, on account of his lameness, and remains hidden for nine years in a cave surrounded by water. By exchanging the reversal, the birth (the fall into the water) is here plainly represented as the termination of the nine months of the intra-uterine life. More common than the cave birth is the exposure in a box, which is likewise told in the Babylonian Marduk-Tammuz myth, as well as in the Egyptian-Phoenician Osiris-Adonis myth (compare Winckler: *Die Weltanschauung des alten Orients, Ex Oriente Lux,* Vol. I., p. 43; and Jeremias, *Die Babylonisches . . . ,* p. 41). Bacchus, according to Pausanius (III, 24), is also removed from the persecution of the king through exposure in a chest on the Nile, and is saved at the age of three months by a king's daughter, which is remarkably suggestive of the Moses legend A similar story is told of Tennes, the son of Cycnus (Siecke: "*Hermes . . .*" loc. cit., p. 48) and of many others.

The occurrence of the same symbolic representation among the aborig-

nifies the process of birth, although it is represented by its opposite.

Those who object to this representation by opposites should remember how often the dream works with the same mechanism.[9] A confirmation of this interpretation of the exposure, as taken from the common human symbolism, is furnished by the material itself, in the dream by the grandfather (or still more convincingly by the mother herself)[1] in the Ctesian version of Cyrus before his birth; in this dream, so much water flows from the lap of the expectant mother as to inundate all Asia, like an enormous ocean.[2] It is remarkable that in both cases the Chaldeans correctly interpreted these water dreams as birth dreams. In all prob-

---

ines is illustrated by the following examples: Stucken (op. cit.) relates the New Zealand tale of the Polynesian Fire (and Seed) Robber, Manitiki-tiki, who is exposed directly after his birth, his mother throwing him into the sea, wrapped in an apron (chest, box). A similar story is reported by Frobenius (op. cit., p. 379) from the Betsimisaraka of Madagascar, where the child is exposed on the water, is found and raised by a rich, childless woman, but finally resolves to discover his actual parents. According to a report of Bab (*Zeitschrift für Ethnologie,* 1906, p. 281), the wife of the Raja Besurjay was presented with a child floating on a bubble of water-foam (from Singapore).

[9] Compare Freud: *Interpretation of Dreams.*

[1] Abraham (op. cit. pp. 22–3) contains the analysis of a very similar although more complicated birth dream, corresponding to the actual conditions: the dreamer, a young pregnant woman awaiting her delivery, not without fear, dreamed of the birth of her son, and the water appeared directly as the amniotic fluid.

[2] This fantasy of an enormous water is extremely suggestive of the large and widespread group of the flood myths, which actually seem to be no more than the universal expression of the exposure myth. The hero is here represented by humanity at large. The wrathful father is the god; the destruction and the rescue of humanity follow each other in immediate succession. In this parallelization, it is of interest to note that the ark, or pitched house, in which Noah floats upon the water is designated in the Old Testament by the same word (*tebah*) as the receptacle in which the infant Moses is exposed (Jeremias: *The Old Testament . . .*, p. 250). For the motif of the great flood, compare Jeremias, p. 226, and Lessmann, at the close of his treatise, "*Die Kyrossage . . .*," loc. cit., where the flood is described as a possible digression of the exposure in the water. A transition instance is illustrated by the flood saga told by Bader, in his Baden folk legends: When the Sunken Valley was inundated once upon a time by a cloudburst, a little boy was seen floating upon the waters in a cradle, and was miraculously saved by a cat (Gustav Friedrich, op. cit., p. 265).

TRANSLATORS' NOTE: The author has endeavored to explain the psychological relations of the exposure myth, the flood legend, and the devouring myth in his article on the "Overlying Symbols in Dream Awakening, and Their Recurrence in Mythical Ideation"—"*Die Symbolschichtung in Wecktraum und ihre Wiederkehr im mythischen Denken,*" *Jahrbuch für Psychoanalyse,* V (1912).

ability, these dreams themselves are constructed out of the knowledge of a very ancient and universally understood symbolism, with a dim foresight of the relations and connections which are appreciated and presented in Freud's teachings. There he says, in referring to a dream in which the dreamer hurls herself into the dark water of a lake: Dreams of this sort are birth dreams, and their interpretation is accomplished by reversing the fact as communicated in the manifest dream; namely, instead of hurling oneself into the water, it means emerging from the water, i.e., to be born.[3] The justice of this interpretation, which renders the water dream equivalent to the exposure, is again confirmed by the fact that precisely in the Cyrus saga, which contains the water dream, the theme of the exposure in the water is lacking, while only the basket, which does not occur in the dream, plays a part in the exposure.

In this interpretation of the exposure as the birth, we must not let ourselves be disturbed by the discrepancy between the succession of the individual elements of the symbolized materialization and the real birth process. This chronological rearrangement or even reversal has been explained by Freud as due to the general manner in which recollections are elaborated into fantasies; the same material reappears in the fantasies, but in an entirely novel arrangement, and no attention whatsoever is paid to the natural sequence of the acts.[4]

Besides this chronological reversal, the reversal of the contents requires special explanation. The first reason for the representation of the birth by its opposite—the life-threatening exposure in the water—is the accentuation of the parental hostility toward the future hero.[5] The creative

[3] *Interpretation of Dreams.* Compare the same reversal of the meanings in Winckler's interpretation of the etymology of the name of Moses, on page 16, footnote 7.

[4] The same conditions remain in the formation of dreams and in the transformation of hysterical fantasies into seizures. See p. 238 (and the annotation on that page) of Freud's *Traumdeutung* (the German edition of *Interpretation of Dreams*); see also his "*Allgemeines über den hysterischen Anfall*" ("General Remarks on Hysterical Seizures") in *Sammlung kleiner Schriften . . .*, 2d series, pp. 146 ff.

[5] According to a pointed remark of Jung's, this reversal in its further mythical sublimation permits the approximation of the hero's life to the solar cycle. Carl G. Jung: "*Wandlungen und Symbole der Libido,*" *Jahrbuch für Psychoanalyse,* V (1912), p. 253.

influence of this tendency to represent the parents as the first and most powerful opponents of the hero will be appreciated when it is kept in mind that the entire family romance in general owes its origin to the feeling of being neglected—namely, the assumed hostility of the parents. In the myth, this hostility goes so far that the parents refuse to let the child be born, which is precisely the reason of the hero's lament; moreover, the myth plainly reveals the desire to enforce his materialization even against the will of the parents. The vital peril, thus concealed in the representation of birth through exposure, actually exists in the process of birth itself. The overcoming of all these obstacles also expresses the idea that the future hero has actually overcome the greatest difficulties by virtue of his birth, for he has victoriously thwarted all attempts to prevent it.[6] Or another interpretation may be admitted, according to which the youthful hero, foreseeing his destiny to taste more than his share of the bitterness of life, deplores in a pessimistic mood the inimical act which has called him to earth. He accuses the parents, as it were, for having exposed him to the struggle of life, for having allowed him to be born.[7] The refusal to let the son be born, which belongs especially to the father, is frequently concealed by the contrast motif, the wish for a child (as in Oedipus, Perseus, and others), while the hostile attitude toward the future successor on the throne and in the kingdom is projected to the outside—it is attributed to an oracular verdict, which is thereby revealed as the substitute of the ominous dream, or better, as the equivalent of its interpretation.

[6] The second item of the schedule here enters into consideration: the voluntary continence or prolonged separation of the parents, which naturally induces the miraculous conception and virgin birth of the mother. The abortion fantasies, which are especially distinct in the Zoroaster legend, also belong under this heading.

[7] The comparison of birth with a shipwreck, by the Roman poet Lucretius, seems to be in perfect harmony with this symbolism: "Behold the infant: Like a shipwrecked sailor, cast ashore by the fury of the billows, the poor child lies naked on the ground, bereft of all means for existence, after Nature has dragged him in pain from the mother's womb. With plaintive wailing he filleth the place of his birth, and he is right, for many evils await him in life" (*De Natura Rerum,* V, 222–7). Similarly, the first version of Schiller's *Robbers,* in speaking of Nature, says: "She endowed us with the spirit of invention, when she exposed us naked and helpless on the shore of the great Ocean, the World. Let him swim who may, and let the clumsy perish!"

From another point of view, however, the family romance shows that the fantasies of the child, although apparently estranging the parents, have nothing else to say concerning them besides their confirmation as the real parents. The exposure myth, translated with the assistance of symbolism, likewise contains nothing but the assurance: this is my mother, who has borne me at the command of the father. But on account of the tendency of the myth, and the resulting transference of the hostile attitude from the child to the parents, this assurance of the real parentage can only be expressed as the repudiation of such parentage.

On closer inspection, it is noteworthy in the first place that the hostile attitude of the hero toward his parents concerns especially the father. Usually, as in the myth of Oedipus, Paris, and others, the royal father receives a prophecy of some disaster, threatening him through the expected son; then it is the father who causes the exposure of the boy and who pursues and menaces him in all sorts of ways after his unlooked-for rescue, but finally succumbs to his son, according to the prophecy. In order to understand this trait, which at first may appear somewhat startling, it is not necessary to explore the heavens for some process into which this trait might be laboriously fitted. Looking with open eyes and unprejudiced minds at the relations between parents and children, or between brothers, as these exist in reality,[8] a certain tension is frequently, if not regularly revealed between father and son, or still more distinctly a competition between brothers. Although this tension may not be obvious and permanent, it is lurking in the sphere of the unconscious, as it were, with periodic eruptions. Erotic factors are especially apt to be involved, and as a rule the deepest, generally unconscious root of the dislike of the son for the father, or of two brothers for each other, is related to be competition for the tender devotion and love of the mother. The Oedipus myth shows plainly, only in grosser dimensions, the accuracy of this interpretation, for the parricide is here followed by

[8] Compare the representation of this relation and its psychic consequences, in Freud's *Interpretation of Dreams*.

the incest with the mother. This erotic relation with the mother, which predominates in other mythological cycles, is relegated to the background in the myths of the birth of the hero, while the opposition against the father is more strongly accentuated.[9]

The fact that this infantile rebellion against the father is apparently provoked in the birth myths by the hostile behavior of the father, is due to a reversal of the relation, known as *projection*, which is brought about by very peculiar characteristics of the myth-forming psychic activity. The projection mechanism—which also bore its part in the reinterpretation of the birth act, as well as certain other characteristics of myth formation, to be discussed presently —necessitates the uniform characterization of the myth as a *paranoid* structure, in view of its resemblance to peculiar processes in the mechanism of certain psychic disturbances. Intimately connected with the paranoid character is the property of separating or dissociating what is fused in the imagination. This process, as illustrated by the two parent-couples, provides the foundation for the myth formation, and together with the projection mechanism supplies the key to the understanding of an entire series of otherwise inexplicable configurations of the myth. As the motor power for this projection of the hero's hostile attitude onto

[9] Some myths convey the impression that the love relation with the mother had been removed, as being too objectionable to the consciousness of certain periods or peoples. Traces of this suppression are still evident in a comparison of different myths or different versions of the same myth. For example, in the version of Herodotus, Cyrus is a son of the daughter of Astyages; but according to the report of Ctesias, he makes the daughter of Astyages, whom he conquers, his wife, and kills her husband (who in the rendering of Herodotus is his father). See Hüsing, op. cit. Also a comparison of the saga of Darab with the very similar legend of St. Gregory serves to show that in the Darab story the incest with the mother which otherwise precedes the recognition of the son is simply omitted; here, on the contrary, the recognition prevents the incest. This attenuation may be studied in the nascent state, as it were, in the myth of Telephus, where the hero is married to his mother but recognizes her before the consummation of the incest. The fairy-tale-like setting of the Tristan legend, which makes Isolde draw the little Tristan from the water (i.e., give him birth), thereby suggests the fundamental incest theme, which is likewise manifested in the adultery with the wife of the uncle.

TRANSLATORS' NOTE: The reader is referred to *Inzestmotiv,* in which the incest theme, which is here merely mentioned, is discussed in detail, picking up the many threads which lead to this theme, but which have been dropped at the present time.

the father, there stands revealed the wish for its justification, arising from the troublesome realization of these feelings against the father. The displacement process that begins with the projection of the troublesome sensation is still further continued, however, and with the assistance of the mechanism of separation or dissociation, it has found a different expression of its gradual progress in very characteristic forms of the hero myth. In the original psychologic setting, the father is still identical with the king, the tyrannical persecutor. The first attenuation of this relation is manifested in those myths in which the separation of the tyrannical persecutor from the real father is already attempted, but not yet entirely accomplished, the former being still related to the hero, usually as his grandfather, for example in the Cyrus myth with all its versions, and in the majority of all hero myths in general. In the separation of the father's part from that of the king, this type signifies the first return step of the descent fantasy toward the actual conditions, and accordingly the hero's father appears in this type mostly as a lowly man (see Cyrus, Gilgamesh, and others). The hero thus arrives again at an approach toward his parents, the establishment of a certain kinship, which finds its expression in the fact that not only the hero himself, but also his father and his mother represent objects of the tyrant's persecution. The hero in this way acquires a more intimate connection with the mother—they are often exposed together (Perseus, Telephus, Feridun)—who is nearer to him on account of the erotic relation; while the renouncement of his hatred against the father here attains the expression of its most forcible reaction,[1] for the hero henceforth appears, as in the Hamlet saga, not as the persecutor of his father (or grandfather) but as the avenger of the persecuted father. This involves a deeper relation of the Hamlet saga with the Persian story of Kaikhosrav, where the hero likewise appears as the avenger of his murdered father (compare Feridun and others).

[1] The mechanism of this defense is discussed in Freud's "Hamlet Analysis," in his *Interpretation of Dreams*. Ernest Jones has also discussed this in an article (1911) in the *American Journal of Psychology*.

The person of the grandfather himself, who in certain sagas appears replaced by other relatives (the uncle, in the Hamlet saga), also possesses a deeper meaning.[2] The myth complex of the incest with the mother—and the related revolt against the father—is here combined with the second great complex, which has for its contents the erotic relations between father and daughter. Under this heading belongs, besides other widely ramified groups of sagas,[3] the story which is told in countless versions of a *newborn boy,* of whom it is *prophesied* that he is to become the *son-in-law* and *heir* of a certain ruler or potentate, and who finally does so in spite of all persecutions (exposure and so forth) on the part of the latter.[4] The father who refuses to give his daughter to any of her suitors, or who attaches to the winning of the daughter certain conditions difficult of fulfillment, does this because he really begrudges her to all others, for when all is told he wishes to possess her himself. He locks her up in some inaccessible spot, so as to safeguard her virginity (Perseus, Gilgamesh, Telephus, Romulus), and when his command is disobeyed he pursues the daughter and her offspring with insatiable hatred. However, the unconscious sexual motives of his hostile attitude, which is later on avenged by his grandson, render it evident that again the hero kills in him simply the man who is trying to rob him of the love of his mother; namely, the father.

Another attempt at a reversal to a more original type consists in the following theme: The return to the lowly father, which has been brought about through the separation of the father's rôle from that of the king, is again nullified through the lowly father's secondary elevation to the rank of a god, as in Perseus and the other sons of virgin mothers (Karna, Ion, Romulus, Jesus). The secondary character of this godly paternity is especially evident in those myths where the virgin who has been impregnated by

[2] In regard to further meanings of the grandfather, see Freud's "Analysis of a Phobia in a Five-Year-Old Boy," *Jahrbuch für Psychoanalyse,* I (1909); also the contributions of Jones, Abraham, and Ferenczi in the March, 1913, issue of *Internationale Zeitschrift für ärtzliche Psychoanalyse.*

[3] See Chapter xi, *Inzestmotiv.*

[4] Detailed literary references concerning the wide distribution of this story are found in R. Köhler: *Kleiner Schriften,* Vol. II, p. 357.

divine conception later on marries a mortal (Jesus, Karna, Ion), who then appears as the real father, while the god as the father represents merely the most exalted childish idea of the magnitude, power, and perfection of the father.[5] At the same time, these myths strictly insist upon the motif of the virginity of the mother, which elsewhere is merely hinted at. The first impetus is perhaps supplied by the transcendental tendency, necessitated through the introduction of the god. At the same time, the birth from the virgin is the most abrupt repudiation of the father, the consummation of the entire myth, as illustrated by the Sargon legend, which does not admit any father besides the vestal mother.

The last stage of this progressive attenuation of the hostile relation to the father is represented by that form of the myth in which the person of the royal persecutor not only appears entirely detached from that of the father, but has even lost the remotest kinship with the hero's family, which he opposes in the most hostile manner, as its enemy (in Feridun, Abraham, King Herod against Jesus, and others). Although of his original threefold character as the father, the king, and the persecutor, he retains only the part of the royal persecutor or the tyrant, the entire plan of the myth conveys the impression that nothing had been changed—as if the designation "father" had been simply replaced by the term "tyrant." This interpretation of the father as a "tyrant," which is typical of the infantile ideation,[6] will be found later on to possess the greatest importance for the interpretation of certain abnormal constellations of this complex.

The prototype of this identification of the king with the father, which regularly recurs also in the dreams of adults,

[5] A similar identification of the father with God ("Heavenly Father," etc.) occurs, according to Freud, with the same regularity in the fantasies of normal and pathological psychic activity as the identification of the emperor with the father. It is also noteworthy in this connection that almost all peoples derive their origin from their god (Abraham, op. cit.).

[6] An amusing example of unconscious humor in children recently appeared in the daily press: A politician had explained to his little son that a tyrant is a man who forces others to do what he commands, without heeding their wishes in the matter. "Well," said the child, "then you and Mama are also tyrants!"

presumably is the origin of royalty from the patriarchate in the family, which is still attested by the use of identical words for king and father, in the Indo-Germanic languages (compare the German *Landesvater*, "father of his country," = king).[7] The reversal of the family romance to actual conditions is almost entirely accomplished in this type of myth. The lowly parents are acknowledged with a frankness which seems to be directly contradictory to the tendency of the entire myth.

Precisely this revelation of the real conditions, which hitherto had to be left to the interpretation, enables us to prove the accuracy of the latter from the material itself. The biblical legend of Moses has been selected as especially well adapted to this purpose.

Briefly summarizing the outcome of the previous interpretation-mechanism, to make matters plainer, we find the two parent-couples to be identical, after their splitting into the personalities of the father and the tyrannical persecutor has been connected—the highborn parents are the echo, as it were, of the exaggerated notions the child originally harbored concerning his parents. The Moses legend actually shows the parents of the hero divested of all prominent attributes; they are simple people, devotedly attached to the child, and incapable of harming him. Meanwhile, the assertion of tender feelings for the child is a confirmation, here as well as everywhere, of the bodily parentage (compare the overseer in the Gilgamesh legend, the charioteer in the story of Karna, the fisherman in the Perseus myth, etc.). The amicable utilization of the exposure motif, which occurs in this type of myth, is referable to such a relationship. The child is surrendered in a basket to the water, but not with the object of killing him (as, for example, the hostile exposure of Oedipus and many other heroes), but for the purpose of saving him (compare also Abraham's early history, page 17). The danger-fraught warning to the exalted father becomes a hopeful prophecy for the lowly father—compare, in the birth story of Jesus, the oracle for Herod and Joseph's dream)—entirely cor-

[7] See Max Müller, op. cit., pp. 20 ff. Concerning the various psychological contingencies of this setting, compare pp. 83 ff. of *Inzestmotiv*.

responding to the expectations placed by most parents in the career of their offspring.

Retaining from the original tendency of the romance the fact that Pharaoh's daughter drew the child from the water, i.e., gave it birth, the outcome is the familiar theme (grandfather type) of the king whose daughter is to bear a son, but who, on being warned by the ill-omened interpretation of a dream, resolves to kill his forthcoming grandson. The handmaiden of his daughter (who in the biblical story draws the box from the water at the behest of the princess) is charged by the king with the exposure of the newborn child in a box, in the waters of the river Nile, that it may perish (the exposure motif, from the viewpoint of the highborn parents, here appearing in its original disastrous significance). The box with the child is then found by lowly people, and the poor woman raises the child (as his wet nurse); when he is grown up, he is recognized by the princess as her son. Just as in the prototype, the fantasy concludes with the recognition by the highborn parents.

If the Moses legend were placed before us in this more original form, as we have reconstructed it from the existing material,[8] the sum of this interpretation-mechanism would be approximately what is told in the myth as it is actually transmitted—namely, that his true mother was not a princess, but the poor woman who was introduced as his nurse, her husband being his father.

This interpretation is offered as the tradition, in the reconverted myth; and the fact that this tracing of the progressive mutation furnishes the familiar type of hero myth, is the proof of the correctness of our interpretation.

It has thus been our good fortune to show the full accuracy of our interpretative technique through the material itself, and it is now time to demonstrate the tenability of the general viewpoint upon which this entire technique is

[8] Compare Eduard Meyer: "*Die Mosessagen und die Lewiten,*" in *Sitzungsberichte der königlich preussischen Akademie der Wissenschaften*, XXXI (1905), p. 640: "Presumably Moses was originally the son of the tyrant's daughter (who is now his foster mother), and probably of divine origin." The subsequent elaboration into the present form is probably referable to national motives.

founded. Hitherto, the results of our interpretation have created the appearance that the entire myth formation started from the hero himself, that is, from the youthful hero. At the start we took this attitude in analogizing the hero of the myth with the ego of the child. Now we find ourselves confronted with the obligation to harmonize these assumptions and conclusions with the other conceptions of myth formation, which they seem to contradict directly.

The myths are certainly not constructed by the hero, least of all by the child hero, but they have long been known to be the product of a people of adults. The impetus is evidently supplied by the popular amazement at the apparition of the hero, whose extraordinary life history the people can only imagine as ushered in by a wonderful infancy. This extraordinary childhood of the hero, however, is constructed by the individual myth-makers—to whom the indefinite idea of the folk-mind must be ultimately traced—from the consciousness of their own infancy. In investing the hero with their own infantile history, they identify themselves with him, as it were, claiming to have been similar heroes in their own personality. The true hero of the romance is, therefore, the ego, which finds itself in the hero, by reverting to the time when the ego was itself a hero, through its first heroic act, i.e., the revolt against the father. The ego can only find its own heroism in the days of infancy, and it is therefore obliged to invest the hero with its own revolt, crediting him with the features which made the ego a hero. This object is achieved with infantile motives and materials, in reverting to the infantile romance and transferring it to the hero. Myths are, therefore, created by adults, by means of retrograde childhood fantasies,[9] the hero being credited with the myth-maker's personal infantile history. Meanwhile, the tendency of this entire process is the excuse of the individual units

[9] This idea, which is derived from the knowledge of the neurotic fantasy and symptom construction, was applied by Professor Freud to the interpretation of the romantic and mythical work of poetic imagination, in a lecture entitled "Der Dichter und das Phantasieren" ("Poets and Imaginings"), reprinted in *Sammlung kleiner Schriften* . . . , 2d series.

of the people for their own infantile revolt against the father.

Besides the excuse of the hero for his rebellion, the myth therefore contains also the excuse of the individual for his revolt against the father. This revolt has burdened him since his childhood, as he has failed to become a hero. He is now enabled to excuse himself by emphasizing that the father has given him grounds for his hostility. The affectionate feeling for the father is also manifested in the same fiction, as has been shown above. These myths have therefore sprung from two opposite motives, both of which are subordinate to the motive of vindication of the individual through the hero: on the one hand the motive of affection and gratitude toward the parents; and on the other hand, the motive of the revolt against the father. It is not stated outright in these myths, however, that the conflict with the father arises from the sexual rivalry for the mother, but is apparently suggested that this conflict dates back primarily to the concealment of the sexual processes (at childbirth), which in this way became an enigma for the child. This enigma finds its temporary and symbolical solution in the infantile sexual theory of the basket and the water.[1]

The profound participation of the incest motif in myth formation is discussed in the author's special investigation of the Lohengrin saga, which belongs to the myth of the birth of the hero. The cyclic character of the Lohengrin saga is referred by him to the *fantasy of being one's own son*, as revealed by Freud.[2] This accounts for the identity of father and son, in certain myths, and for the repetition of their careers; it explains the fact that the hero is sometimes not exposed until he has reached maturity, and also the intimate connection between birth and death in the exposure motif.[3] Jung, who regards the typical fate of the hero as the portrayal of the human libido and its typical

[1] For ethno-psychologic parallels and other infantile sexual theories which throw some light upon the supplementary myth of the hero's procreation, compare the author's treatise in *Zentralblatt für Psychoanalyse*, II (1911), pp. 392–425.

[2] Rank: *Die Lohengrin Saga*.

[3] Concerning the water as the "water of death," compare especially ibid., Chapter iv.

vicissitudes, has made this theme the pivot of his interpretation, as the fantasy of being born again, to which the incest motif is subordinated. Not only the birth of the hero, which takes place under peculiar symbolic circumstances, but also the motif of the two mothers of the hero, are explained by Jung through the birth of the hero taking place under the mysterious ceremonials of a rebirth from the mother consort.[4]

Having thus outlined the contents of the birth myth of the hero it still remains for us to point out certain complications within the birth myth itself, which have been explained on the basis of its paranoid character, as "splits" of the personality of the royal father and persecutor. In some myths, however, and especially in the fairy tales that belong to this group,[5] the multiplication of mythical personages—and with them, of course, the multiplication of motifs, or even of entire stories—are carried so far that sometimes the original features are altogether overgrown by these addenda. The multiplication is so variegated and so exuberantly developed that the mechanism of the analysis no longer does it justice. Moreover, the new personalities here do not show the same independence, as it were, as the new personalities created by splitting, but they rather present the characteristics of a copy, a duplicate, or a "double," which is the proper mythological term. An apparently very complicated example, namely, Herodotus' version of the Cyrus saga, illustrates that there doubles are not inserted purely for ornamentation, or to give a semblance of historical veracity, but that they are insolubly connected with myth formation and its tendency. Also, in the Cyrus legend, as in the other myths, a confrontation

[4] Loc. cit., p. 356.

[5] The fairy tales, which have been left out of consideration in the context, precisely on account of these complications, include especially: "The Devil with the Three Golden Hairs" (Grimm, No. 29), and the very similar "Saga of Emperor Henry III" (Grimm, *Deutsche Sagen*, Vol. II, p. 177); "Water-Peter," with numerous variations (Grimm, Vol. III, p. 103); "Fundevogel," No. 51; "The Three Birdies" (No. 96); "The King of the Golden Mountain" (No. 92), with its parallels; as well as some foreign fairy tales, which are quoted by Bauer, at the end of his article (loc. cit.). Compare also, in Hahn: *Greek and Albanese Fairy Tales* (Leipzig, 1864), the review of the exposure stories and myths, especially No. 20 and No. 69.

occurs. The royal grandfather, Astyages, and his daughter, with her husband, are confronted by the cattle herder and his wife. A checkered gathering of other personalities which move around them, are readily grouped at sight: Between the highborn parent-couple and their child stand the administrator Harpagos with his wife and his son, and the noble Artembares with his legitimate offspring. Our trained sense for the peculiarities of myth structure recognizes at once the doubles of the parents in the intermediate parent-couples and all the participants are seen to be identical personalities of the parents and their child; this interpretation being suggested by certain features of the myth itself. Harpagos receives the child from the king, to expose it; he therefore acts precisely like the royal father and remains true to his fictitious paternal part in his reluctance to kill the child himself—because it is related to him—but he delivers it instead to the herder Mithradates, who is thus again identified with Harpagos. The noble Artembares, whose son Cyrus causes to be whipped, is also identified with Harpagos; for when Artembares with his whipped boy stands before the king, to demand retribution, Harpagos at once is likewise seen standing before the king, to defend himself, and he also is obliged to present his son to the king. Thus Artembares himself plays an episodal part as the hero's father, and this is fully confirmed by the Ctesian version, which tells us that the nobleman who adopted the herder's son, Cyrus, as his own son, was named Artembares.

Even more distinct than the identity of the different fathers is that of their children, which of course serves to confirm the identity of the fathers. In the first place, and this would seem to be conclusive, *the children are all of the same age*—not only the son of the princess, and the child of the herder, who are born at the same time; but Herodotus specially emphasizes that Cyrus played the game of "Kings" (in which he caused the son of Artembares to be whipped) with boys of the same age as Cyrus. He also points out, perhaps intentionally, that the *son of Harpagos,* destined to become the playmate of Cyrus, whom the king had recognized, was likewise apparently of the same age as

Cyrus. Furthermore, the remains of this boy are placed before his father, Harpagos, in a basket; it was also a basket in which the newborn Cyrus was to have been exposed, and this actually happened to his substitute, the herder's son, whose identity with Cyrus is obvious and tangible in the version of Justin given on page 36. In this report, Cyrus is actually exchanged with the *living* child of the herders; but this paradoxical parental feeling is reconciled by the consciousness that in reality nothing at all has been altered by this exchange. It appears more intelligible, of course, that the herder's wife should wish to raise the living child of the king, instead of her own *stillborn* boy, as in the Herodotus version (page 30); but here the identity of the boys is again evident, for just as the herder's son suffered death instead of Cyrus in the past, twelve years later the son of Harpagos (also in a basket) is killed directly for Cyrus, whom Harpagos had allowed to live.[6]

The impression is thereby conveyed that all the multiplications of Cyrus, after having been created for a certain purpose, are again removed, as disturbing elements, once this purpose has been fulfilled. This purpose is undoubtedly the exalting tendency that is inherent in the family romance. The hero, in the various duplications of himself and his parents, ascends the social scale from the herder Mithradates, by way of the noble Artembares (who is high in the king's favor), and of the first administrator, Harpagos (who is personally related to the king)—until he has himself become a prince; so his career is shown in the Ctesian version, where Cyrus advances from the herder's son to the king's administrator.[7] In this way, he con-

[6] A connection is here supplied with the theme of the twins, in which we seem to recognize the two boys born at the same time—one of which dies for the sake of the other, be it directly after birth, or later—and whose parents appear divided in our myths into two or more parent-couples. Concerning the probable significance of this shadowy twin brother as the afterbirth, compare the author's discussion in his *Inzestmotiv* (pp. 459 ff).

[7] The early history of Sigurd, as it is related in the Völsungasaga (compare Rassmann, op. cit., Vol. I, p. 99), closely resembles the Ctesian version of the Cyrus saga, giving us the tradition of another hero's wonderful career, together with its rational rearrangement. For particulars, see Bauer, loc. cit., p. 554. Also the biblical history of Joseph (Exodus 37–50)—with the exposure, the animal sacrifice, the dreams, the sketchy brethren, and the fabulous career of this hero—seems to belong to this type of myth.

stantly removes, as it were, the last traces of his ascent, the lower Cyrus being discarded after absolving the different stages of his career.[8]

This complicated myth with its promiscuous array of personages is thus simplified and reduced to three actors —the hero and his parents. Entirely similar conditions prevail in regard to the "cast" of many other myths. For example, the duplication may concern the daughter, as in the Moses myth, in which the princess-mother (in order to establish the identity of the two families)[9] appears among the poor people as the daughter Miriam, who is merely a split of the mother, the latter appearing divided into the princess and the poor woman. In case the duplication concerns the father, his doubles appear as a rule in the part of relatives, more particularly as his brothers, as for example in the Hamlet saga, in distinction from the foreign personages created by the analysis. In a similar way, the grandfather, who is taking the place of the father, may also appear complemented by a brother, who is the hero's granduncle, and as such his opponent, as in the myths of Romulus, Perseus, and others. Other duplications, in ap-

[8] In order to avoid misunderstandings, it appears necessary to emphasize at this point the historical nucleus of certain hero myths. Cyrus, as is shown by the inscriptions which have been discovered (compare Duncker, op. cit., p. 289; and Bauer, loc. cit., p. 498) was descended from an old hereditary royal house. It could not be the object of the myth to elevate the descent of Cyrus, nor must the above interpretation be regarded as an attempt to establish a lowly descent. Similar conditions prevail in the case of Sargon, whose royal father is also known (compare Jeremias: *The Old Testament . . .*, p. 410 *n.*). Nevertheless a historian writes about Sargon as follows (Ungnad: "*Die Anfänge der Staatenbildung in Babylonien,*" *Deutsche Rundschau,* July 1905): "He was evidently of noble descent, or no such saga could have been woven about his birth and his youth." It would be a gross error to consider our interpretation as an argument in this sense. Again, the apparent contradiction which might be held up against our explanation, under another mode of interpretation, becomes the proof of its correctness, through the reflection that it is not the hero but the average man who makes the myth and wishes to vindicate himself in it. The people imagine the hero in this manner, investing him with their own infantile fantasies, irrespective of their actual compatibility or incompatibility with historical facts. This also serves to explain the transference of the typical motifs, be it to several generations of the same hero-family, or be it to historical personalities in general (concerning Caesar, Augustus and others, compare Usener, *Rhein. Mus.*, LV, p. 271).

[9] This identification of the families is carried through to the minutest detail in certain myths, as for example in the Oedipus myth, where one royal couple is offset by another, and where even the herdsman who receives the infant for exposure has his exact counterpart in the herdsman to whom he entrusts the rescue of the boy.

parently complicated mythological structures—as for ex ample in Kaikhosrav, Feridun, and others—are easily recognized when envisaged from this angle.

The duplication of the fathers (or the grandfathers) by a brother may be continued in the next generation, and concern the hero himself, thus leading to the *brother myths,* which can only be hinted at in connection with the present theme. The prototypes of the boy (who in the Cyrus saga vanish into thin air after they have served their purpose, the exaltation of the hero's descent), if they were to assume a vitality of their own, would come to confront the hero as competitors with equal rights, namely, as his brothers. The original sequence is probably better preserved through the interpretation of the hero's strange doubles as shadowy brothers who, like the twin brother, must die for the hero's sake. Not only the father (who is in the way of the maturing son) is removed, but also the interfering competitor (the brother), in a naïve realization of the childish fantasies, for the simple reason that the hero does not want a family.

The complications of the hero legends with other myth cycles include (besides the myth of the hostile brothers, which has already been disposed of) also the actual incest myth, such as forms the nucleus of the Oedipus saga. The mother, and her relation to the hero, appear relegated to the background in the myth of the birth of the hero. But there is another conspicuous motif: the lowly mother is so often represented by an animal. This motif of the helpful animals[1] belongs in part to a series of foreign elements, the explanation of which would far exceed the scope of this essay.[2]

The animal motif may be fitted into the sequence of

[1] Compare Gubernatis: *Zoological Mythology* (London, 1872); and Hartmann: *Die Tiere in der indogermanischen Mythologie* (Leipzig, 1874). Concerning the significance of animals in exposure myths, see also the contributions by Bauer (loc. cit., pp. 574 ff.); Goldziher (op. cit., p. 274); and Liebrecht: *Zur Volkskunde, Romulus und die Welfen* (Heilbronn, 1879).

[2] Compare Freud's article on the infantile recurrence of totemism, in *Imago*, Vol. II (1913). Concerning the totemistic foundation of the Roman she-wolf, see Jones's writings on nightmares (*Älptraume*). The woodpecker of the Romulus saga was discussed by Jung (loc. cit., pp. 382 ff.).

our interpretation, on the basis of the following reflections. Much as the projection onto the father justifies the hostile attitude on the part of the son, so the lowering of the mother into an animal is likewise meant to vindicate the ingratitude of the son who denies her. As the persecuting king is detached from the father, so the exclusive rôle of wet nurse assigned to the mother—in this substitution by an animal—goes back to the separation of the mother into the parts of the child-bearer and the suckler. This cleavage is again subservient to the exalting tendency, in so far as the childbearing part is reserved for the highborn mother, whereas the lowly woman, who cannot be eradicated from the early history, must content herself with the function of nurse. Animals are especially appropriate substitutes, because the sexual processes are here plainly evident also to the child, while the concealment of these processes is presumably the root of the childish revolt against the parents. The exposure in the box and in the water asexualizes the birth process, as it were, in a childlike fashion; the children are fished out of the water by the stork, who takes them to the parents in a basket.[3] The animal fable improves upon this idea, by emphasizing the similarity between human birth and animal birth.

This introduction of the motif may possibly be interpreted from the parodistic point of view if we assume that the child accepts the story of the stork from his parents, feigning ignorance, but adding superciliously: If an ani-

[3] The stork is known also in mythology as the bringer of children. Siecke (*Liebesgeschichten des Himmels*, p. 26) points out the swan as the player of this part in certain regions and countries. The rescue and further protection of the hero by a bird is not uncommon; compare Gilgamesh, Zal, and Cycnus (who is exposed by his mother near the sea and is nourished by a swan, while his son Tennes floats in a chest upon the water). The interpretation of the leading motif of the Lohengrin saga also enters into present consideration. Its most important motifs belong to this mythical cycle: Lohengrin floats in a skiff upon the water, and is brought ashore by a swan. No one may ask whence he has come; the sexual mystery of the origin of man must not be revealed, but it is replaced by the suggestion of the stork fable; the children are fished from the water by the swan and are taken to the parents in a box. Corresponding to the prohibition of all inquiries in the Lohengrin saga, we find in other myths (for example, the Oedipus myth), a *command to investigate*, or a riddle that must be *solved*. For the psychological significance of the stork fable, compare Freud: *Infantile Sexual Theories*. Concerning the hero myth, see also the author's *Die Lohengrin Saga*.

mal has brought me, it may also have nursed me.[4]

When all is said and done, however, and when the cleavage is followed back, the separation of the childbearer from the suckler—which really endeavors to remove the bodily mother entirely, by means of her substitution through an animal or a strange nurse—does not express anything beyond the fact: The woman who has suckled me is my mother. This statement is found directly symbolized in the Moses legend, the retrogressive character of which we have already studied; for precisely the woman who is his own mother is chosen to be his nurse (similarly also in the myth of Hercules, and the Egyptian-Phoenician Osiris-Adonis myth—where Osiris, encased in a chest, floats down the river and is finally found under the name Adonis, by Isis, who is installed by Queen Astarte as the nurse of her own son).[5]

Only a brief reference can here be made to other motifs which seem to be more loosely related to the entire myth. Such themes include that of playing the fool, which is suggested in animal fables as the universal childish attitude toward grownups. They include, furthermore, the physical defects of certain heroes (Zal, Oedipus, Hephaestus), which are meant perhaps to serve for the vindication of individual imperfections, in such a way that the reproaches of the father for possible defects or shortcomings are incorporated into the myth, with the appropriate accentuation—the hero being endowed with the same weakness which burdens the self-respect of the individual.

This explanation of the psychological significance of the myth of the birth of the hero would not be complete without emphasizing its relations to certain mental diseases. Even readers without psychiatric training—or these perhaps more than any others—must have been struck with

[4] Compare Freud: "Analysis of a Phobia in a Five-Year-Old Boy," loc. cit.

[5] Usener (*Stoff des griechischen Epos,* p. 53) says that the controversy between the earlier and the later Greek sagas concerning the mother of a divinity is usually reconciled by the formula that the mother of the general Greek saga is recognized as such, while the mother of the local tradition is lowered to the rank of a nurse. Thero may therefore be unhesitatingly regarded as the mother, not merely the nurse, of the god Ares.

these relations. As a matter of fact, the hero myths are equivalent in many essential features to the delusional ideas of certain psychotic individuals who suffer from delusions of persecution and grandeur—the so-called paranoiacs. Their system of delusions is constructed very much like the hero myth, and therefore indicates the same psychogenic themes as the neurotic family romance, which is analyzable, whereas the system of delusions is inaccessible even for psychoanalytical approaches. For example, the paranoiac is apt to claim that the people whose name he bears are not his real parents, but that he is actually the son of a princely personage; he was to be removed for some mysterious reason, and was therefore surrendered to his "parents" as a foster child. His enemies, however, wish to maintain the fiction that he is of lowly descent, in order to suppress his legitimate claims to the crown or to enormous riches.[6] Cases of this kind often occupy alienists or tribunals.[7]

[6] Abraham, loc. cit., p. 40; Riklin, op. cit., p. 74.

[7] Brief mention is made of a case concerning a Frau von Hervay, because of a few subtle psychological comments upon the same by A. Berger (*Feuilleton der Neue Freie Presse,* Nov. 6, 1904), which in part touch upon our interpretation of the hero myth. Berger writes as follows: "I am convinced that she seriously believes herself to be the illegitimate daughter of an aristocratic Russian lady. The desire to belong through birth to more distinguished and brilliant circles than her own surroundings probably dates back to her early years; and her wish to be a princess gave rise to the delusion that she was not the daughter of her parents, but the child of a noblewomen who had concealed her illegitimate offspring from the world by letting her grow up as the daughter of a sleight-of-hand man. Having once become entangled in these fancies, it was natural for her to interpret any harsh word that offended her, or any accidental ambiguous remark that she happened to hear, but especially her reluctance to be the daughter of this couple, as a confirmation of her romantic delusion. She therefore made it the task of her life to regain the social position of which she felt herself to have been defrauded. Her biography manifests the strenuous insistence upon this idea, with a tragic outcome."

The female type of the family romance, as it confronts us in this case from the asocial side, has also been transmitted as a hero myth in isolated instances. The story goes of the later Queen Semiramis (in Diodorus, II, 4) that her mother, the goddess Derceto, being ashamed of her, exposed the child in a barren and rocky land, where she was fed by doves and found by shepherds, who gave the infant to the overseer of the royal flocks, the childless Simnas, who raised her as his own daughter. He named her Semiramis, which meant "dove" in the ancient Syrian language. Her further career and autocratic rulership, thanks to her masculine energy, is a matter of "history."

Other exposure myths are told of Atalanta, Cybele, and Aërope (see Röscher, op. cit.).

This intimate relationship between the hero myth and the delusional structure of paranoiacs has already been definitely established through the characterization of the myth as a paranoid structure, which is here confirmed by its contents. The remarkable fact that paranoiacs will frankly reveal their entire romance has ceased to be puzzling, since the profound investigations of Freud have shown that the contents of hysterical fantasies, which can often be made conscious through analysis, are identical up to the minutest details with the complaints of persecuted paranoiacs; moreover, the identical contents are also encountered as a reality in the arrangements of perverts for the gratification of their desires.[8]

The egotistical character of the entire system is distinctly revealed by the paranoiac, for whom the exaltation of the parents, as brought about by him, is merely the means for his own exaltation. As a rule the pivot for his entire system is simply the culmination of the family romance, in the apodictic statement: I am the emperor (or god). Reasoning in the symbolism of dreams and myths—which is also the symbolism of all fancies, including the "morbid" power of imagination—all he accomplishes thereby is to put himself in the place of the father, just as the hero terminates his revolt against the father. This can be done in both instances, because the conflict with the father—which dates back to the concealment of the sexual processes, as suggested by the latest discoveries—is nullified at the instant when the grown boy himself becomes a father. The persistence with which the paranoiac puts himself in the father's place, i.e., becomes a father himself, appears like an illustration to the common answers of little boys to a scolding or a putting off of their inquisitive curiosity: You just wait until I am a papa myself, and I'll know all about it!

Besides the paranoiac, his equally asocial counterpart must also be emphasized. In the expression of the identical

[8] Freud: *Three Contributions to the Theory of Sex;* also *Psychopathologie des Altagslebens;* and *Hysterische Phantasien und ihre Beziehung zur Bisexualität.*

fantasy contents, the hysterical individual, who has suppressed them, is offset by the pervert, who realizes them; and just so the diseased and passive paranoiac—who needs his delusion for the correction of the actuality, which to him is intolerable—is offset by the active criminal, who endeavors to change the actuality according to his mind. In this special sense, this type is represented by the anarchist. The hero himself, as shown by his detachment from the parents, begins his career in opposition to the older generation; he is at once a rebel, a renovator, and a revolutionary. However, every revolutionary is originally a disobedient son, a rebel against the father.[9] (Compare the suggestion of Freud, in connection with the interpretation of a "revolutionary dream.")[1]

But whereas the paranoiac, in conformity with his passive character, has to suffer persecutions and wrongs which ultimately proceed from the father—and which he endeavors to escape by putting himself in the place of the father or the emperor—the anarchist complies more faithfully with the heroic character, by promptly himself becoming the persecutor of kings, and finally killing the king, precisely like the hero. The remarkable similarity between the career of certain anarchistic criminals and the family romance of hero and child has been elsewhere illustrated by the author, through special instances.[2] The truly heroic element then consists only in the real justice or even necessity of the act, which is therefore generally endorsed and admired;[3] while the morbid trait, also in criminal

[9] This is especially evident in the myths of the Greek gods, where the son (Cronus, Zeus) must first remove the father, before he can enter upon his rulership. The form of the removal, namely through castration—obviously the strongest expression of the revolt against the father—is at the same time the proof of its sexual provenance. Concerning the revenge character of this castration, as well as the infantile significance of the entire complex, compare Freud: "Infantile Sexual Theories," and "Analysis of a Phobia in a Five-Year-Old Boy (loc. cit.).

[1] Freud; *Tramdeutung* (German edition of *Interpretation of Dreams*), 2d edition, p. 153.

[2] *"Belege zur Rettungsphantasie," Zentralblatt für Psychoanalyse,* I (1911), p. 331; also *"Die Rolle des Familienromans in der Psychologie des Attentäters," Internationale Zeitschrift für ärtzliche Psychoanalyse,* I (1913).

[3] Compare the contrast between Tell and Parricida, in Schiller's *Wilhelm Tell,* which is discussed in detail in the author's *Inzestmotiv.*

cases, is the pathologic transference of the hatred from the father to the real king, or several kings, when more general and still more distorted.

As the hero is commended for the same deed, without asking for its psychic motivation, so the anarchist might claim indulgence from the severest penalties, for the reason that he has killed an entirely different person from the one he really intended to destroy, in spite of an apparently excellent (perhaps political) motivation of his act.[4]

For the present let us stop at the narrow boundary line where the contents of innocent infantile imaginings, suppressed and unconscious neurotic fantasies, poetical myth structures, and certain forms of mental disease and crime lie close together, although far apart as to their causes and dynamic forces. We resist the temptation to follow one of these divergent paths that lead to altogether different realms, but which are as yet unblazed trails in the wilderness.

[4] Compare in this connection the unsuccessful homicidal attempt of Tatjana Leontiew, and its subtle psychological illumination, in Wittels: *Die sexuelle Not* (Vienna and Leipzig, 1909).

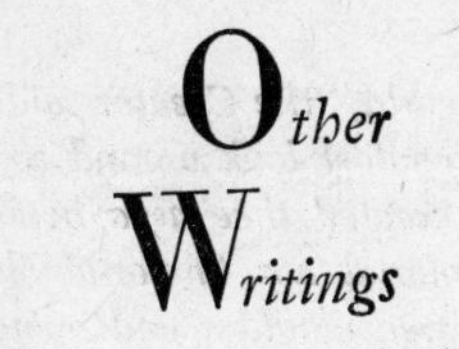
Other
Writings

"In the midst of the world," the Creator said to Adam, "I have placed thee, so thou couldst look around so much easier, and see all that is in it. I created thee as a being neither celestial nor earthly, neither mortal nor immortal alone, so that thou shouldst be thy own free moulder and overcomer; thou canst degenerate to animal, and through thyself be reborn to godlike existence. Animals bring forth from the womb what they should have; the higher spirits, on the other hand, are from the beginning, or at least soon after, what they remain in all eternity. Thou alone hast power to develop and grow according to free will: in one word, thou hast the seeds of all-embracing life in thyself!" PICO DELLA MIRANDOLA

I Introduction (to ART AND ARTIST)

In art, as in everything living, there is no progress, but only varieties of one stimulus.

—HEBBEL

EDITOR'S NOTE: *In his opening remarks Rank pays tribute to the archaeological discoveries and researches of the late nineteenth century and the first quarter of the twentieth century. He comments that the mass of this new material—such as the Paleolithic wall-paintings in Spain and the magnificent Mayan monuments in Central America—throw new light on the art history of the Western world. Especially, a Northern culture is elevated by them to a rank alongside the ancient high cultures of the South and particularly of the East, from which it was once thought that all artistic stimulus had come. These facts call for a new approach in art-criticism, and this he proposes to undertake. Rank mentions the work of the cultural historian Carl Schuchhardt, and continues his Introduction as follows:*

. . . Only one of Schuchhardt's opinions essentially needs concern us here: namely that, even in prehistoric times, he finds definite evidence of the same contrast between North and South that is found in the historical periods of artistic development, as, for instance, in the struggle between Gothic and Renaissance. And this dualism is not limited to Europe, at any rate as the term is understood in our present historical geography. Southern France, for instance, shows a stone age similar to that of North

Africa, and, in the East, the radiation from the Southern cultural zone of the Mediterranean races did not stop short at the borders of Asia. If, for a start, we admit the distinctiveness and independence of the three culture zones—Northern, Southwestern, and Eastern—as they are indicated by nature and established by achaeological discoveries, we get a new picture of cultural development which will be full of significance for the understanding of the forms and styles of art as well.

These three great culture zones, differentiated even in prehistoric times, were bound, sooner or later, to meet in the Mediterranean and create a mixed culture, which in its turn was quite distinctive and, as is not surprising, brought forth a human type of many and varied talents. The culture which we have recently come to know as the Cretan-Mycenaean leaves us in no doubt that historic Greece also was a result of these cultural mixings in "the Balkans," although at the same time we see something greater, too—the birth of a new and more harmonious type of human being that was at once the end product and the conqueror of the old. Whether the now undeniable existence of Northern influence side by side with that of the Southwest and the East is a justification of the theory of an Indo-Germanic penetration of Hellas is of little importance, compared with the fact that the influences of Northern and Southwestern cultural elements are now taking their rightful place along with those of the once unchallengeable East. All the same, it would be premature to throw overboard without more ado the old formula *Ex oriente lux;* rather does it seem that a new meaning can be given to it if we limit its application to a particular world outlook that with good reason we may call the prescientific. For that which has undeniably enlightened our culture from the East is the intellectual penetration of phenomena with the tendency to bring them into a system, whether it be of a mythological, religious, or philosophical nature. In other words, it is intellectualism that we have taken from the East, while the North shows the opposite tendency toward the mystic, the nebulous, and the spiritual, as against the intellectual. The South, again, shows a pretty definite leaning toward naturalism, which is alien to both the other cultures, in its direct association with nature; nay, more in the oneness of its human type with nature, which climatic reasons, not to mention others, cause the Northerner to reject, while the East is antipathetic to nature precisely on account of its hyperintellectuality.

Be this as it may, there is one point on which almost all our scholars, writers of cultural history, and art critics are agreed: that the North has produced an abstract, geometrical style of art, whereas the peculiar characteristic of the Southern style is naturalism. Only the East has proved difficult to "place"; for, from having been overestimated as the prime source of all human culture, it is now denied any influence whatever. And so it comes about that we have Pan-Babylonians and Pan-Germanics opposing each other, each school trying to prove the superiority or independence of its own culture instead of taking trouble to analyze its specific characteristics. We shall presently be able to demonstrate, in connection with a particular problem, not only how each of the three cultural zones excelled in the production of different art-forms, but how even today an intelligent comparison of the respective cultural materials may throw light on one and the same problem from different sides. For instance, in accounting for the widespread spiral ornament, we shall find the most and the best historical data in the North, while the South will contribute the nature myths necessary to its interpretation, and the East an explanation of it that borders on the scientific. While art- and culture-history are, quite rightly, interested in the succession in time of the phenomena and the different influences under which they come into being, we, on the other hand, regard it as our task to establish, not the spatial "whence" or the temporal "since when," but *the spiritual why*. This does not imply any intention of denying the effect of culture-drift or the importance of historical sequence; we merely think that the problem as to how the phenomenon in question arose at all—no matter when and where—is entitled to be considered at least as worthy of an attempt at solution.

We have discussed the cultural-historical aspects of the

art-problem somewhat in detail here, because by implication they contain the style-problems within themselves. For if we identify the North with abstract and the South with naturalistic art, we present at the same time the psychological characterization of a corresponding human type who will produce just this kind of style. It is true that "North" and "South" are terms essentially referring to climate and the economic conditions dependent on climate; but these things do, after all, contribute definitely to the production of the human type concerned. And we must not forget that man is not *only* a product of his natural environment, since the essence of every culture is determined by the greater or less degree of its domination of nature and independence of her influences. In looking at art from the ethnological or economic standpoint, we are apt to overlook the fact that art is produced by man and not by nature, although it is nature that helps to form and educate man. Here, again, the artist with his creative personality is almost eliminated, as he is from the spiritual and scientific history of art and the aesthetic which borders on psychology. Not only does this apply to the prehistoric age, for which no report on the individual man can reach us; it applies also to the artistic development that works itself out in the full light of history. When writers on art speak of a Gothic artist or an Impressionist, they refer of course to the laws of style revealed in his work. But the individual artist who employs this style as a form of expression is something more than a mere representative of this tendency; and one often wonders what psychological significance such an aesthetic classification really has. To put it in another way, does the Gothic artist stand for a particular type of man? And, supposing that he has found his expression in the North, what is his spiritual structure, and can it perhaps take root elsewhere than in Northern mother earth—as was the case, we take it, with Michelangelo? And will not a strong personality, like Michelangelo in the South, or Goethe in the North, be inclined in any case to take over the given art-forms, indeed, and even to develop them, but also to break through, to overcome, these forms, to mix them with others, to supplant them by others?

The fact that this not only is possible, but does actually occur in the case of almost every great artist-personality, brings us back to our *spiritual* dualism and to the experience that at any rate the two tendencies—call them what one will—must be potentially present in the artist, even though both do not always find expression. In mentioning the following treatises on the derivation of the creative impulse from this conflicting dualism, I would remind my readers that even cool-eyed art-historians are forced in the end to some such conception of the transmutation of the laws of style. Two important critical studies on art which appeared in the same year (1923) arrive from totally different starting points at the one conclusion: that the two opposing tendencies of style (which Scheltema in *Altnordische Kunst* calls "mechanical" and "organic," and Herbert Kühn in *Kunst der Primitiven* "imaginative" and "sensory") coexist side by side and even develop each out of the other. Kühn starts from economic factors—wherein he had been anticipated by Grosse and to some extent Hörnes—and connects naturalistic art with the nomadic hunter's existence, and the abstract art-form with that of the farmers and cattle-breeders who have settled on the soil. These simple parallels between economic forms and art-forms, which have been extended by others to the family organization (matriarchal = naturalistic; patriarchal = abstract), are applied by Kühn to a psychological opposition of consumption and production on the basis of the Marxian theory. He sees the hunter as leading an existence which mainly absorbs from outside and having in consequence a naturalistic conception of art-forms; whereas agrarian culture is one of fruitfulness in creative art as in other respects. Kühn does not, indeed, as we have seen, accept any opposition of principle between the two tendencies, but deduces the one by a dialectical process from the other. But in one culture zone it will be a development from the sensory to the imaginative, as in the South Seas or in Africa, where the natural model becomes geometricized; and another time—say, in the North—it will be the other way round, a development from the geometric style to the organic.

A similar process of development is recognized by

Scheltema in his deep and subtle analysis of the style of specifically Northern art-forms. These he does not derive from economic forms, like Kühn, or technical-practical motives, like Schuchhardt, but accounts for on a principle of spiritual development. While Scheltema, who has confined his special research to a strictly limited and definite field, sees the same development from abstract to organic repeated in every single phase of development of Northern art, from the stone age to the bronze and iron ages, Kühn, with a wider scope, has managed to establish the recurrence of one law of development at different times and different places almost throughout the history of art. Thus in Crete a peak period of imaginative art was followed by frank sensorialism. "Altered in form, and yet quite similar, was the change which took place under the same laws, thousands of years afterwards, in America among the Aztecs and Incas, and again, centuries later, in Africa among the conquering races of Benin and Yoruba. In all these cultures the way leads unmistakably from imaginative to sensorial art, from collectivism to individualism, from the dualist outlook to the unitary, and from the strongly religious world to the practical everyday society."[1] The only exception to this rule that development leads from abstract to concrete appears to occur in the case of paleolithic man's naturalistic art. Scheltema excludes this art from his survey on the ground that no further artistic development from it is possible, and that the abstract art-form of the Neolithic age is primary and intrinsic in the North. But I do not think the question can be disposed of so simply. For one thing, we cannot divide off the Northern Neolithic so sharply from the Southern, for all their differences; and, for another, it remains doubtful whether the naturalism of the glacial age really represents the beginning of all artistic activity, whether, in fact, there are not more abstract art-forms, completely lost to us, which preceded it. It is risky to reconstruct the mentality of these people on no other evidences than the artistic remains of the glacial age that have been accidentally preserved. But it is nevertheless noteworthy that the sole explanation of the

[1] Herbert Kühn: *Kunst der Primitiven,* p. 120.

appearance of such highly developed drawing and pictorial art as this Paleolithic has handed down to us comes from a physiologist, Max Verworn. In his book *Zur Psychologie der primitiven Kunst* (1908), the scholar declares this art to be a "physioplastic" reproduction of nature that, in contrast to the later "ideoplastic" treatment, has a certain spontaneity, instinctiveness, and non-reflectiveness. It does not seem to me that this view does much more than give us a terminology that strikingly expresses the dualism lying at the base of all artistic production, although it does at least imply an attempt at evaluation instead of a mere description. For even if we accept Verworn's terminology, we are still obliged to assume that glacial man, although in the main physioplastic in his rendering, must also have had ideoplastic possibilities of no rudimentary order; otherwise he would not have been in a position to produce a work of art intuitively. All art, whether primarily naturalistic or primarily abstract, unites both elements within itself, and indeed itself arises (as we shall see) from a conflict between the two tendencies, of which first one, then the other, gains the upper hand. The decision does not, however, depend only on the culture and its economic environment, but equally upon the creative individual, in whom the same dualistic conflict exists, whether, as at a primitive stage, between life and death, or at a later one, between body and soul, matter and spirit, individual and society.

Leaving aside, therefore, for the moment all attempts such as those above mentioned to assign values to the style-contrasts, and looking at the problem from its psychological aspect, we may say (following up an idea of Kühn's) that naturalistic art has always flourished where and when individualism was the order of the day or had obtained the mastery. This was not the case only in definite master-cultures with whose structure we are familiar, such as Crete, Mycenae, Classical Greece, and the Renaissance; it applies also to primitive man—at least in the wider sense of the term. For even if this primitive man was no individualist in the sense in which those masterful natures were so —or even in the sense of our decadent psychologism—he was a lordly person relying upon his own strength before he became sedentary and united to collective bodies of men through agriculture. In any case, abstract art, in contrast to sensory or organic art, is usually collective, as is demonstrated by Northern and also primitive ornamentation, as well as by religious Gothic. In these facts a paradoxical phenomenon discloses itself, which will not startle the psychologist and indeed will facilitate our approach to the understanding of the spiritual dynamism in artistic creativity. The autonomous individualism of primitive man, as well as that of the lordly masters, appears to be more dependent on nature in its artistic creativeness than is the sedentary collective type of man, who, though depending to a great extent on nature's moods and his own environment (of commerce), can yet rise to abstractions in art which are quite independent of reality. We shall see presently how this compensatory function of the art-form brings the development of personality and its dynamic need of equalization into unison. Here I would merely point out—in pursuance of an idea already put forward—that in neither of the two art-forms is it a question of an absolute style-principle, but only of a more or a less, while at the same time both style-forms alike possess the tendency to reproduce something absent, which in certain cases happens to be a natural object, while in others it pictures an idea. The obvious purpose in this tendency is domination, whether this takes the form of a naturalistic representation of an animal as a hunting spell or of the symbolic representation of a human abstraction. Behind both there is the creative will of the personality, which only now and then manifests itself directly, and at other times reacts to the compulsion of collective society and gives expression thereto. Undoubtedly this second art-form—here one agrees with Scheltema—is more capable of development, not only for stylistic and aesthetic but for psychological reasons as well. For the abstraction at the base of this mechanical art represents even in itself a rising above nature, and it can be still further intensified and varied, whereas in naturalistic or organic art the objects within a given cultural environment are limited, so that the artistic effort to deal with them otherwise than in their natural setting does not find them very malleable. In a word, art consists in the latter case of arbitrary re-creation (not copying) of the given objects; in the other, of the new creation of ever-changing ideas. Nevertheless, for both we must assume a creative force in the individual himself, which has to be studied in its various forms before we can arrive at a deeper understanding of the art-forms produced by it.

II *Creative Urge and Personality Development*

Socrates appears before us as one of those great plastic figures, all of a piece, such as we are accustomed to see at his period—a complete, classical work of art, which has risen of itself to that height. These figures are not made; they form themselves completely into what they are; they become that which they will to be, and to that they remain true. Thus Socrates, by his art and power of conscious will, formed himself for his own character and his life's task.

—HEGEL

SINCE I originally approached the art-problem from the psychological side, and wish now, too, to study it in relation to the development of personality, the historical method of presentation, which is usual in art-histories, is barred. Yet even for the psychological approach it is not the one side or the other that matters, but the fundamental dualism which appears as the basis of all cultural development in man. For if this dualism is as fundamental as we have assumed, it must make itself evident in the various stages of artistic creation as well as in the growth of personality, and will very likely reveal certain essential relations between the two. This, however, only becomes possible by taking a genetic view of the significances of the various ideologies from which both the style of a period and the artistic creativeness in it are born. This comparative method, which we shall frequently adopt in all parts of this work, seeks, however, not so much to establish similarities or dependences as to establish a concatenation of meaning extending from the prehistoric cave man to the individualistic artist-type of today with his "neurotic" psychology. If such a dualism really does exist in human nature, its existence must be just as demonstrable psychologically in the modern artist as it has been shown *aesthetically* in the history of style or *ethnically* in the history of culture. We use psychology, therefore, not as an exclusive principle of elucidation, but as an auxiliary that has been provided for us by the study of the modern artist-type (not by his art); just as we use primitive art in order to understand the collective ideologies which condition creativity, and Oriental and Classical art in order to discover its intellectual interpretation. Our account may thus put readers off—the more that we ourselves shall often have to wrestle with certain cultural phenomena before we can apply the understanding thus won to the study of art.

Fortunately we have at least this much start, that a recent discovery has taken us up to the threshold of our own problems. I refer to the revolution in the understanding of artistic creativity which was set going by the Viennese art-historian Alois Riegl, and which since its first appearance in his *Stilfragen* (1893) has dominated all modern studies of art. Riegl posed it as a principle which illuminates the artistic creation of every age, that the peculiarities of style at various epochs are not to be explained by defective ability, but are only intelligible as the expression of a particular *will-to-form*. This view may seem self-evident to the psychologist, but it was unattainable either by psychology proper or by a psychologizing aesthetic. It could only come from viewing style, as Riegl does, as a manifestation of collective ideology. Unfortunately, Riegl only lived long enough to illustrate his subtle and far-reaching theory in a single specialized department, that of Late

Roman arts and crafts.[1] But the fact that so historically limited and artistically subordinate a domain should have given room for this form of description and presentation shows the brilliant achievement of Riegl in all its greatness. Rejecting the traditional mode of regarding art as a matter of objects and iconography, and understanding it as "form and color in surface and in space," he ascribed to these crafts, even to the ornamentation prevailing in them, the same significance as vessels of the will to form as he did to sculpture, painting, and architecture—thus opening a wholly new chapter in art-history as well as giving a wholly new method of approach. When we remember what an important part was played in prehistory by this form of art, hitherto a neglected stepchild, we may well admit that without Riegl's magnificent achievement the essence of primitive ornament and thus of abstract art in general would have remained unintelligible. Of course further work was necessary in order to give Riegl's idea the broad historical and aesthetic foundation which was far beyond the attainment of a single—and all too short—life.

It is therefore comprehensible that Riegl himself should not have been able to free himself entirely from the shackles of his own tradition and the aesthetic views of his age, and that in the application of his ideas he was restricted by academic prejudice. Though his account of the Classical art as an antithesis to Late Roman remains a permanent achievement of an almost spiritual attitude to art, he nevertheless succumbed to historicism in summarily declaring everything "Late Roman" which showed the same criteria of style, without thinking of the possibility of a psychological content in this conception. On the other hand he took the "denaturalization of the art-form," as it developed from the Classical to the decadent Late Roman civilization, as a law inherent in all artistic development, again without considering the possibilities of various other conjunctures influencing it. As Scheltema—who fully appreciates Riegl's main achievement—has shown, there are in

[1] *Die spätrömische Kunstindustrie, nach den Funden in Österreich-Ungarn, im Zusammenhange mit der Gesamtentwicklung der bildenden Künste bei den Mittelmeervölkern* (Vienna, 1901).

the North similar abstract forms which have developed, not from any desiccation of natural forms, but in the reverse direction. This similarity of forms is explained by the similarity of the will, but this was not "Late Roman" in the North, nor "Nordic" in the South, but in both cases resulted from a collective ideology which characterized in the South the end, and in the North the beginning, of the development of a culture.

Thus, though this absolute art-will of Riegl remains the basis of all treatment of art, yet obviously a great deal, if not everything, depends on which manifestations of the culture as a whole we take for the study of the art-will of this particular period. Riegl did so on the craft-art, and thus at any rate remained within the sphere of art himself, which has obvious advantages, but (as we have seen from his mistakes) disadvantages as well. Other students also have discussed the collective ideology of particular periods, which decides its will-to-form also, in terms of its religious or philosophical tendencies, in order later to show these as taking effect in the art-forms. All these works of the Riegl school, which go more or less beyond their master's, are extremely valuable contributions to a new view of art, and will come to be regarded as such. But they all suffer from a certain one-sidedness, which is the more intelligible that the idea of Riegl's art-will, however collectively we may take it, yet contains in its very name a strong psychological element which absolutely demands the inclusion of the personality of the creative artist. Certainly we do not mean a psychological interpretation of the laws of style, by which their importance would be reduced to mere psychologizing; but we can only hope for a real step forward in our understanding of art if we can settle more definitely the part played by the creative individual in the collective work and then put the result into the great equation of all the factors which have any bearing, direct or indirect, on the creation of the art-forms.

Of course, for such an undertaking, which tackles the problem of art primarily from the psychological end, a different starting point is required from that called for in a study of art from the stylistic or cultural-historical angle.

Even if by art we understand, not the part played by the creator in the psychological sense, but the product, the work, or even the content of all art—at least for the particular period—we can for the time being sum up the relation of the artist to his art as follows: the artist, as a definite creative individual, uses the art-form that he finds ready to his hand in order to express a something personal; this personal must therefore be somehow connected with the prevailing artistic or cultural ideology, since otherwise he could not make use of them, but it must also differ, since otherwise he would not need to use them in order to produce something of his own. While this aspect brings us again to the dualism in the artist, there is, as we know already, a similar dualism at the bottom of the cultural ideology, as one of the manifestations of which the style of the age must be regarded. But the general ideology of the culture—which determines its religion, morals, and society, as well as its art—is again only the expression of the human types of the age, and of this the artist and the creative personality generally are the most definite crystallization. The circular argument here is only apparent, for we may not disregard the creative process, which presents itself as an essential factor between the ideology of the art, the style, and the creative personality, the artist. We must admit, however, that we know almost nothing of this process in the artist, since here, more than anywhere, the hopes held out by modern psychology have proved delusive.

We shall quote later the authors who have been honest enough to admit the failure of scientific psychology to explain artistic creativity; but we would say at once here that this fact has been contributory to our own attempt to understand the problem of the artist purely in relation to that of art—the artist representing only one, the individual factor, while we have to regard art as the collective expression of their contemporary cultural ideology. The artist, as it were, takes not only his canvas, his colors, or his model in order to paint, but also the art that is given him formally, technically, and ideologically, within his own culture; this probably emerges most clearly in the case of the poet, whose material is drawn from the cultural possessions already circulating and is not dead matter, as is that used by the plastic arts. In any case, we can say of all artistic creation that the artist not only creates his art, but also uses art in order to create. Withal, there remains still (quite apart from the cultural problem of the origin of style) the purely psychological problem as to what is the type, the individual, that for the creative expression of its personality takes this or that art-ideology in particular, what are the motives and processes that transform a creative impulse into art achievements of high aesthetic value.

For the solution of this fundamental psychological question we have naturally to keep to the present, where we have a definite artistic type before us as a living phenomenon, and not merely his historical biography and completed work. But the prevalent psychology has already failed in the task of finding a satisfactory explanation for the birth of an individual work, even when the artist is historically known and his artistic personality has been studied biographically—where in fact the stages of growth can still be traced. Still less, then, is it likely that it could achieve an understanding of primitive collective art or the amazing achievements of the psychologically crude stone age man. If any psychology is to explain this at all adequately, it will in any case have to be a new one and one that, while taking its bearings by primitive art, avoids, on the one hand, the predication of our own feelings in it and, on the other, the interpretation of our own aesthetic sensibility by reference to it.

The merit of developing Riegl's ideas to their logical issue and placing the aesthetic understanding of alien styles on a new basis goes in particular to a historian, Wilhelm Worringer; and his fundamental work, *Abstraktion und Einfühlung, ein Beitrag zur Stilspsychologie*,[2] is doubly important for us as a starting point because it also works out the psychological core of Riegl's attitude, at least as far as is necessary and possible in relation to the aesthetic problem. And if Worringer, as I should like to remark at once, was limited in his purely psychological penetration of the problem by the natural boundaries of his own interests, he

[2] Munich, 1908; quoted according to the tenth edition, 1921.

did take aesthetic to the very verge beyond which it must give place to psychology.

For myself I became acquainted with Worringer's ideas when I had already settled my own interpretation of the problem of art; still I owe him many valuable suggestions, though yet again I should have been unable to use these had I not of myself gone beyond the traditional view of aesthetic, which Worringer so splendidly criticizes and so fruitfully completes. The idea of the will-to-form, when I came across it in the form in which Riegl first expounded it and Worringer extended it, sounded to me at once like something familiar. Not only had I long ago come to the conclusion from my analysis of creative artists that their productivity and the varying quality of their work were not a matter of capacity; but I had got beyond the individual psychology in my ideas about the creative personality and of the determining ideology, before I returned to the problem of art. For me the problem of willing, in a philosophical sense of the word, had come to be the central problem of the whole question of personality, even of all psychology, and it only remained to apply it to the particular case of the creative artist. Riegl's revolutionary treatment of art, in the aesthetic and psychological form in which Worringer formulated it, gave me the courage to attempt an understanding of the specific ideology of the artist—that is, his style—in a similar sense to that which my psychology of the will had opened up in dealing with other ideologies. The general principles and interpretation which are valid for the growth and meaning of general ideologies must be applicable to the ideology of art, which we had recognized the peculiarities of style to be. Further, the aesthetic laws deduced from the history of style must either coincide to a considerable extent with, or at least be somehow related to, both the significance of the whole cultural ideology and the manifestations of the creative personality.

There was one point in particular in Worringer's work which seemed to me to confirm my own notion of the origin and significance of the general cultural ideology for the problem of artistic creation. In my *Seelenglaube und Psy-*

chologie, I had, as mentioned above, sought to establish as the primary ideology the belief in immortality that seemed to express itself in artistic creation in the same ways as in religion and social institutions. The particular way in which this showed itself in style, however, remained, for the time being, beyond my grasp, until I had come to know Riegl's views of style and Worringer's aesthetic. For Riegl, it is true, who deals particularly with collective phenomena, the art-will is purely instinctive; according to the materialistic conception of Verworn, it is "physioplastic"; while for Worringer, who interprets it more philosophically, it is an almost "cosmic something" arising spontaneously from the abstract linear art which corresponds to crystalline form. So far, therefore, it has nothing to do with the individual will of the conscious artistic personality, though we might regard it as being in a Schopenhauerian sense its precursor. But the matter is not quite so simple that we could assume this instinctive art-impulse to have merely become individually conscious; for increasing individualization alters the whole cultural ideology and therefore art with it; and consequently abstract linear ornament is not now created consciously by the individual will of the artists as heretofore instinctively by the primitive impulse to abstraction, but replaced by new forms of expression.

For with this individualization the general art-form changes in its essence (some authorities think, in the direction of naturalism), but the creative personality also becomes other than it was. The question, How did the individual artist-type grow up at all in our Western culture if the artistic creation of earlier men and times was abstract and collective? is almost identical with the problem of the development of individuality and personality itself. But this is not a problem that can be solved by psychology alone; rather we may hope for a deeper knowledge of the development of personality from a better understanding of the development of art. As I have shown elsewhere, the immortality-belief in its various forms and cultural variations has certainly participated in it; and it is here, as already remarked, that I find the decisive point of contact with Worringer's aesthetic to which we may relate our study. Its merit seems to me to be that it has shown this individual *urge to eternalization* of the personality, which motivates artistic production, to be a principle *inherent in the art-form itself,* in fact its essence. He says of primitive and also of Oriental cultures, whose style he is discussing: "The kind of satisfaction which they looked to obtain from art was not, as in Western art, that of sinking themselves in the external world, and finding enjoyment in it, but that of depriving the individual thing in the external world of its arbitrary and apparently haphazard character; that is to immortalize the object in giving it an abstract form and so finding a resting place in the flight of phenomena. Their strongest impulse was to bring it close to its absolute value." [3]

If, with this "instinctive urge to abstraction" as it appears very early in art, we compare the growth of other collective ideologies at a primitive level, we find to our surprise that, correspondingly, the other ideologies also become the more abstract the further we pursue them backward. The most important as well as the best-authenticated instance of this is the development of religion, as I have tried to expound it in *Seelenglaube und Psychologie.* Primitive religion, as a belief in souls (as we know it), is originally so abstract that it has been called irreligious by comparison with higher religions, in which the gods have already assumed concrete form. But from a study of these abstract preliminary stages of religion, which are a matter of spirits and demons, we see also that the urge for abstraction in primitives is rooted in the soul-belief that, in the intellectualized form of the East, culminates in the absolute abstract of the soul. Compared with the idea of the soul or its primitive predecessors, even the abstractest form of art is concrete, just as on the other hand the most definite naturalism in art is abstract when compared with nature.

[3] Worringer, op. cit., p. 21. We cannot at present enter upon the criticism of Worringer's exaggeration of his own principle of elucidation, which in essence he seeks to exemplify by reference to the Gothic style. He appears therein to have succumbed to the same compulsion as Riegl, in that he calls everything "Gothic" that comes within the style-criteria of his own "Gothic," and thus reaches a "universal Gothic," which perhaps ought to be defined in terms of personality rather than in those of aesthetics.

If primitive art, then, is in its origins a concreted representation of an abstract idea of the soul and is at the same time the nucleus of what becomes at a later stage the figuration of God, we cannot possibly understand the change and growth of art-forms without following the change of the idea of the soul in human history. Here we may state, more definitely than we have as yet, that the main task of this book is to expound the *development and change in meaning of art-forms from similar changes in the idea of the soul,* which decides the development of personality, even as it is itself influenced thereby. Though we have later to give an account of the relation between the prevailing style in art and the contemporary belief in the soul, we can even now see how religion has always drawn art along in its wake from the earliest times to the present day.

The urge for abstraction, which owed its origin to a belief in immortality and created the notion of the soul, created also the art that served the same ends, but led beyond the purely abstract to the objectivizing and concretizing of the prevailing idea of the soul. Everything produced objectively in any period by the contemporary idea of the soul was beautiful, and the aesthetic history of the idea of the beautiful is probably no more than a reflection of the changes in the idea of the soul under the influence of increasing knowledge. The most illuminating demonstration that the source of the beauty-ideal lies in the contemporary ideal of the soul is found in the religious art of all times and peoples, but most conspicuously in the higher cultures, where the already unified idea of the soul was ideally embodied in the forms of their gods. Thus Anubis with his animal head was as much an ideal of beauty for the Egyptians as was Zeus with a leonine mane for the Greeks, or the tortured and martyred body of Jesus for the Christians. The concept of the beautiful, which inspires the works of art of a period, is derived, not from the abstract significance of the soul-concept (in the way in which, for instance, the Romantics spoke of the "beautiful soul"), but from its concretization. That is, the religious art portrayed the idea of the soul in concrete form for the men of the time, in the shape of gods, and so, psychologically speaking, proved their existence. It is precisely the concreteness of art as compared with the idea of the soul that makes it convincing; for it creates something visible and permanent in contrast to something which was merely thought or felt, which was at first handed down from one generation to another only by means of mystic tradition and was only fixed in literature of religious form at a very late stage.

This close association, in fact fundamental identity, of art and religion, each of which strives in its own way to make the absolute eternal and the eternal absolute, can be already seen at the most primitive stages of religious development, where there are as yet neither representations of gods nor copies of nature. Almost all students of the art of primitive peoples get the unanimous impression that, as the first historian of primitive art, Franz Kugler, put it as early as 1842, "the intention of primitive art was far less toward the imitation of nature than toward the representation of particular ideas." More than fifty years later so great an authority as Leo Frobenius says the same of African art: "We cannot say that there was any direct extrovert effort at the attainment of some perfection of form.[4] All the objects of art come only out of the need to give plastic expression to ideas." We shall show later in detail how almost all these "ideas" turn more or less on the idea of the soul, which itself arises from the problem of death. Here we need only note that the redeeming power of art, that which entitles it to be regarded aesthetically as beautiful, resides in the way in which it lends concrete existence to abstract ideas of the soul. Art, then—at least in its beginning—was not the satisfaction of the desire of the individual artist to attain immortality for himself in his work, but the confirmation of the collective immortality-idea in the work itself as a picture of the soul. Thus primitive art must be, like the primitive idea of the soul, collective in order to achieve its aim, the continuation of the individual existence in the

[4] Following Ernst Vatter: *Die religiöse Plastik der Naturvölker* (Frankfurt, 1926). Vatter shows that the plastic of primitive peoples is unintelligible unless it is regarded as an expression of religious ideas.

species. And it follows, too, that primitive art must be abstract in order to reproduce this abstract idea of the soul as faithfully as may be.

Worringer was certainly right in denying that art began with the imitation of nature, or even had this object; but it was imitation all the same, though in a wider sense. The most definite representation possible of an idea *is* imitation, in the ideoplastic sense; and we might explain this very character of abstraction of primitive art by the fact that it faithfully represents an idea that is itself abstract. That is, the soul was depicted as abstractly as possible, in order that it might be like this abstract, and the further the divinizing of the soul in different personifications proceeded, the more concrete, or, as we should say, naturalistic, art became. If in this wise the obstinately defended theory of imitation (though not strictly in the sense of imitation of nature) is found to have a deeper significance in the soul, we may use the second disputed principle of the old aesthetic also to support our new structure. The accusation of aimlessness made against an art that exists only for beauty's sake cannot be sustained, either in respect of primitive art or in respect of the individual creative dynamism of the modern artist. Art unquestionably has an end, probably even serves a variety of ends—but the ends are not concrete and practical; they are abstract and spiritual. Primitive art above all has obviously some object, as Vatter points out[5] as deterrent, magic, charm; and it obtains it by making the supernatural ideology of primitive men tangible and comprehensible. In this is its value, its function, and hence comes the satisfaction it provides, which at later stages of aesthetic appreciation is deduced from the idea of beauty —an idea which originally, and even in Greek philosophy, was coincident with the idea of the good, the satisfying, and the useful.

The relations of art and religion, though so often discussed, would thus seem to call for a new treatment from our point of view; this we cannot give here, although in the course of a discussion centered on the development of personality we may be able to throw some light on hitherto

[5] Op. cit., p. 193.

unsuspected linkages. There is no doubt that even in the historical times of art, religion used it as a means to represent, in objective and concrete form, the contemporary idea of the soul; but not, so to say, "illustratively," as if mankind were too immature to form abstract ideas of the soul. It *had* to be made concrete, pictorial, and real, so as to *prove* its existence, and had to be presented in matter to demonstrate its indestructibility. Not only, therefore, have we in the art-form (style) the expression of a will that varies from time to time under the influence of changes in the soul-idea, but the same principle holds even of the content of art—so far as it is religious—and, indeed, it is religious from the start, if we may give this name to the supersensible, even where it has not condensed into the idea of a god. It is therefore not a defective faculty of abstraction that drives to the concretization of the soul and its pictorial representation in the god, *but the will to objectify it and thus to impart to it existence and, what is more, eternity.*

Here we come to the interesting question as to what extent the development of primitive art and its frank use by religion has itself contributed to the formation of a religion, and how far it was essential to it; in other words, whether the transition from animism to religion (that is, from the belief in the soul to the belief in God) was only possible through art, because in art lay the only mode of exhibiting the soul in objective form and giving personality to God.[6] It seems certain that art was at one time more abstract, since its purpose was to give existence to the non-existent by the truest possible copying. In the course of development it merely became more concrete, a destiny it shares with all other ideologies, as I have shown elsewhere, and with the development of human institutions out of these ideologies. Its culmination came in the individual art-creation of the Classical style as we have it in Greek work. There man himself—in his own full naturalness, yet in idealized beauty too—had become the vehicle of an immortal soul and was not, like the Oriental gods, a mere

[6] We shall refer later to the apparent exception of the Jewish people, who condemned every representation of Deity as idolatrous, and consequently produced no art.

representative of the belief in the soul. *In this sense not only did the development of the soul begin with art, but the process of humanization of the soul completed itself in art and not in religion.* It was art, by its embodiment of man in lasting material, that finally gave him the courage to reassume the soul which, because of the transitoriness of its bodily form, he had abstracted into an absolute idea of the soul.

From a point of view such as this, art, though born from the same spirit as religion, appears not only as outlasting it, but actually as fulfilling it. If religion, as is hardly disputable, could develop beyond soul-belief only by the help of art, and if, moreover, as I would believe, the humanization of the soul, which implies the completion of religion, is accomplished by art, religion would almost sink to a transition stage of art. This is, of course, a matter of attitude—but it does seem certain that the development of art has always striven beyond religion, and that its highest individual achievements lie outside purely religious art, until in modern times it completely emancipates itself from that influence and even takes its place. But this tendency toward independence corresponds to an irreligiosity (or even an anti-religiosity) that is inherent and essential in all artistic creation, and that we must admit, in spite of its logically contradicting our own discussion, unless we are to sacrifice a decisive, and perhaps the most important, side of the creative impulse to a one-sided theory. Personal creativity is antireligious in the sense that it is always subservient to the individual desire for immortality in the creative personality and not to the collective glorification of the creator of the world. The individual artist of course uses collective forms, among which the religious, in the widest sense, take first place, so as to overcome his personal dualism by a social compensation. But at the same time he tries to save his individuality from the collective mass by giving his work the stamp of his own personality. Hence it is quite rightly that Rudolf Kautzsch, in his brief but valuable paper *Die bildende Kunst und das Jenseits* (Jena, 1905), emphasizes the fact that on one side religion is a handicap on art; and we too have seen in our survey of prevalent theories of art that the periods of strong development of personality, or of constructive individualism like that predicated of the superman, have always been among the highest periods of artistic productivity.

Among these periods of *floraison* we have mentioned the prehistoric art of self-dependent Paleolithic man, Classical Greek art, and the Renaissance. All these periods, which either are individualistic or are carried along by a definite cult of personality, show—in contrast to the abstract and rigid style of Egyptian, Christian, and to a certain extent even Gothic art—a vivid naturalism *that is certainly no imitation of nature, but rather an organic vitalization of fossilizing art-forms.* We have indicated in the Introduction the psychical significance of this antithesis and how it may be psychologically understood. Religion is the collective ideology par excellence, which can only spring from a powerful group-need and mass-consciousness, which itself springs from the need of the individual for dependence and implies his subjection to higher forces. Art also, which sprang originally from self-feeling, is then subordinated to religion, just as the creative personality is subordinated to the creator. *Religion springs from the collective belief in immortality; art from the personal consciousness of the individual.* The conflict between art and religion, which we can so easily trace in the individual artist, is thus ultimately a conflict between individuality and collectivity, the dualistic struggle within the creative artist of the two impulses of his own self. In this sense there is a reciprocal dependence between art and religion, but, concurrent with it from the outset, an opposition between them. For, on the one hand, the artist has need of religion so as to make his own impulse toward immortality collective, while religion needs the artist in order to make concrete its abstract notion of the soul; on the other hand, the artist seeks to eternalize his individuality apart from the collective ideologies, while religion would deny the individual in favor of the community. Thus though art is in the last resort anti-collectivist—in spite of the fact that it makes use of the various communal ideologies, especially of contemporary religion and the style dependent on it—it yet needs these collective ideologies, even if only to overcome them from time to time by the force of personality. This fact may perhaps explain why the present age, with its strong individualism, has failed to produce any great art like other periods marked by strong personality and consequent alienation from religion. These other periods had strength in their religious and antireligious currents, as well as other powerful collective ideologies, which our present-day society in its disruption lacks. Even if nowadays, with the decay of religious faith, the artist is immeasurably overvalued, this seems only a last effort at re-establishing a similarly decaying cult of the personality, of which we are just as incapable as we are of collective faith.

True, there was probably a time when the artist did play the part of the religious hero on earth, being the creative representative of a humanized god: the time, that is, when there arose content and concept of genius wherein dwelt the divine spark, the immortal soul. But if we want to understand the personality of the creative artist, we must turn for a while to the history of this idea of genius; for this idea has not always existed, though there were geniuses before it. The necessity for the birth of this idea, and its elaboration into a cult of personality, whose last stages only are known to us, seem to me to have arisen from the incessant conflict with, and final conquest of, these collective ideologies by a new type of humanity, which appeared first in Greece, but had to be reborn for western Europe in Italy. For Greece had, in spite of its extraordinary personality-culture, a strong national idea which defined the type, while in the Renaissance a new European personal consciousness arose that towered above religious and national boundaries and established a world reign of humanism which could vie with collective Christianity.

The notion of genius as it grew up between the Renaissance and the eighteenth century was created by the artist as a new ideology, and henceforth it was as much a means toward production as had previously been the abstract idea of style derived from the collective belief in the soul. But this new "religion of genius," as Zilsel calls it,[7] centered on a type and no longer on a collectivity; it was indeed individual and even psychological, in its emphasis, based wholly on the artist and no longer on art, on style. At the Renaissance, out of which this genius was born, the Middle Ages were freed from the collective spirit of Christianity and fought through once more to personality. Now for the first time there appears the creative artist of the modern age, whose inferior imitators today produce their art without possessing either the collective ideology of earlier ages or the individual religion of genius that has produced the greatest of our great artists, a Michelangelo, a Shakespeare, a Rembrandt, a Goethe. Such men as these, being tied to their age, stand in sharp opposition to a collective art such as had still ruled in the Gothic. They are alone and unique—in spite of their countless imitators—for they are individual, and not only in their personality and the works born from it; their whole ideology is individual, since it springs from the notion of genius and is only possible through it. These men who are for us the representatives of the type "genius" embody the same process and achievement, on earth and individually, that in its religious form we saw beginning with the image of God. The idea of genius is, in its mythical origin, a *representation* of the immortal soul, that part of the personality which can beget (*gignere*) what is immortal, be it a child or a work.

The idea of the "Genius" comes originally from early Roman times, when it means the personal protecting spirit, of man, as opposed to woman, where it is called "Juno" and corresponds to the Egyptian "ka" and Greek "daimon." Without discussing this notion of a psychical double of man, which is represented in different forms in the different doctrines of the soul, let us note here that the Roman Genius, in keeping with the cultural idea of Rome that was built up on the right of the father, acquired the

[7] Edgar Zilsel: *Die Geniereligion; ein kritischer Versuch über das moderne Persönlichkeitsideal* (Leipzig, 1918). See also, in connection with what follows, the older work of Jacob Cahan: "Zur Kritik des Geniebegriffs" (diss., Berne, 1911).

literal meaning of "begetter." But Otto is right in maintaining that the current explanation of Genius as a deified incarnation of masculine reproductive power does not fully explain the idea.[8] Thus, Genius is also the god of one's birthday—and Otto concluded that the idea contains, as well as the notion of begetting, that of the descent also and indeed that of the continuity of all life. It is hard to see why philologists find this view so difficult, since it is precisely the stage of father-right that is characterized by the collectivizing of the personal reproductive impulse. And so the Roman idea of Genius contains from the beginning, in addition to the individual urge to reproduction, a collective element which points beyond the individual, in a way that is not true of the Egyptian ka and the Greek daimon, both of which are purely personal.[9] For this reason it was specially fitted to become a social conception of genius that should include both individual and collective elements. Still the artist's concept of genius is more personal than collective and thus needs a new ideology. This could no longer be a personal peculiarity of style deduced from a collective idea of the soul, but had to become an *aesthetic of feeling* dependent on consciousness of personality.

Thus the eighteenth century, which was completely sterile of any collective art and was distinguished only by a few dominant artistic individualities, produced an aesthetic as abstracted from the art-products of earlier ages. This was not, however, the universally valid "science of art" that it was for so long supposed to be, but was itself a new ideology of art, which was to replace the now decadent religious collective ideology by a psychological artistic ideology corresponding to the new genius-type. Aesthetic is thus the psychological ideology of art, born from the notion of the genius-type and not from the collective—and religious—notion of style. Our Classicist aes-

[8] W. Otto: *Die Manen oder von den Urformen des Totenglaubens* (Berlin, 1923).

[9] E. Bickel shows brilliantly (*Homerischer Seelenglaube: geschichtliche Grundzüge menschlicher Seelenvorstelungen;* Berlin, 1925) how all these various soul-ideas eventually, in the late period of Greece, passed into the new concept of *psyche,* which prepared the way for the Christian idea of the soul.

thetic in fact directs its gaze much more to the individual art-product of Classical artists, while the abstract style of which Worringer speaks appears much more as a collective product. When Worringer explains the incongruence of art-history and aesthetic by the fact that our aesthetic is nothing more than a psychology of the Classical way of feeling art, he is certainly right; but there will probably always be a similar incongruence between every ideology and its concretization, as indeed there actually is between our aesthetic and the corresponding intuitive (*einfühlende*) art, as also between the religious art of Egypt and medieval Christianity and the works respectively produced by them.

In addition to this natural divergence between an ideology and its concretization, there is in artistic creation yet another decisive factor which aesthetic would have to neglect entirely if it sought to make its laws absolute, and this is the personality of the artist, with his own system of ideology, which perhaps runs largely parallel with the general, but by no means coincides with it. These problems of the boundaries between psychology and aesthetics we will postpone until a later chapter; here we need only state that even Worringer underestimates the influence of the creative personality when he is dealing with art- and style-forms from the standpoint of their aesthetic effects, however he may emphasize the importance of abstract art as well as intuitive.

True, in a summing-up which is perhaps the culminating point of his magnificent argument, Worringer says that the psychological victory over this aesthetic dualism is found in the demand for self-renunciation which lies at the root of all aesthetic experience and which is achieved now by intuition (*Einfühlung*), now by abstraction. But it is just these ultimate psychological problems of art that will trip us up if we have neglected or inadequately understood the creative personality, an understanding that is an inherent necessity in all aesthetic, however far it may advance into the domain of psychology. For aesthetic, by its nature, can only deal with the effect of a work of art, and it takes account of its creation by an artist only by arguing theoretically back from the contemplator to the creator. But this conclusion, apart from its indirect nature, is a fallacy; for as we (or at least as I, myself) have been convinced by a study of the productive personality, there is between that and the unproductive type not only a quantitative but a qualitative difference. The quantitative difference, which is obvious, would be enough in itself to throw doubt on the soundness of thus arguing back from the receptive to the creative; and the qualitative demands a wholly new orientation to the problem, which we shall attempt at least to suggest in the chapter on the play-impulse and aesthetic pleasure. But even at the outset it seems to me clear that the idea of intuition (*Einfühlung*) as fashioned by psychological aesthetic has been attained as from a viewpoint of reception, while the notion of abstraction that Worringer contrasts with it refers rather to the spiritual attitude of the creative artist. In any case, there is here a vagueness of concepts, though it is not attributable to Worringer's unitary interpretation, but belongs to all aesthetic. Ever since Aristotle's day this seems to me to have begun with the tacit assumption that the artist intended to present the effect he aimed at in his phenomenal form, and that therefore there were involved in the creation, at least potentially, the same psychological experiences and psychical processes as are to be observed in the contemplator of the work and especially in the aesthetic critic.

Without disputing that in some cases the artist does aim at a definite idea effect in his work, it is certainly not the rule, especially with the individual work of the creative artist, since here the work of art is essentially an expression of his personality. Nor need we doubt that the artist occasionally does find pleasure and satisfaction in his creation, though the confessions of great artists themselves generally tell rather of the struggle and suffering of creating it. But the fundamental difference in essence between the creative and the receptive types, which are psychologically complementary, is not affected by such evidences. While aesthetic pleasure, whether in the creator or in the contemplator, is ultimately a renunciation of self, the essence of the creative impulse is the exactly opposite tendency toward assertion of self. Here again, however, we must be careful not to set up this opposition, in the form in which we have to state it, as if it were absolute. There may be periods in which a strong individualism or a particular development of personality expresses its tendency toward a self-assertion in creativity as opposed to other periods of collective subordination that involve rather a self-negation. In other words, the dualism of the individual and the community, which we showed to be the fundamental conflict, appears here also in a psychological form and in its relation to various forms of art. Even though we found religion with its collectivizing tendency to be ultimately restrictive of art, this really means only that under its influence another art grows and flourishes in which the individual art-expression, being alien, is thwarted and that this again reacts to force collective art into new paths. All the same, it seems psychologically indispensable to set an impulse of self-assertion against that of self-negation if we are to understand the creative personality as it develops out of the idea of genius.

Though this artistic type, as such, was only born with the Renaissance and developed from the idea of genius, yet it must have existed previously as a creative type in the sense of an urge to self-assertion, since otherwise no art, and least of all the strongly marked naturalistic art of prehistoric man, would have been possible. Our psychological knowledge of the type begins only with the Renaissance; and there already it denotes—artistically, sociologically, and psychologically—something different, which we can only conjecturally assume in the artists of earlier epochs. *Psychologically,* the notion of genius, of which we see the last reflection in our modern artist-type, is the apotheosis of man as a creative personality: the religious ideology (looking to the glory of God) being thus transferred to man himself.[1] *Sociologically,* it meant the creation and recognition of "genius" as a type, as a culture-

[1] See the extract, on page 98, from Pico della Mirandola's oration on human dignity, which is described by Burckhardt (*Die Kultur der Renaissance in Italien*) as "one of the noblest achievements of this cultural period."

factor of highest value to the community, since it takes over on earth the rôle of the divine hero. *Artistically,* it implies the individual style, which indeed still holds on to the exemplars that later appear in aesthetic as formulated law, but which is already free and autonomous in its divine creative power and is creating new forms from out of itself. This artist, liberated from God, himself become god, soon overleaps the collective forms of style and their abstract formulation in aesthetic and constructs new forms of an individual nature, which cannot, therefore, be subsumed under laws. And so our Classicist aesthetic of the eighteenth century appears as a final attempt to save the Classical forms—if not wholly, at any rate in abstract formulae—before they were shattered by the individual *Sturm und Drang* effort of the self-creative personality. Aesthetic appears here as the last endeavor to find art's psychological justification in itself, which corresponds exactly to the self-justification of the artist in the psychological type of the genius.

Here begins the "art for art's sake" ideology, and here too is the source of all artistic psychology, both of which began with the birth of the genius-notion. Psychology is, of course (at least as dealing with the problem of the personality), a young science, so that it will be best to start with its latest results that we may be clear as to what it has contributed to the elucidation of these problems and what still remains obscure. Now, the latest statements in this field show with astonishing frankness and unanimity that the psychology of personality has helped little or not at all to the understanding of genius or (as it is termed scientifically) the productive personality;[2] moreover, that it probably never will contribute anything, since ultimately we are dealing with dynamic factors that remain incomprehensible in their specific expression in the individual personality. This implies that they can be neither predetermined nor wholly explained even ex post facto; as, indeed, we cannot understand, in my view, personality at

[2] E. Kretschmer: *Geniale Menschen* (Berlin, 1929; reprinted lectures of 1919); W. Lange-Eichbaum: *Genie-Irrsinn und Ruhm* (Munich, 1928); P. Plaut: *Psychologie der produktiven Persönlichkeit* (Stuttgart, 1929).

all, even man as such, by a purely individual psychology.[3] In any event, the notion of art had always proved too narrow to include under one aspect the varieties of productive personality or their manifold achievements; and on the other hand the psychological idea of the productive personality was far too wide to explain artistic production. For, psychologically speaking, there are productive personalities who never produce a work of art, or indeed anything creative at all; and, again, the poet may be so different from the plastic artist, the musician, or the scientifically productive type that it is impossible to bring them all under one head.

The study of a certain neurotic type, which I had already regarded as *artiste manqué* in my youthful work, gave me a new approach, on the basis of that analysis, to the problem of the creative personality. We have in such cases either individuals who, though they are really productive (since they possess the productive force of dynamism), produce nothing, or else artistically productive men who feel themselves restricted in their possibilities of expression. Pure psychoanalysis of such types, undertaken for the removal of inhibitions as indicated by Freud's therapy, did not help at all for the psychological understanding of the creative process, although it established a fair amount regarding their behavior as individuals. The only tangible statement which Freud's theory could give us about the artistic process was that which asserted that the impulse to artistic productivity originated in the sex-impulse. But it is easy to see that this explanation (which I myself accepted in my first work on the psychology of artists) takes us no further in reality, being a pure paraphrase of the individual meaning already obvious in the very concept of genius (*gignere* = to beget). But psychology could not explain how from the sex-impulse there was produced, not the sex-act, but the art-work, and all the ideas called in to bridge this infinite gulf—"compensation," "sublimation," etc.—were only psychological

[3] One may be unable, for example, to arrive at an individual psychological explanation of homosexuality in the artist (Michelangelo, Shakespeare) and yet understand why a particular artist-type is, and almost necessarily must be, homosexual (see pages 153 ff.).

transcriptions for the fact that we have here something different, higher and symbolical.

Dreams, too, which in the new interpretation of Freud seemed to promise so much for the elucidation of artistic creativity, proved, on a more careful comprehension of the problem, to be incapable of taking us beyond a superficial analogy.[4] The fact that we all dream and, in dreams, are all (in the fine comparison of Schopenhauer) poets of the stature of Dante or Shakespeare is sufficient by itself to force to our notice the fact that we do not know what it is which allows a Dante or a Shakespeare to do in waking life what we all, according to Schopenhauer, do in our sleep. They all (as I expressed it) superadd, to their equipment and their creative dream-fantasy, a particular ideology of art. And so we are back at our question, What individuals are driven and able to do this and what psychological presuppositions make it possible? If we approach the problem from the study of the productive neurotic type—that is, if we start with the artistic type living today—we arrive at the following condition for creative art. The neurotic, no matter whether productive or obstructed, suffers fundamentally from the fact that he cannot or will not accept himself, his own individuality, his own personality. On one hand he criticizes himself to excess, on the other he idealizes himself to excess, which means that he makes too great demands on himself and his completeness, so that failing to attain leads only to more self-criticism. If we take this thwarted type, as we may do for our purposes, and compare him to the artist, it is at once clear that the artist is in a sense the antithesis to the self-critical neurotic type. Not that the artist does not criticize himself, but by accepting his personality he not only fulfills that for which the neurotic is striving in vain but goes far beyond it. The precondition, then, of the creative personality is not only its acceptance but its actual glorification of itself.

The religion of genius and the cult of personality thus begin, in the creative individual, with himself; he, so to

[4] On the subject of dreams and art, see also Friedrich von Hausegger: *Das Jenseits des Künstlers.*

say, appoints himself as an artist, though this is only possible if the society in which he lives has an ideology of genius, recognizes it, and values it. This leads straight to the realization that the productive personality, if it has once accomplished this self-appointment by the aid of his community's ideology of the artist, must justify this self-assertion under compulsion by its work and by ever higher achievement. And so the problem of the process of artistic creation, which is no more than a compulsory dynamic, shifts to its precondition, which is the glorification of the individual personality. At this point we have a fruitful parallel to the "absolute will-to-art" which Riegl talks of and Worringer defines as a lifting of the object out of nature and its eternalization in an abstract schematic form that reproduces the essential. We see that the very same process that at the primitive stage of the collective abstract style relates to the object, takes place at the developed stage of individual art, in relation to the subject; in other words, the individual raises himself from out of the community by his inclusion in the genius-type in just the same way as the object is torn from its natural surroundings by its artistic stylization. The individual, as it were, abstracts himself in the style demanded by the genius-ideology and so concentrates the essence of his being, the reproductive urge, in the genius-concept. He says, more or less, that he needs only to create and not to beget.[5] The novelty of our present view lies, however, in this: that we have good reason for assuming that *this creativity begins with the individual himself—that is, with the self-making of the personality into the artist,* which we have described previously as his appointment to the genius-type. The creative artistic personality is thus the first work of the productive individual, and it remains fundamentally his chief work, since all his other works are partly the repeated expression of this primal creation, partly a justification by dynamism.

I regard it as the double advantage of this insight into

[5] Here, perhaps, there is a most suggestive link with Schulte-Vaerting's theory of the "sexual superman" (1928), which he regards as a biological throwback phenomenon.

artistic personality-development that is gained from a study of the modern type, not only that it is applicable to the understanding of all cultural genesis, but that, moreover (according to a theory of art which I only came across after the event), artistic personality appears to subsist already in the beginning of all artistic production. Certain modern art-historians assume that the origin of primitive art is to be found neither in the imitation of nature nor in the impulse to abstraction, but in bodily ornament. As far as I know, Ernst Grosse was the first, in his book on the beginnings of art (1894), to insist on the priority of body-painting over ornamental decoration; and Adam van Scheltema particularly has tried to extend the idea even to prehistoric art (*Die altnordische Kunst;* 1923). It is sufficient here to refer the reader to a later exposition and to quote the (to the best of my belief) latest author who champions this view; according to which we should be justified in saying that the tendency toward self-creation which is brought to light in modern artist-psychology is one of the essential components of artistic creation even in primitive times. E. von Sydow accepts the view that "the beginning of art lay in its application to the body."[6] He does not, however, mention his predecessors, so that it is apparently psychoanalysis which led him to this idea. Yet, if this were so, the psychoanalysts interested in the problem of art would not have needed to wait for Sydow in order to introduce this principle of explanation into the history of art, and anyhow it would be a confirmation on their part of a view which is alien to them. For this view of art presupposes a voluntaristic psychology, which in my own case I was only able to reach after passing beyond the libido theory of Freud, and which takes Sydow also far beyond his sexualization of the artistic impulse.

Sydow, it is true, appeals to the deliberate interference with the natural form of the body in primitive tribes, which in some cases, although not always, is sexual in character: for instance, the deformation of the skull, the piercing of ears, lips, nose, etc But even in the artificial painting of the body and the tattooing which is to be found

[6] Op. cit., pp. 173 ff.

all over the world, the sexual explanation fails completely; and so Sydow's generalization looks more like an instance of our self-conscious impulse to creation than a proof that art in particular has a sexual origin. "Art rose, not in any isolated and self-contained work, but by the moulding of the human body, to a formative plasticity, urged thereto by an idealized instinct of will to style. It is true, indeed, that even at this stage the art-form not only serves to give a close support to the human form, as it is found in nature, *but impresses and enforces a dominant form on the natural material of bone, flesh, and blood, as an assertion of its own independence;* so that art in this application of it to man himself achieves or seeks to achieve a truly *new creation.* It is only when the art of the body has been perfected that it separates itself from the body and becomes self-dependent in a permanent work." [7] Yet again, to make this view sound, we must give a plausible explanation of why body-art passed over to ornament proper, a problem of which there have been some preliminary explanations, but which, if we assume the priority of "body-art," more than ever demands a clear psychological understanding of the development of personality—to which accordingly we must now pass.

Whatever the meaning of the much-disputed tattooing as the essential expression of body-art may be, it is at least certain that practical objects, such as hardening the skin or the attraction or repulsion of others, do not have a great bearing. The purely sensual interpretation of tattooing, as suggested by W. Joest,[8] has nowadays given place to the magic interpretation, as emphasized in Jane Harrison's well-known *Ancient Art and Ritual* and as has been admitted by W. D. Hambly in his most recent discussion of the subject.[9] But there is no sort of consensus as to the real point of this magical painting of the body. We shall have opportunity later to give our own view; here it is enough to state the general conclusion that an artistic achievement is also part of the business. It seems, too,

[7] Op. cit.; italics mine.
[8] *Tâtowiren, Narbenzeichnen, und Körperbemalen* (Berlin, 1887).
[9] *The History of Tattooing and its Significance* (London, 1925).

worth mentioning in this connection that certain linguists connect the German word *malen* (to paint) with the drawing-in of body-marks (*Mal*) or signs, just as the Tahitian word *tatu* is derived from *ta,* which means "mark" or "sign." Among the American Indians as well as the Australians and other peoples, a typical form of painting is, in fact, the sign of the tribe, which indicates membership of a particular totem, and is therefore in a sense a collective badge of the individual that robs him of his personality in order to include him in a community, and yet on the other hand does not merely label him, but enhances his individual significance by marking it off from certain others. Both would explain why tattooing follows on the puberty ceremonies at which the individual becomes both a personality and a member of a community. On the other hand, the belief held by the Fijians and the Eskimos alike that to remain untattooed is to hazard one's future happiness in the world beyond throws a light on the religious significance of tattooing, a significance that inheres also in membership of a particular totem-society. We have thus, along with the enhancement of (and even emphasis on) the self, its leveling-down by means of the collective symbol; so that in fact we should find the fundamental dualism of art even at the primary stage of human creative instinct. This discovery loses much of its strangeness and gains considerably in probability when we remember that the same thing is found in the medieval guild uniforms, and still exists today in the uniform of various professions, which marks out the individual above his neighbors, but makes him, as beyond himself, a member of a great professional group or class.

From this point of view, of course, we cannot admit it to be mere chance that the "Bohemian" artist of modern times, even as late as the close of last century, had a definite costume, even a conventional mode of doing the hair and beard, which were to mark him out as a "genius." The proper artist, who had chosen art as his profession, had a special manner, almost a special life, laid down for him; and in actual fact he had to play a definite part determined by an ideology; so also, according to Dessoir, the actor nowadays represents this pristine type of artist, where object and subject coincide, and the body forms the material in which and through which the artist creates. So, even at this last stage of the individual "artist's art," we have the genius-type to which the artist tries to suit himself even in costume and manner, serving as an ideology for artistic creation; just as earlier aesthetic, and still earlier religion, had provided the art-ideologies of their various times and places. Yet, be it observed, these were ideologies of *art*—that is, collective style-laws, as in religious art, or psychological laws of feeling in aesthetes' art—but at this latest stage of individual artist's art we are concerned no longer with an ideology of *art,* whether abstract or emotional, but an ideology of the artist; and this means a justification of *art-creation* in the creative personality itself that struggles for eternalization, and not a justification of *art* by some abstract impulse of the soul, as in religion, or in aesthetic of sensation, as in psychology.

Now, though Worringer quite rightly opposes linear art, which develops from the impulse to abstraction, to the Classical art, which is intuitive, this is obviously not enough, for we have here a third type of art, which is as different from the other two as the one is from the other. If we want a word to set in parallel with "abstraction" and "intuition" as expressing the spiritual attitude of modern art, based on an individual, we may talk of an art of "expression"—in fact, the word, as "expressionism," has been taken as their slogan by a group of modern artists (according to Sydow, called also "psychic vitalism"). But since we are ourselves living in the midst of this art, it is doubly difficult to pass from a purely aesthetic judgment to a psychological valuation. It is too tempting to look for a historical comparison and a cultural valuation of this "modern art"; Worringer, strangely enough, does not admit modern art to be the expression of any "will-to-form" of its own, but regards it rather as an expression of "inability," which he does, however, concede to the result of an excessive urge to equal—or to outdo—earlier epochs.[1]

We shall have to discuss in a later chapter the reasons

[1] Wilhelm Worringer: *Künstlerische Zeitfragen* (Munich, 1921).

for which our present-day culture had to come out at the art that it has done. At the moment it is more important to notice in these art-forms only the exaggeration (or, if you like, the distortion) of a quality common to all creative art, which entitles such an art as this to its place with the rest in the development of forms; in the same way as we tried to understand abstract and naturalistic styles not only as art-forms but as psychical expressions. Then we shall see that we have here to deal, not with a third type of art, nor indeed with a type of art or a style at all, but with spiritual needs that at one time are abstract, at another naturalistic, at a third individualistic. It is not our business to attempt an aesthetic judgment—least of all before we have studied the question how far the psychical basis of the modern artist can be traced up in the origins and development of Classical and abstract art. Yet it may be that the genesis of the creative personality, which is the problem that this book is seeking to unravel, will throw a new light on the form of art that is included under the aesthetic law of intuition (*Einfühlung*) and may even contribute to the elucidation of other, still obscure points in that abstract style of primitive art that so purely expresses the absolute will-to-form.

III *Life and Creation*

What would live in song immortally
Must in life first perish. . . .
—SCHILLER

BEFORE we trace the rise and significance of this "artist's art," if one may so call it, as it grows out of the primitive art-ideologies, it is perhaps desirable to characterize more clearly its essential precondition: the creative personality itself. In spite of all "unconsciousness" in artistic production (a point to which we shall return later), there can be no doubt that the modern individualist type of artist is characterized by a higher degree of consciousness than his earlier prototype: the consciousness not only of his creative work and his artist's mission, but also of his own personality and its productiveness. If, as it should seem, the instinctive will-to-art (Riegl), which creates abstract forms, has in this last stage of artistic development become a conscious will-to-art in the artist, yet the actual process that leads a man to become an artist is usually one of which the individual is not conscious. In other words, the act we have described as the artist's self-appointment as such is in itself a spontaneous expression of the creative impulse, of which the first manifestation is simply the forming of the personality itself. Needless to say, this purely internal process does not suffice to make an artist, let alone a genius, for, as Lange-Eichbaum has said, only the community, one's contemporaries, or posterity can do that. Yet the self-labeling and self-training of an artist is the indispensable basis of all creative work, and without it general recognition could never arise. The artist's lifelong work on his own productive personality appears to run through definite phases, and his art develops in proportion to the success of these phases. In the case of great artists, the process is reflected in the fact that they had either a principal or a favorite work, at which they labored all their lives (Goethe's *Faust*, Rodin's *Porte d'enfer*, Michelangelo's Tomb of Julius, and so on), or a favorite theme, which they never relinquished and which came to be a distinct representation of themselves (as, for example, Rembrandt's self-portraits).

On the other hand, this process of the artist's self-forming and self-training is closely bound up with his life and his experiences. In studying this fundamental problem of the relation between living and creating in an artist, we are therefore again aware of the reciprocal influence of these two spheres. All the psychography and pathography (with its primary concern to explain the one through the other) must remain unsatisfactory as long as the creative impulse, which finds expression equally in experience and in productiveness, is not recognized as the basis of both. For, as I already showed in my essay on Schiller (written in 1905), creativeness lies equally at the root of artistic production and of life experience.[1] That is to say, lived experience can only be understood as the expression of volitional creative impulse, and in this the two spheres of artistic production and actual experience meet and overlap. Then, too, the creative impulse itself is manifested first and chiefly in the personality, which, being thus perpetually made over, produces art-work and experience in the same way. To draw the distinction quite drastically between this new standpoint and earlier ones, one might put it that the artist does not create from his own experience (as Goethe, for instance, so definitely appears to do), but almost in spite of it. For the creative impulse in the artist, springing from the tendency to immortalize himself, is so powerful that he is always seeking to protect himself against the transient experience, which eats up his ego. The

[1] *Das Inzestmotiv in Dichtung und Sage* (Chapters iii and xvi). I found the same conception later in Simmel's *Goethe* (Berlin, 1913).

artist takes refuge, with all *his own* experience only from the life of *actuality*, which for him spells mortality and decay, whereas the experience to which he has given shape imposes itself on him as a creation, which he in fact seeks to turn into a work. And although the whole artist-psychology may seem to be centered on the "experience," this itself can be explained only through the creative impulse—which attempts to turn ephemeral life into personal immortality. In creation the artist tries to immortalize his mortal life. He desires to transform death into life, as it were, though actually he transforms life into death. For not only does the created work not go on living; it is, in a sense, dead, both as regards the material, which renders it almost inorganic, and also spiritually and psychologically, in that it no longer has any significance for its creator, once he has produced it. He therefore again takes refuge in life, and again forms experiences, which for their part represent only mortality—and it is precisely because they are mortal that he wishes to immortalize them in his work.

The first step toward understanding this mutual relation between life and work in the artist is to gain a clear idea of the psychological significance of the two phenomena. This is only possible, however, on the basis of a constructive psychology of personality, reaching beyond the psychoanalytical conception, which is a therapeutic ideology resting on the biological sex-impulse. We have come to see that another factor must be reckoned with besides the original biological duality of impulse and inhibition in man; this is the psychological factor par excellence, the individual will, which manifests itself both negatively as a controlling element, and positively as the urge to create. This creator-impulse is not, therefore, sexuality, as Freud assumed, but expresses the antisexual tendency in human beings, which we may describe as the deliberate control of the impulsive life. To put it more precisely, I see the creator-impulse as the life-impulse made to serve the individual will. When psychoanalysis speaks of a sublimated sexual impulse in creative art, meaning thereby the impulse diverted from its purely biological function and directed toward higher ends, the question as to what diverted and what directed is just being dismissed with an allusion to repression. But repression is a negative factor, which might divert, but never direct. And so the further question remains to be answered, What, originally, led to such repression? As we know, the answer to this question was outward deprivation; but that again suggests a merely negative check, and I, for my part, am of opinion that (at any rate from a certain definite point of individual development) positively willed control takes the place of negative inhibition, and that it is the masterful use of the sexual impulse in the service of this individual will that produces the sublimation.

But even more important for us than these psychological distinctions is the basic problem of why this inhibition occurs at all, and what the deliberate control of the vital impulse means to the individual. Here, again, in opposition to the Freudian conception of an external threat as the cause of the inhibition, I suggest that the internal threatening of the individual through the sexual impulse of the species is at the root of all conflict. Side by side with this self-imposed internal check, which is taken to be what prevents or lessens the development of fear, there stands the will as a positive factor. The various controls that it exercises enable the impulses to work themselves out partially without the individual's falling completely under their influence or having to check them completely by too drastic repression. Thus, in the fully developed individual, we have to reckon with the triad Impulse-Fear-Will, and it is the dynamic relationship among these factors that determines either the attitude at a given moment or—when equilibrium is established—the type. Unsatisfactory as it may be to express these dynamic processes in terms like "type," it remains the only method of carrying an intelligible idea of them—always assuming that the inevitable simplification in this is not lost sight of. If we compare the neurotic with the productive type, it is evident that the former suffers from an excessive check on his impulsive life, and according to whether this neurotic checking of the instincts is effected through fear or through will, the picture presented is one of fear-neurosis or compulsion-neurosis. With the productive type the will dominates, and exercises a far-reaching control over (but not check upon) the instincts, which are pressed into service to bring about creatively a social relief of fear. Finally, the instincts appear relatively unchecked in the so-called psychopathic subject, in whom the will affirms the impulse instead of controlling it. In this type—to which the criminal belongs—we have, contrary to appearances, to do with *weak*-willed people—people who are subjected to their instinctive impulses. The neurotic, on the other hand, is generally regarded as the weak-willed type, but wrongly so, for his strong will is exercised upon himself and, indeed, in the main repressively, so it does not show itself.

And here we reach the essential point of difference between the productive type who creates and the thwarted neurotic; what is more, it is also the point from which we get back to our individual artist-type. Both are distinguished fundamentally from the average type, who accepts himself as he is, by their tendency to exercise their volition in reshaping themselves. There is, however, this difference: the neurotic, in this voluntary remaking of his ego, does not get beyond the destructive preliminary work and is therefore unable to detach the whole creative process from his own person and transfer it to an ideological abstraction. The productive artist also begins (as a satisfactory psychological understanding of the "will-to-style" has obliged us to conclude) with that re-creation of himself which results in an ideologically constructed ego; this ego is then in a position to shift the creative will-power from his own person to ideological representations of that person, and thus to render it objective. It must be admitted that this process is in a measure limited to within the individual himself, and that not only in its constructive, but also in its destructive, aspects. This explains why hardly any productive work[2] gets through without morbid crises of a "neurotic" nature; it also explains why the relation between productivity and illness has so far been unrecognized or

[2] This applies, not only to most artists, but also, as Wilhelm Ostwald for one has convincingly proved, to the scientific creative type (*Grosse Männer;* Leipzig, 1909).

misinterpreted, as, for instance, in Lombroso's theory of the insanity of genius. Today this theory appears to us as the precipitate left by the old endeavors to explain genius on rational-psychological lines, which treated such features as depart from the normal as "pathological." However much in the Italian psychiatrist's theory is an exaggeration of the materialism of nineteenth-century science, yet undeniably it had a startling success, and this I attribute to the fact that genius itself, in its endeavor to differentiate itself from the average, has probably dramatized its pathological features also. But the psychologist should beware of deducing from this apparent factor any conclusions as to the production or total personality, without taking into account the feeling of guilt arising from the creative process itself; for this is capable of engendering a feeling of inferiority as a secondary result, even though the primary result may be a conviction of superiority. As I have said elsewhere, the fundamental problem is *individual difference*, which the ego is inclined to interpret as inferiority unless it can be proved by achievement to be superiority.

Even psychoanalysis in its turn did not succeed in surmounting Lombroso's materialist theory of insanity or supplementing his rational explanation by a spiritual one. All it did was to substitute neurosis for insanity (which was at bottom Lombroso's own meaning), thus tending either to identify the artist with the neurotic—this is particularly the case in Sadger's and Stekel's arguments—or to explain the artist on the basis of an inferiority feeling. (Alfred Adler and his school took the latter view.)[3] It is characteristic that during the last few years the psychiatrists (such as Lange-Eichbaum, Kretschmer, Plaut) who have contributed most towards clearing up the position of genius are precisely those who have managed to keep clear of the one-sidedness of these psychoanalytic schools. And if these researches have not made any important contribution

[3] A characteristic instance of how, in avoiding the Scylla of Lombroso, one may fall a victim to the Charybdis of analytical psychology is afforded by Victor Jonesco's book *La Personalité du génie artiste* (Paris, 1930), which I read only after the completion of my own work. A praiseworthy exception is Bernard Grasset's original essay *Psychologie de l'immortalité* (Paris, 1929).

to the understanding of the process of creating, psychoanalysis, even in its exaggerations, must at least be credited with having discovered that experience, in so far as it is the antithesis of production, embraces not only the relations of love and friendship, but also those morbid reactions of a psychic and bodily nature that are known as "neurotic." A real understanding of these neurotic illnesses could not, however, be satisfactorily obtained as long as we tried to account for them in the Freudian sense by thwarted sexuality. What was wanted in addition was a grasp of the general problem of fear and of the will-psychology going therewith that should allow for the exercise of the will, both constructively and destructively, affecting the ego and the work equally. Only through the will-to-self-immortalization, which rises from the fear of life, can we understand the interdependence of production and suffering and the definite influence of this on positive experience. This does not preclude production being a creative development of a neurosis in objective form; and on the other hand, a neurotic collapse may follow as a reaction after production, owing either to a sort of exhaustion or to a sense of guilt arising from the power of creative masterfulness as something arrogant.[4]

Reverting now from the production-process to experience, it does not take long to perceive that experience is the expression of the impulse-ego, production of the will-ego. The external difficulties in an artist's experience appear, in this sense, but as manifestations of this internal dualism of impulse and will, and in the creative type it is the latter which eventually gains the upper hand. Instinct presses in the direction of experience and, in the limit, to consequent exhaustion—in fact, death—while will drives to creation and thus to immortalization. On the other hand, the productive type also pays toll to life by his work and to death by bodily and spiritual sufferings of a "neurotic"

[4] How this feeling of guilt can hinder or, on the other hand, further productivity, I have shown in my book *Wahrheit und Wirklichkeit* (1929), in the section on the sense of guilt in creation. [EDITOR'S NOTE: In English translation, this may be found in the one-volume edition of *Will Therapy and Truth and Reality* (New York: Alfred A. Knopf; 1945), pp. 270–91.]

order; and conversely, in many cases, the product of a type that is at bottom neurotic may be his sole propitiatory offering to Life. It is with reason, therefore, that from the beginning two basic types of artist have been distinguished; these have been called at one time Dionysian and Apollonian, and at another Classical and Romantic.[5] In terms of our present dynamic treatment, the one approximates to the psychopathic-impulsive type, the other to the compulsion-neurotic volitional type. The one creates more from fullness of powers and sublimation, the other more from exhaustion and compensation. The work of the one is entire in every single expression, that of the other is partial even in its totality, for the one lives itself out, positively, in the work, while the other pays with the work —pays, not to society (for both do that), but to life itself, from which the one strives to win freedom by self-willed creation, whereas for the other the thing created is the expression of life itself.

This duality within one and the same type is of outstanding significance in the psychology of the productive type and in the work it produces. For, while in the two classes of neurotics (frustrated by fear and by the will, respectively) the form of the neurosis is of minor matter compared with the fact of breaking down the inhibition itself, by the curative process of dynamic equilibration, in the productive type the dynamism itself determines not only the kind but the form of his art. But this highly complicated problem is only mentioned here with a view to discussion later, and we will turn from the two artist-types, which Müller-Freienfels, in his *Psychologie der Kunst,* characterizes as "expressive artists" and "formative artists,"[6] back to the problem of experience that is common to both. This problem, as was pointed out at the beginning of this chapter, only becomes intelligible through the conception of immortality. There appears to be a common impulse in all creative types to replace collective immortality—as it is represented biologically in sexual propaga-

[5] E. von Sydow distinguishes these polar opposites, from the standpoint of aesthetic, as "eros-dominated" and "eros-dominating" (op. cit., p. 164).

[6] Vol. II, pp. 100 ff.

tion—by the individual immortality of deliberate self-perpetuation. This is, however, a relatively late stage of development in the conception of immortality, after it has already become individualized—a stage preceded by attempts to create conceptions of collective immortality, of which the most important is religion. I have tried in another connection[7] to show how, within religious development itself, the idea of the collective soul was gradually transformed into the idea of the individual god, whose heir the artist later became. In the foregoing pages likewise, I have indicated that the initial conception of an individual god, subsequently to be humanized in the genius, had itself been helped on, and perhaps even only rendered possible, by art. But there was an early stage of artistic development, which was at the same time the climax of religious development, in which the individual artist played no part because creative power was still the prerogative of the god.

The individual artist, whose growth from the creative conception of a god has been sketched out, no longer uses the collective ideology of religion to perpetuate himself, but the personal religion of genius, which is the precondition of any productions by the individual artist-type. And so we have *primitive art*, the expression of a collective ideology, perpetuated by abstraction which has found its *religious* expression in the idea of the soul; *Classical art*, based on a *social* art-concept, perpetuated by *idealization*, which has found its purest expression in the conception of beauty; and, lastly, *modern art*, based on the concept of individual genius and perpetuated by *concretization*, which has found its clearest expression in the personality-cult of the artistic individuality itself. Here, then, in contrast to the primitive stage, it is the artist and not art that matters, and naturally therefore the experience of the individual takes on the significance characteristic of the Romantic artist-type.[8] Here, obviously, not only do we see the tendency—in our view the basic tendency—of the artist-type

[7] *Seelenglaube und Psychologie.*

[8] What interests us today in Byron, for instance, is his romantic life, and not his out-of-date poetry.

to put oneself and one's life into one's creative work; but we see also how, in the eyes of this type, the problem of the relation between experience and creation[9] has become an artistic (aesthetic) one; whereas it is really only a psychological one, which discloses, indeed, important points of contact with art (considered as an ideological conception), but differs from it in essence.

For the Romantic dualism of life and production, which manifests itself as a mixture of both spheres, has, as a typical conflict within the modern individual, nothing to do with art, although obliged like art to express itself creatively. This Romantic dualism of life and creation, which corresponds to our psychological dualism of impulse and will, is, in the last resort, the conflict between collective and individual immortality, in which we have all suffered so acutely since the decay of religion and the decline of art. The Romantic type, flung hither and thither between the urge to perpetuate his own life by creating and the compulsion to turn himself and life into a work of art, thus appears as the last representative of an art-ideology which, like the religious collective-ideology, is in process of dying out. This does not prevent this final attempt to rescue the semi-collective "religion of genius" by taking it into modern individualism from bringing forth outstanding and permanently valuable works of art; perhaps, indeed, (as Nietzsche himself, the ultraromantic, recognized), it requires that it should. On the other hand, it is just the appearance of this decadent type of artist which marks the beginning of a new development of personality, since the tendency to self-perpetuation is in the end transferred to the ego from which it originally sprang.[1]

On this issue the Romantic becomes identical, as a psychological type, with the neurotic—this is not a valuation, but merely a statement of fact—and for that matter

[9] See W. Dilthey *Erlebnis und Dichtung.* The artist-personalities examined there in relation to this problem are, as is natural, chiefly Romantic types (Lessing, Goethe, Novalis, Hölderlin).

[1] EDITOR'S NOTE: This aspect is discussed in greater detail in "The Artist's Struggle," a later chapter in *Art and Artist,* not included in this selection of excerpts.

the comparison may even be reversed, since the neurotic likewise has creative, or, at least, self-creative, forces at command. We can thus understand the experience-problem of the individualist type of artist also only by studying the nature of neurosis, just as the therapy of the neurotic requires an understanding of the creative type.[2] Now, the neurotic represents the individual who aims at self-preservation by restricting his experience, thus showing his adherence to the naïve faith in immortality of the primitive, though without the collective soul-ideology that supports that faith. The productivity of the individual, or of the thing created, replaces—for the artist as for the community—the originally religious ideology by a social value; that is, the work of art not only immortalizes the artist ideologically instead of personally, but also secures to the community a future life in the collective elements of the work. Even at this last stage of individual art-creativity there function ideologies (whether given or chosen) of an aesthetic, a social, or a psychological nature as collective justifications of the artist's art, in which the personal factor makes itself more and more felt and appreciated.

If the impulse to create productively is explicable only by the conception of immortality, the question of the experience-problem of the neurotic has its source in failure of the impulse to perpetuate, which results in fear, but is also probably conditioned by it. There is (as I have shown) a double sort of fear: on the one hand the fear of life that aims at avoidance or postponement of death, and on the other the fear of death that underlies the desire for immortality. According to the compromise that men make between these two poles of fear, and the predominance of one or the other form, there will be various dynamic solutions of this conflict, which hardly permit of description by type-labeling. For, in practice, both in the neurotic and in the productive type—the freely producing and the thwarted—all the forces are brought into play, though with varying accentuation and periodical

[2] This is a point of view I have endeavored to present in my last technical work: *Die Analyse des Analytikers und seine Rolle in der Gesamtsituation* (1931) [included in English translation in *Will Therapy and Truth and Reality*].

balancing of values. In general, a strong preponderance of the fear of life will lead rather to neurotic repression, and the fear of death to production—that is, perpetuation in the work produced. But the fear of life, from which we all suffer, conditions the problem of experience in the productive type as in other people, just as the fear of death whips up the neurotic's constructive powers. The individual whose life is braked is led thereby to flee from experience, because he fears that he will become completely absorbed in it—which would mean death—and so is bound up with fear. Unlike the productive type, who strives to be deathless through his work, the neurotic does not seek immortality in any clearly defined sense, but in primitive fashion as a naïve saying or accumulation of actual life. But even the individualist artist-type must sacrifice both life and experience to make art out of them. Thus we see that what the artist needs for true creative art in addition to his technique and a definite ideology is life in one form or another; and the two artist-types differ essentially in the source from which they take this life that is so essential to production. The Classical type, who is possibly poorer within, but nearer to life, and himself more vital, takes it from without: that is, he creates immortal work from mortal life without necessarily having first transformed it into personal experience as is the case with the Romantic. For, to the Romantic, experience of his own appears to be an essential preliminary to productivity, although he does not use this experience for the enrichment of his own personality, but to economize the personal experiences, the burden of which he would fain escape. Thus the one artist-type constantly makes use of other life than his own—in fact, nature—for the purpose of creating, while the other can create only by perpetually sacrificing his own life. This essential difference of attitude to the fundamental problem of life throws a psychological light on the contrast in styles of various periods in art. Whatever aesthetic designation may be applied to this contrast, from the spiritual point of view the work of the Classicist, more or less naturalistic, artist is essentially *partial,* and the work of the Romantic, produced from within, *total.*[3] This totality-type spends itself perpetually in creative work without absorbing very much of life, while the partial type has continually to absorb life so that he may throw it off again in his work. It is an egoistical artist-type of this order that Ibsen has described in so masterly a fashion. He needs, as it were, for each work that he builds, a sacrifice that is buried alive to insure a permanent existence to the structure, but also to save the artist from having to give himself. The frequent occasions when a great work of art has been created in the reaction following upon the death of a close relation seem to me to realize those favorable cases for this type of artist in which he can dispense with the killing of the building's victim because that victim has died a natural death and has subsequently, to all appearances, had a monument piously erected to him.[4]

The mistake in all modern psychological biography lies in its attempt to "explain" the artist's work by his experience, whereas creation can only be made understandable through the inner dynamism and its central problems. Then, too, the real artist regards his work as more important than the whole of life and experience, which are but a means to production—almost, indeed, a by-product of it. This refers, however, to the Classical type only, for to the Romantic type his personal ego and his experience are more important than, or as important as, his work; sometimes, indeed, production may be simply a means to life, just as to the other type experience is but a means to production. This is why Romantic art is far more

[3] These types, evolved from a study of psychological dynamics (see my *Die Analyse des Analytikers*), are, as I have since discovered, accepted as the essential key-concepts of all polar contrasts of style by P. Frankl in his *Entwicklungsphasen der neueren Baukunst.* True, Frankl's work is not merely limited to architecture, but more narrowly still to the contrast in style between Renaissance and Baroque. We shall presently see, however ("*Schönheit und Wahrheit*"), that this contrast between totality and partiality is a general spiritual distinction between the Classical-naturalistic and the primitive-abstract styles.

[4] Shakespeare's *Hamlet* and Mozart's *Don Juan* are familiar examples of the reaction after a father's death, while Wagner's *Lohengrin* followed on the death of the composer's mother. These works are supreme examples of artists negotiating with the problem of the Beyond. To these instances may be added Ibsen's epilogue *When We Dead Awaken;* here the death is that of the artist himself.

subjective, far more closely bound up with experience, than Classical, which is more objective and linked to life. In no case, however, will the individual become an artist through any *one* experience, least of all through the experiences of childhood (which seem pretty universal). The becoming of an artist has a particular genesis, one of the manifestations of which may be some special experience. For the artistic impulse to create is a dynamic factor apart from the content of experience, a will-problem that the artist solves in a particular way. That is, he is capable of forming the given art-ideology—whether of the collective kind (style) or the personal (genius-idea)—into the substance of his creative will. He employs, so to say, personal will-power to give form or life to an ideology, which must have not only social qualities like other ideologies, but purely artistic ones, which will be more closely specified from the point of view of aesthetics.

The subjective character of modern art, which is based on the ideology of a personal type of artist, imposes also a special outlook in the artist toward his own creative power and his work. The more production is an essential means to life (and not just a particular ideological expression of it), the more will the work itself be required to justify the personality—instead of expressing it—and the more will this subjective artist-type need individuals to justify his production. From this point of view as well as others it is easy to see that experience, in its particular form of love-experience, takes on a peculiar significance for the Romantic artist, whose art is based on the personality-cult of the genius-concept. The primitive artist-type finds his justification in the work itself; the Classical justifies the work by his life; but the Romantic must justify both life and experience by his work and, further, must have a witness of his life to justify his production. The fundamental problem of the Romantic artist is thus the self-justification of the individual raised above the crowd, while the Classical artist-type expresses himself in his work—which receives a social justification by way of general recognition. But the Romantic needs, further, whether as contrast or as supplement to this social approval, a personal approbation of his own, because his feeling of the guilt of creation can no longer be allayed by a collective ideology any more than he can work effectively in the service of such an ideology. In this sense his artistic work is rather a forcible liberation from inward pressure than the voluntary expression of a fundamentally strong personality that is capable of paralyzing the subjective element to a great extent by making collective symbolism his own. The artist who approximates more nearly to the Classical type excels less, therefore, in the creating of new forms than in perfecting them. Further, he will make much more frequent use of old traditional material, full of a powerful collective resonance, as the content of his work, while the Romantic seeks new forms and contents in order to be able to express his personal self more completely.

Thus, as the artist-type becomes more and more individualized, he appears on the one hand to need a more individual ideology—the genius-concept—for his art, while on the other his work is more subjective and more personal, until finally he requires for the justification of his production an individual "public" also: a single person for whom ostensibly he creates. This goes so far in a certain type of artist, which we call the Romantic, that actual production is only possible with the aid of a concrete Muse through whom or for whom the work is produced. The "experience" which arises in this manner is not, like other sorts of experience, an external phenomenon set over against creative work, but is a part of it and even identical with it, always providing that the Muse—in practice, usually a real woman—is suited to this rôle or at least makes no objection to it, and so long as the artist can maintain such a relation on the ideological plane without confusing it with real life. It is this case, in which the conflict between life and creation reaches extreme intensity, that we so often see actualized in the modern type of artist. Here the woman is expected to be Muse and mistress at once, which means that she must justify equally the artistic ego, with its creativeness, and the real self, with its life; and this she seldom (and in any case only temporarily) succeeds in doing. We see the artist of this type working off on the woman his inward struggle between life and production or, psychologically speaking, between impulse and will. It is a tragic fate that he shares with the neurotic, who suffers from the same inner conflict. Another way out of the struggle is to divide its elements between two persons, of whom one belongs to the ideological creative sphere, and the other to the sphere of actual life. But this solution also presents difficulties of a psychological as well as a social order, because this type of artist has a fundamental craving for totality, in life as in work, and the inner conflict, though it may be temporarily eased by being objectivized in such an outward division of rôles, is as a whole only intensified thereby.

The same applies to another solution of this ego-conflict which the artist has in common with the neurotic, and one which shows more clearly even than the complicated love-conflict that it is at bottom a question not of sexual but of creative problems. From the study of a certain class of neurotic, we have found that in many cases of apparent homosexual conflicts it is less a sexual perversion than an ego-problem that underlies them, a problem with which the individual can only deal by personifying a portion of his own ego in another individual. The same applies, it is true, to heterosexual love-relations, from which the homosexual differs only in that the selfward part of this relation is stronger, or at any rate more distinct. If the poet values his Muse the more highly in proportion as it can be identified with his artistic personality and its ideology, then self-evidently he will find his truest ideal in an even greater degree in his own sex, which is in any case physically and intellectually closer to him. Paradoxical as it may sound, the apparently homosexual tendencies or actual relationships of certain artists fulfill the craving for a Muse which will stimulate and justify creative work in a higher degree than (for a man) a woman can do. It is only as the result of the artist's urge for completion, and his desire to find everything united in one person, that it is mostly a woman that is taken as, or made into, a Muse, although instances of homosexual relations between artists are by no means rare.

Greece, in particular, with its high development of purely intellectual ideologies in art and philosophy, was of course the classical country of boy-love; and there is nothing contradictory in this, particularly if we understand the boy-friendship in the Greek spirit.[5] For it was in the main, or at least collaterally, a high spiritual relation which had as its basis and object a "pedagogic" training for the boy. The master—whether philosopher or sculptor, or, in other words, artist in living or in shaping—was not content to teach his pupil or protégé his doctrines or his knowledge: he had the true artistic impulse to transform him into his own image, to create. And this, by the way, was the form of personal immortality characteristic of Greek culture at its height, which not only found expression in works of art or spiritual teaching, but sought fulfillment in a personal, concrete successor. This successor was no longer (or not yet, if we think of Rome) the physical son, but the like-minded pupil. This is why the spiritual relation of pupil-and-master—which Christianity was to set up again as the center of its doctrine of life—has remained a more important thing to the creative artist than the juridical father-and-son relation which psychoanalysis seeks to regard as fundamental, whereas it is spiritually of a secondary order. And in Greece, therefore, the state of being a pupil did not mean the mere acquiring of a certain discipline and the mastery of a certain material knowledge, as in the civilization of father-right, but the forming of a personality—which begins by identification with the master and is then "artistically" developed and perfected on the pupil's own lines. In this sense the Greek was creative before he arrived at creating works of art, or, indeed, without ever shaping anything but himself and his pupil. Socrates is the best known of many examples of this.

This educative ideology of the artistic Greek nation, which is manifested also in boy-love in all its aspects, brings up the question, Did that Greek art, which may seem to us today the main achievement of the Greek

[5] See my account in *Modern Education* (New York: Alfred A. Knopf; 1932), pp. 24–6.

civilization, perhaps represent to the Greek a mere by-product thereof, an auxiliary, in fact, to the education of the men, who as the real vessels of the culture were thus enabled *inter alia* to practice art for its own sake? This brings us to another question, Was not every great art, whether of primitive or cultivated peoples, bound up with some such cultured task, which lies beyond the bounds of aesthetics, but also beyond all individual artist-psychology? In any case, there are numerous literary proofs of the high degree to which the Greeks were conscious of this national importance of their art. They said that men should learn from works of art and try themselves to become as beautiful and perfect as the statues around them. This gives us an insight into the characteristic way in which the Greeks extended their own creation of individual personalities to include a whole nation, which was not content to produce works of art for their own sake but strove to create an artistic human type who would also be able to produce fine works of art. Seen in this light, boy-love, which, as Plato tells us, aimed perpetually at the improvement and perfection of the beloved youth, appears definitely as the Classical counterpart of the primitive body-art on a spiritualized plane. In the primitive stage it is a matter of physical self-enhancement; in the civilized stage, a spiritual perfecting in the other person, who becomes transferred into the worthy successor of one's self here on earth; and that, not on the basis of the biological procreation of one's body, but in the sense of the spiritual immortality-symbolism in the pupil, the younger.

Christianity took over this ideal of personal character-formation in the symbol of the Exemplar-Master, but, in proportion as it became a world-wide religion of the masses, it was unable to carry it out at the personal level. The collective immortality-dogma, which became symbolized in Christ, relieved the individual of this task of personal self-creation; Christ instead was no longer a model, but became a victim who took upon himself voluntarily the development of everyone's personality. Correspondingly, Christian art remained stationary in the abstract collective style of the religious ideology, until in the

Renaissance it was freed by the emergence of a new type of personality. It was not mere imitation of Classical Greece, but the expression of a similar ideology of personality that led the artists of the Renaissance to try to re-experience the Greek ideal of boy-love. We see, for instance, two of the really great artists, of entirely different social environment, expressing the identical spiritual ideology, with such far-reaching similarity that the notion that the mere accident of a personal experience produced both cases must be dismissed. They both, Michelangelo and Shakespeare, found almost identical words in their famous sonnets for the noble love which each of them felt for a beautiful youth who was his friend. Michelangelo's case is the simpler in that we at least think we know to whom his sonnets were addressed, although it might equally well be the short-lived Ceccino Bracchi or Tommaso de Cavalieri, the object of a lifelong adoration. It is not even clear in some of his later sonnets whether his "idol" refers to his younger friend or to Vittoria Colonna, whose platonic friendship came later. The content of Shakespeare's sonnets is a far more complicated matter. His ideal has been sought among the widely differing persons among the aristocracy of his day. His adoring friendship for the youth in question was not, as with Michelangelo, followed by a soothing maternal friendship, but was broken in upon by a young and beautiful woman. Here, as in his dramas also, woman figures as an evil, disturbing daemon that the Elizabethan dramatist never succeeded in transforming into a helpful Muse, but always felt to be an obstacle to creative work; whereas in his young friend he found the ideal which spurred him on and aided him. But whatever the decision reached by zealous scholars concerning the identity of the person addressed in his immortal sonnets, this "biographical" fact seems to me unimportant as compared with the psychological evidence that this glorification of a friend is, fundamentally, self-glorification just as was the Greek boy-love. In this sense, not only are the sonnets in fact self-dedicated—as is creative work of every description—but they reveal that peculiar attitude of the creative instinct toward the creative ego which seeks to glorify it by artistic idealization and at the same time to overcome its mortality by eternalizing it in art.

The fact that an idealized self-glorification in the person of another can take on physical forms, as in the Greek boy-love, has actually nothing to do with the sex of the beloved, but is concerned only with the struggle to develop a personality and the impulse to create which arises from it. This impulse is at bottom directed to the creator's own rebirth in the closest possible likeness, which is naturally more readily found in his own sex; the other sex is felt to be biologically a disturbing element except where it can be idealized as a Muse. But the likeness to himself will not only be found in the bodily form of his own sex, but also be built up with regard to the spiritual affinity, and in this regard the youthfulness of the beloved stands for the bodily symbol of immortality. In this manner does the mature man, whose impulse to perpetuate himself drives him away from the biological sex-life, live his own life over again in his youthful love; not only seeking to transform him into his intellectual counterpart, but making him his spiritual ideal, the symbol of his vanishing youth. The sonnets of both Renaissance artists are full of such laments over the vanishing youth of the beloved, whose glorious picture it is the duty of the poem to preserve to all eternity. Just as we know, from the psychology of the creative genius, that his impulse to create arises from precisely this tendency to immortalize himself in his work, so we can be in no doubt as to whose transitoriness it is that the poet deplores with almost monotonous reiteration. In these sonnets there is so complete a revelation of the meaning and content of the whole output of their authors, and indeed of the nature of the artist's creative instinct in general, that their high valuation and, no less, their intriguing ambiguity become comprehensible. Yet they are easy to understand if we regard them as the subjective completion of their author's objective creations, for in their naïve self-projection they admit their own transitoriness to be the reason for their own perpetuation in poetry.

From this point of view, then, the biographical presentation, even when it can be done with certainty, seems to us inessential. We are by no means cast down when this method fails, for we can understand that beyond a certain point failure is unavoidable, since the creation of a work of art cannot be explained even by the reconstruction of an inspirer. Thus the factual and concrete biography of Michelangelo or Shakespeare does not enable us to understand their work the better; rather we are left more amazed than before at their coincidence. Vasari, anyhow, declares that the one and only portrait by Michelangelo which was true to nature was that of his young friend Tommaso Cavelieri, "for he detested copying the actual appearance of anyone who was not completely beautiful." The same ideal fashion in which he immortalizes the beloved in poetry corresponds exactly with Shakespeare's attitude to *his* ideal. For the English poet also has the conscious intention of immortalizing his friend's beauty at least in his verse, if time is bound to destroy his bodiliness. This is the constantly reiterated theme in the Shakespeare sonnets, and Michelangelo had the same feeling in the presence of the beloved youth: that his beauty should be incorporated into eternity. Not only is it evident from this self-immortalization in the work that the matter is at bottom one of self-immortalization expressed in another (in the ideal), but both these artists have expressed with great clearness, and to the point of monotony, the idea of oneness with the friend. Shakespeare says in Sonnet XXXIX:

> What can mine own praise to mine own self bring?
> And what is 't but mine own when I praise thee?

Michelangelo not only says in one of his sonnets that a lover "transforms himself" into the beloved, but in a letter presses this transformation of the beloved into his own image, so far as to call his friend Tommaso "a genius who is a stranger in this world." [6]

This psychological solution of the much-disputed sonnet problem shows how experience, and still more the whole attitude toward life, grows out of the struggle to create

[6] The references are taken from Emil Lucka's book on Michelangelo (1930).

and so reduces the problem of experience to the problem of creativity. For the extent to which the artist succeeds in actualizing his love-ideal, in the service of his own self-immortalization, is of minor importance compared with the basic attitude that his work discloses—namely, one originating in dissatisfaction with artistic creation and so urging the creator in some form or other toward life—that is, toward the actual experiencing of his fundamental self. In any case, his impulse to form man in his own image or in the image of his ideal inevitably brings him into conflict with real life and its conditions. These conditions are not artistic, but social, conditions, in which one individual has to respect another and is not permitted to remake him. Now, a certain measure of conflict is, of course, necessary to creative work, and this conflict is, in fact, one of the fields in which an artist displays his greatness, or, psychologically speaking, the strength of his creative will-power. By means of it he is able to work off a certain measure of his inner conflict in his art without entirely sacrificing the realities of life or coming into factual conflict with them. In any case, the destructive results of this ensemble of realities upon the neurotic, as we are able to observe them in his neurosis, show that what distinguishes him from the artist is that the latter constructively applies his will-power in the service of *ideological* creation. A certain type of artist, for whom Goethe may stand as the model, will learn to deal with his experiences and conflicts economically and in the end wisely, while another type exhausts his strength in chasing after stimulating experiences so that his conflict does not come out in production. For the artist himself the fact *that* he creates is more immediately important than *what* he produces, although we are inclined to make his classification as a particular type depend upon the result, his art-work. Here again we find ourselves at a point where art as the result of production must be sharply differentiated from the artist as a creative individual. There is, in fact, no norm for the artist as a type, although we are constantly tempted to set up more or less precisely formulated norms both for art and for the individual work of art. Production is a vital process which happens within the individual and is independent at the outset from the ideology manifested in the created work. On the other hand, the work can show an equal independence toward the artist who has created it, and can in favorable instances be compared with other works within the categories of art; but it can never be compared with its author or with the artist as a psychological type. Between the two—artist and art—there stands Life, now dividing, now uniting, now checking, now promoting.

Here we must return once more to the relation of the artist to woman (or to the opposite sex). In the life of many an artist this is a disturbing factor, one of the deepest sources of conflict, indeed, when it tends to force or beguile him into closer touch with life than is necessary or even advantageous to his production. To make a woman his Muse, or to name her as such, therefore, often amounts to transforming a hindrance into a helper—a compromise which is usually in the interest of productiveness, but renders no service to life. Here, again, everything naturally depends on the artist's dynamic type and his specific conflict over life and production. There are artists for whom even a feminine Muse represents nothing but a potential homosexual relation; for they see in her not so much the woman as a comrade of like outlook and like aims, who could equally well—and possibly better—be replaced by a male friendship. On the other hand, there is an artist-type that is totally unable to produce at all without the biological complement of the other sex and, indeed, depends directly on the sexual life for its stimulus. For the type that is creative in and by means of sexual abstinence has its opposite in another type that, strange to say, is not only not exhausted by the sexual act but is definitely stimulated to create thereby. Schulte-Vaerting has described this type as the "sexual superman," but it seems to me rather that here too some hidden mechanism of fleeing from life is involved, which impels the artist from biological mortality to individual immortality in production after he has paid his tribute to sexuality.

This leads us to the profoundest source of the artistic

impulse to create, which I can only satisfactorily explain to myself as the struggle of the individual against an inherent striving after totality, which forces him equally in the direction of a complete surrender to life and a complete giving of himself in production. He has to save himself from this totality by fleeing, now from the Scylla of life, now from the Charybdis of creation, and his escape is naturally accomplished only at the cost of continual conflict, both between these two spheres and within each of them separately. How this conflict and the triumph over it is manifested in creative working we shall seek to show in the chapter on "The Artist's Fight with Art." For the moment we are dealing only with manifestations and attempted solutions within the sphere of life, irrespective of whether these are concerned with persons of the same or of the opposite sex. In every case the artist's relation to woman has more of an ideological than of a sexual significance, as Emil Lenk has demonstrated in a study on creative personalities.[7] Usually, however, he needs two women, or several, for the different parts of his conflict, and accordingly he falls into psychological dilemmas, even if he evades the social difficulties. He undoubtedly loves both these persons in different ways, but is usually not clear as to the part they play, even if—as would appear to be the rule—he does not actually confuse them one with the other. Because the Muse means more to him artistically, he thinks he loves her the more. This is seldom the case in fact, and moreover it is psychologically impossible. For the other woman, whom, from purely human or other motives, he perhaps loves more, he often enough cannot set up as his Muse for this very reason: that she would thereby become in a sense defeminized and, as it were, made into an object (in the egocentric sense) of friendship. To the Muse for whom he creates (or thinks he creates), the artist seldom gives himself; he pays with his work, and this the truly womanly woman often refuses to accept. But if his relation takes a homosexual form, this giving is still more obviously a giving to himself—that

[7] *Das Liebesleben des Genies* (Dresden, 1926).

is, the artistic form of giving through production instead of surrendering the personal ego.

True, from the standpoint of the ego, the homosexual relation is an idealizing of oneself in the person of another, but at the same time it is felt as a humiliation; and this is not so much the cause as the actual expression of internal conflicts. For, in the dynamism that leads him to create, the artist suffers from a struggle between his higher and his lower self that manifests itself equally in all the spheres and utterances of his life and also characterizes his attitude to woman. She can be for him at once the symbol of the highest and the lowest, of the mortal and the immortal soul, of life or death. The same applies too, as we shall see, to the work itself or to creation, for which the artist is prepared to sacrifice everything, but which, in the hour of disappointment and dejection, he frequently damns and curses. There is in the artist that fundamental dualism from which we all suffer, intensified in him to a point that drives him with dynamic compulsion from creative work to life, and from life back to new and other creativity. According to the artist's personal structure and spiritual ideology, this conflict will take the form of a struggle between good and evil, beauty and truth, or, in a more neurotic way, between the higher and the lower self. It is a struggle that, as we shall presently see, determines the cultural-genetic start and development of the creative instinct itself. In the personal conflicts of the individual artist, the fundamental dualism which originally led to cultural development and artistic creation persists in all its old strength. It cannot, however, be reconstructed and understood as a matter of individual psychology from an analysis of the artist's personal past, because the modern individual not only comes into the world with humanity's fundamental dualism, but is also potentially charged with all the attempts to solve it, so that his personal development no longer provides any parallels with the development of the race.

For if we inquire into the relation between work and production in the artist, we must bear in mind that there are two kinds of experience, just as there are at least two ways of artistic production. Whereas in preanalytical biography it was chiefly the artist's later and proportionately more active experience that was brought into relation with his creativeness, psychoanalysis, with its emphasis on the decisive importance of infantile impressions, brought this more passive stage of experience into the foreground. This conception got no further, however, than the banal statement that even the artist was not immune from those typical experiences of childhood one had come up against in analyzing the adult. Just as Freud saw the cause of neurosis in these typical childhood experiences themselves and not in the individual's particular reaction to them, so did his school claim to see in those same childhood impressions the experiences that led to artistic creativity, though without being able to explain the difference between one outcome of them and another. An inexplicable "remainder" had therefore to be admitted, but this remainder embraced no more and no less than the whole problem of artistic creativity. Beyond this statement, analytical psychography has to this day not progressed, as the latest comprehensive publication in this province shows.[8] And although the Oedipus complex, and the sexual problem of the child that is bound up with it, still forms the center, this is rather the sign of a fatal stoppage than a proof of the superlative importance of this family problem. The whole of analytical pathography has battened for more than a quarter of a century on the Oedipus problem, which was first applied to artistic creation by Freud (in his *Interpretation of Dreams*), without, however, reaching even the point at which I came out when I published my book *Das Inzestmotiv in Dichtung und Sage* (1912, planned in 1905), to which I gave the subtitle: *Grundsüge einer Psychologie des dichterischen Schaffens.*

In this book, as already mentioned, the Oedipus problem is treated mainly as a motive and only in a minor degree as an individual complex; hence its ideological significance

[8] *Die psychoanalytische Bewegung,* Vol. II, No. 4 (July-August 1930), which also contains a bibliography of pyschoanalytical biography. In his introduction Dr. E. Hitschmann describes my book on the incest theme as fundamental for the analytical survey of art and the understanding of artistic creativity.

was considered as well as its psychological. Although, under the spell of the Freudian idea, I gave pride of place to the individual as against the collective psychology which I have since learned to appreciate as "ideology,"[9]) yet with respect to the latter, too, I certainly did not steer clear of psychological premises in dealing with this collective motive that we find in myth and saga before the poets made a theme of it. But, be this as it may, the book has even now not been superseded; indeed, analytical art-criticism has not yet put itself in face of its problems—to which I must at this point return. That the poets struggled so intensely with the Oedipus complex was regarded at the time as a proof of its ubiquity, and so it actually was so far as concerned individual psychology. But from the standpoint of the psychology of artistic production, the poets' wrestling with the Oedipus experience seems to me to mean something essentially different: namely, that the artist reacts more strongly than, and certainly in a different way from, the normal person to this unavoidable average experience of the parental relation. This is not, however, because of the experience, but because of his peculiar reactivity, which in the case of artistic expression we call "creative." Now, from the comparison that I drew in my generalized formulation of "the artist" (also in 1905)[1] between artist and neurotic, it results that the latter also reacts differently from the average person to these and similar experiences. Only, this distinctive reaction does not, with him, lead to production, but to inhibition or to fixation. The artistic reaction is thus distinguishable from the neurotic by an *overcoming of the trauma* or of the potentiality of inhibition resulting therefrom, no matter whether this is achieved by a single effort or is spread over the whole lifework. This overcoming, however (so far as my researches have taken me), is only possible—or at any rate only psychologically explicable—in one way, and this, as we have learned from the therapy which helps to overcome these development-inhibitions, is through volitional affirmation of the obligatory, which in every case not only

[9] *Seelenglaube und Psychologie.*
[1] *Der Künstler.*

works usefully but is also definitely creative. Applied to the special case of the Oedipus conflict, it appears to me today that it is the willed affirmation of the inhibitive family ties that is the creative and at the same time liberating factor. But this affirmation of the given, which in relation to family symbols manifests itself as erotic desire (toward mother and sister) and thirst for battle (with father or brother), corresponds on the one hand to creative appropriation and on the other to a constructive victory over it.

And with this we are back again at the fundamental process of artistic production, which consists in just this deliberate appropriation of that which happens and is given (including passive experiences) in the form of individual new creation. The Oedipus complex forms one of the cultural symbols of this conflict because it synthesizes the biological, psychological, and characterological sides of it. But, even so, it only symbolizes—even in the case of a child, for whom the Oedipus complex is already the expression of an inner experience and not merely adaptation to an outward destiny. It even seems to me as if the Oedipus myth itself, if taken in the Greek spirit,[2] were an experience of this same striving for independence in human development: namely, the deliberate affirmation of the existence forced on us by fate. That which is dimly but unequivocally preordained for the hero by his birth, in the mythical account, he deliberately makes his own by embodying in action and experience. This experience is a creative experience, for it serves to create the myth itself, and the sagas, poems, and tragedies based on it, whose various representations of the one theme are determined by the collective ideological outlook of the moment and the interpretation appropriate thereto. But the life of the individual hero himself will inevitably be destroyed, whether this human destiny be interpreted in terms of heroism, fatalism, or tragedy.

[2] See my explanations in *Die analytische Reaktion* (1929), pp. 68 ff., and also in *Modern Education*, Chapter vii. [The latter is reprinted as the final essay in this collection.]

IV *Art-Form and Ideology*

What am I myself? What have I done? All that I have seen, heard, noted I have collected and used. My works are reverenced by a thousand different individuals. . . . Often I have reaped the harvest that others have sown. My work is that of a collective being and it bears Goethe's name.

—GOETHE

AS SOON AS we interpret the Oedipus material as the collective symbol of a development-process which permeates both the single individual and humanity, and which the creative individuality overcomes in its artistic expression—as the creative Greek nation overcame it in myth—we have revealed to us one of the deepest laws of all artistic productivity: the fact that, in works of art, form and content not only constitute an inseparable unity, but actually express one and the same thing in two different ways. We have seen likewise that the process that goes on in the creative personality during the artistic shaping of this content finds its symbol in the content of the Oedipus myth. Only, the various art-styles differ as to the manner in which an artist achieves both the unity that constitutes a work of art and harmonious combination of the current ideology with his personal one. *Primitive creative art*, which is based on the collective soul-ideology, achieves unity through abstraction in style, that is, by neglecting everything incidental, temporal, and individual; *Classical art,* which is based on the aesthetic ideology of beauty, achieves unity through conformity between and sheer identity of the specific ideology of art and the general ideology of the people, the one unrepeatable example of which is the Greek culture. Finally, *modern Romantic art,* which is based on the psychological ideology of the artist-type, achieves this unity in art through his *reaction* to the discrepancies existing both within the artist himself and between his personal ideology and the prevailing collective ideology. The first of these unities, therefore—that of primitive art, attained through abstraction—is *static;* the second—that of Classical art, based on projection—is *harmonious;* and the third—that of Romantic art, as the outcome of victorious conflict—is *dynamic.* Thus the first is predominantly one of flat drawing (ornamental); the second, predominantly plastic and figuring (vital); and the third, essentially poetical and musical (rhythmical). These classifications are, of course, to be taken in a very general sense and, like all attempts to set up a historical, critical, or other hierarchy in the fine arts, must always remain unsatisfactory. It may be, indeed, that the real giants in art are just those who somehow exceed the limits of their art's proper sphere. For instance, Rembrandt stands out from the ranks of painters by reason of a dynamism which really is characteristic of literature and music; Homer was lauded, even by the ancients, as the greatest of painters; Dante, in words, is distinguished by a genius for rhythmical presentation, which is one of the features of pictorial art, and in this he has near rivals in Shakespeare the dramatist and Wagner the musician, while the sculptor Michelangelo was at bottom an architect who built with human bodies, and his modern successor, Rodin, discloses very strong painter-qualities such as the Florentine despised.

Taking everything into account, however, the course taken by art-history forces us to regard primitive art as flat and linear, Classical art as essentially plastic and figuring, and modern art as verbal and rhythmical; and the fact that in each of these epochs great things were also produced in other spheres of art is to be ascribed to just such overleapings of frontiers by outstanding artist-personalities, who are to be found at all stages of development, but particularly of artistic development—where they step out of the frame of the prevailing art-ideology and achieve incomparable masterpieces, not only in their own domain but in the realm of art generally. For although they made use of a given ideology, they rose so high above themselves that the result was a work of art that fell into no category and yet was more than personal, a superindividual achievement which thereupon its imitators invested with an ideological significance corresponding to the general recognition accorded to it. If, however, we look at the three kinds of art—graphic, plastic, and rhythmic—from the viewpoint of the artist and his psychological dynamism, we discover other categories, bearing on the problem of artistic creativity, which extend beyond the individual artist and are linked with the great general problems of cultural history.

Whereas primitive art is perpetuated through abstraction, and Classical art achieves immortality through idealization, Romantic art rounds off this immense transformation-process of spiritual development in making vivification its chosen mode of overcoming that fear of death from which the immortality-idea and urge to eternalization first sprang. Primitive art looks beyond individual, mortal life toward an everlasting life of the soul. And the essence of Classical art lies in the fact that it renders life itself everlasting—that is, tries to conserve the actual man as he is and lives—the very thing that the primitive Egyptian sought to do by mummification, save that in Greek art the conservation was achieved symbolically by the aesthetic idealization of the human body in a permanent material such as marble. But modern art, with its dynamic of expression, differs from both these style-forms; neither starts from an abstract of the living nor aims at an ideal conservation of it, but its style-form consists in a vivification of the essence of the actual. This can, however, only be achieved at the cost of real life.

The three art-ideologies, as we thus differentiate them—the abstract, the aesthetic, and the realistic—are based therefore on varying attitudes to life itself, and these attitudes, although determined by the prevailing collective ideology, will still be found to vary in the different individuals of the same epoch. Now, it is my belief that a noncontemporary outlook on vital problems is always essential to the artist, an outlook that deviates more or less from the prevailing ideology and its art-style. In other words, I believe that the artist's personality, however strongly it may express the spirit of the age, must nevertheless bring him into conflict with that age and with his contemporaries; and this again explains why he is obliged, in his work, to convert the collective ideology into one of his own.[1] In this sense, not only does a work of art represent unity of form and content, but it achieves also a unification of personal and collective ideologies of immortality. The artist is, after all, primarily an individual who is unable or unwilling to adopt the dominant immortality-ideology of his age—whether religious, social, or other—and that, not because it differs ideologically from his own, but because it is collective, whereas what he aspires to is an individual immortality. In fact, art sets out to secure this individual immortality by collective methods, while the neurotic clings to the naïve immortality of the individual, which leads to fear of life and terror of death. But the artist obtains his individual immortality by using the collective ideology for his personal creativity and, in this way, not only re-creates it as his own but presents it to humanity as a new collective ideology on an individual basis. Thus he himself becomes immortal along with his work.

According to whether immortality is sought collectively, socially, or individually, the various culture-ideologies differ among themselves, as also do their religious and artistic forms. The primitive artist overcomes individual mortality both by the abstract art-form that is man's spiritual proxy and by his collective soul-ideology. In contrast to this, the modern artist has, as we have pointed out, actually to sacrifice life to make his work live, and this sacrifice in-

[1] The different aspects of this problem are further dealt with in the sections "Beauty and Truth," "The Artist's Fight with Art," and "Success and Fame."

volves both his own life and that of others. In the modern work of art, therefore, the personality of the artist or of his model really lives on dynamically, again an effect which can be achieved only at the cost of real life. But in the primitive work of art it is not the whole being that lives on as an individual, but only his abstraction—corresponding to the collective idea of the soul, which does not vivify that being dynamically, but abstracts him into a timeless form.

If, then, on the one hand, the artist's ideology is in complete harmony with the collective ideology of his time —is, indeed, the most complete expression of it—it is possible that the essential factor of his creative dynamism arises from a personal conflict between the individual death-problem and the collective immortality-idea of the particular cultural period. Yet, as we have already remarked, the primitive artist too—of whom we know nothing—would seem to have broken away, as an individual, from the collective soul-ideology, to the extent of finding the pure abstraction of the soul-idea (or its psychic representative) inadequate and being driven to concrete expression, even though it were of an abstract order. The Classical artist, also, as seen at the height of the Greek culture, was not content merely to accept the national or political immortality-ideology of Hellenism, but stayed it, so to speak, with its religious genesis, in that his sculpture lifted the human being out of the social and replaced him in the spiritual-religious domain. And, lastly, the modern artist, into whose individuality we can gain an insight (not only on the basis of historical data, but also because it expresses itself in its creative work), falls, as an artist-type to itself, outside the social, technical, and scientific ideology which characterizes our contemporary collectivism. He conserves, in his own type, the type rationalized by the conception of genius, the *art*-ideologies of past ages, just as the Classical and the primitive artists preserved the immortality-concepts of culture-epochs which were either dead or decaying. Thus, the unity of form and content, which must be regarded as the essence of creative work, comes into question even at this, the most general level of treatment: art preserves even dead or dying cultures, the epochs of human development, and not only the single creative individual and his limited period; it also vitalizes them—that is, renders them immortal in the particular art-form.[2]

Having reached this level, it is perhaps worth while looking downward onto the plane of purely technical problems, although these, again, can only be detached artificially from the general problem. Material is an essential factor of art-form, and to material in its turn belong the technical means of handling it and the capacity of the craftsman. The fact that, in German, the word *art* (*Kunst*) is allied with *can* (*können*) does not, as we now know, prove that even in practice art was primarily the being able to do a thing. The root relationship is perhaps characteristic rather of German mentality than of art. Be that as it may, for all the emphasis we lay on the will-to-art as against technical ability, we must admit that the material and its treatment represent an essential factor of artistic creativity and the work produced. The Greek sculptures are unthinkable without the supernatural splendor of the marble and equally so without its durability, and this is meant not only in the material sense, but in the ideal sense of the collective immortality-ideology. In the same way, not only are Rembrandt's dynamic portraits unthinkable without the high stage of development that had been reached in oil painting; but in his "Anatomy," as in Leonardo's anatomical studies, there is evidence of some medical knowledge of the body, living and dead.[3]

[2] In this connection it is important to note what Hermann Bahr (*Sendung des Künstlers;* Leipzig, 1923; p. 137) says, in support of his views, that actually in all the arts of all the nations of all times it is the same work of art that is created over and over again. "Not all of Greece is autochthonous: its art is a renaissance of Egypt, just as Rome is a renaissance of Athens, and the history of the Christian West nothing more than a renaissance of Rome." With reference to Goethe, too, he writes: "Thus he lived in art as if in the memory of the true art: his writing became an aid to memory and to the understanding of former art-periods long since expired." Very appropriate, too, is his mention of Nietzsche's deep-rooted condemnation, in *Human, All Too Human,* of the "revolution in poetry," for in poetry's break with tradition he sees the end of art.

[3] The dissection of corpses was first permitted by the ecclesiastical authorities in the Renaissance, and then only occasionally in the case of executed criminals. It was not until the middle of the sixteenth century

The lyrical power of expression of a Goethe, a Hölderlin, or a Stefan George is only possible on the basis of a highly developed and refined cultural language, which has not only technical, but human aspects. We are justified, however, in asking how far these technical advances in the use and treatment of the material are not also themselves attributable to a genuine will-to-art, which previously—or simultaneously—creates the medium the will-to-form needs for its execution. In oil painting, this relation to material is clearly visible in the experiments of Leonardo, Rembrandt, and other painters; but in principle we can draw the same psychological conclusion with regard to sculpture, poetry, and music—even without a close acquaintance with the history of the material—namely, that the actual individual art-will is manifested primarily and essentially in the choice and treatment of the material, while the content of what is presented has more relation to the collective ideologies—although these of course are in a high degree individualized in the work of art produced.

---

that Vesalius (1514–64) introduced the thorough anatomical study of the human body, although information has recently reached us of the astonishing anatomical knowledge possessed by the ancients. (See chapters: "Microcosm and Macrocosm" and "The Formation and the Creation of Speech.")

The rise of the science of anatomy probably influenced Renaissance art and undoubtedly had a definite effect upon its ideology. Apart from Leonardo's personal anatomical studies, which are an outgrowth of his whole scientific ideology, it seems to me probable that Rembrandt was also reacting to the new science of the human body when, in 1632, at the age of twenty-six, he painted his "Anatomy." I have the feeling that this young artist, who in his earlier youthful works had shown more "Rembrandtesqueness," was making a concession to the materialistic and realist ideology of his day in painting this "Anatomy Lecture of Professor Nicolaes Pietersz Tulp." It is as if he wished to show that he, too, knew something about anatomy, and that it was pure choice that made him forgo this "imitative art" in favor of dynamic expression. As we know, Rembrandt's whole life and work were torn by a conflict between the two, which brought him into serious disfavor with his patrons, who were paying for portraits true to nature and not for studies in light- and color-effects. The second anatomical picture, "Doctor Joan Deyman's Anatomy Class" (1656), of which, unfortunately, only a fragment is preserved, in the Rijks Museum, is more of a "real" Rembrandt, as Karl Scheffler in his book: *Holland* (Leipzig, 1930; English translation, New York, 1932) regards it too.

However that may be, Rembrandt's "Anatomy" is an illustration of the ideal case in which the picture not only represents anatomy but actually *is* the anatomy, ideologically expressed, to which the artist demonstrates his attitude by painting it in his own manner.

These reflections bring us once more to the question of the hierarchy of the arts in respect of their historical and aesthetic valuation. In stating that the essence of modern art lies in its living dynamism, we did not forget that the primitive expressions of art known to us are likewise based on live rhythm (as are also dancing, song, and music), nor that ornament, with its recurring motive, shows a distinctly rhythmic character although, by contrast, the rhythm itself is, as it were, frozen, abstract, or dead. Yet this, again, is but a contradiction in logic that is inherent in our conception of artistic development; for, psychologically considered, it merely proves the oft-quoted relationship between modern and primitive art, in spite of the fact that their ideologies are basically different and indeed almost diametrically opposed. For primitive art is still entirely at one with life, forming, indeed, with regard to dance and ritual (singing and music) an essential component of the collective communal life, out of which there develops only gradually the productive artist and the onlooker-community in a passive rôle as two separate spheres.[4] Modern art, on the other hand, even in its most vivid dynamic expression, stands *opposed* to life. It is in the position, so to say, of having taken refuge in art-form rather than, like primitive art, having found in it the expression of life.

The primitive-art ideology is the religious belief in the soul, which leads, on the one hand, to a symbolic abstraction of the forms of life in linear-ornamental art and, on the other, to a concrete presentation of that abstraction. The tendency to concretize arises out of the individual-immortality concept, while the craving for abstraction corresponds to the *collective*-immortality concept. Modern art on the other hand is based on no such consoling idea of immortality, whether of a collective or individual nature. Its compelling motive is *fear of life and experience,* and this motive it carries over into the creative sphere, in the course of which process the individual will binds the biological driving force in the art-form in order to conserve

[4] See Jane Harrison: *Ancient Art and Ritual.*

it. It must be confessed that not only is the unity of the modern work of art (which it shares with art in general) the result of a reaction on emerging victorious from a struggle, but its dynamic vitality is also a reaction to the fear of life characteristic of the modern individual; for since the decay of our collective ideologies relative to religion and state, we suffer from this fear more than any previous generation has done.

Not only is primitive art at one with life as an essential part of it, but the artist is, if not wholly in harmony with the collective ideology, yet far more so than is the case, or even can be, in our modern society. Beginning with the Classic art of the Greek *floraison,* through the links that join it to our modern art-developments, and right into the latter, we find in increasing measure that it is just the very highest work that the productive artist achieves in response to pressure from the most diverse influences, so that this work, though certainly the typical expression of his individuality and epoch, is, over and above this, that of other cultures and alien ideologies. It is this fact that raises it to the timeless sphere of pure art. Classical Greece itself, though definitely influenced by Egypt, Crete, and the North, still seems to us today to be the pure product of the Hellenic spirit, in contrast to the art-development of medieval Europe, where the ideologies are clearly a mixed product with Italian Renaissance and Northern Gothic as the two chief ingredients. Yet the great artists who were born of this epoch experienced in themselves and reproduced in their works the struggle of these different cultural ingredients, in both its constructive and its destructive aspects. Into this category come Shakespeare's mixture of imported Renaissancism and the rising spirit of the Reformation in England; Dürer's Italian and Leonardo's French experiences; Goethe's flight from the *Sturm und Drang* ideology of Gothic to the more harmonious sphere of Southern Mediterranean art; also Nietzsche's struggle on the one hand with Hellenism and on the other with the Christian in him; Hölderlin, ruined by diversity of ideologies; and Kleist's inability to win through from Romantic unsteadiness to the Classical ideal.[5] These, and many other great modern examples, might be quoted as proofs of the disunity of the artist with himself and with his environment that differentiates the modern artist from the primitive and, in a sense, from the Classical. But these problems cannot be discussed without including questions of mixed races, the influence of the country, and other biological, social, and economic conditions.[6]

We now return from the problem of the creative artist's mixing of ideologies to the fact of the occurrence of various art-forms within one and the same cultural epoch. From the creative artist's point of view this is naturally no problem, for the matter is one of specially favorable conditions for production characterizing a particular period of development, or even of some vital necessity providing the stimulus for creative work in great variety during that period. Neither is it a problem from the ideological standpoint—at least not an insistent enigma—that different art-forms should come into existence and actually mature simultaneously. For here problems arise only as the result of the co-operation at any given time of the creative urge and the ideologies that are at its disposal. The artist creates essentially by reason of an inward urge which we may describe as the individual will-to-form, and whether he objectifies this in a picture, a statue, or a symphony is rather a technical and formal matter than an individual problem. This is particularly the case with the great artist whose poem is plastic, whose portrait is poetical, and

[5] Arthur Burkhard, professor of literature at Harvard University, has in a preliminary study—*German Quarterly*, Vol. II, No. 4 (November 1929)—described this conflict between two opposed elements—in the artist and his work—as the hallmark of *German* art, which he formulates as, in the last analysis, a conflict between expression and form. In my opinion, however, this is the characteristic of modern art in general, and in so far as art today is still national—in France or Italy, for instance—it is derived from Classical ideologies.

[6] Of basic importance is Reibmayr's *Die Entwicklungsgeschichte des Talents und Genies* (Munich, 1908). Kretschmer has also a very good summary in the two chapters: "*Die Züchtung der Begabung*" and "*Genie und Rasse*" of his *Geniale Menschen* (Berlin, 1929). See also the general survey in Paul Schultze-Naumburg's *Kunst und Rasse* (Munich, 1928) and, for German literature in particular, Josef Nadler's *Literaturgeschichte der deutschen Stämme und Landschaften* (3 vols., Regensburg, 1914–18).

whose music is architectonic in effect.[7] Nevertheless it may be said that drawing was characteristic of primitive art, while sculpture is the Classical expression-medium, and the rhythmic arts (poetry and music) the modern. Poetry in particular can be proved historically to be of relatively recent date—relatively not only to the vast spaces of time which separate us from the prehistoric cave-paintings, but even to those covered by historical evidence within our reach. Moreover, poetry as a species of art is bound up with writing, as its material, and this particular immortality-technique was a very late discovery, which reached sure fulfillment only with the printing of books. The form in which the art of poetry existed before its fixation through writing can only be conjectured from a few traditional magic formulae and the prayer-like songs which were performed chiefly in honor of some godhead or hero. With such primitive peoples as we are still able to observe, singing appears to play an inferior rôle as against dancing and instrumental music, possibly because they are too fearful of pronouncing the "word" that is still identical with the thing that it designates. This magical effect of the spoken word, which here asserts itself as a dread of the evoking call, may on the other hand be *salutary*, as when it forms the basis of songs and hymns—in which we recognize the oldest form of prayer and which we must also regard as the original form of the art of poetry.[8] For the

[7] The Innsbruck archaeologist Heinrich Sitte has demonstrated in his synthetic essay on Bach's *Chromatic Fantasia and Fugue* (No. 5 of the manuscript series, *Preussische Jahrbücher*, Berlin, 1921) that "its thematic content contains the Parthenon frieze, Giotto's frescoes in the Scrovegni Chapel, Dante's *Divine Comedy*, Beethoven's *Ninth Symphony*, and Goethe's *Faust*. All these works, therefore, although uttered in different languages, are really all the time one and the same composition" (Bahr, op. cit., p. 137). Sitte's discovery that Bach set his own family name to music in this fugue is another striking example of the inseparable unity of the form and content of a work of art. The fugue is not only by Bach: it *is* Bach, the whole Bach, as man and as triumphant artist. "Out of the double cry of anguish: B [flat]—A—C—H [= B natural]," continues Sitte, "there grew an uninterrupted cry of higher and higher triumph: A—B—H—C. And this motif, so unique in origin, he made . . . without any trickery into the boldest fugue which he ever wrote, and which comprises his whole human existence, in joy and in sorrow, as if it were his portrait."

[8] In a preliminary introduction to a history of American literature, Ludwig Lewisohn very rightly lays stress on the "sacred" origin and character of literature (*This Quarter*, Summer 1929). The book has appeared since (*Expression in America*).

rest, the earliest poetical products of the primitives, as of civilized peoples, are *epic* in character; either they are mythical stories of gods which are reminders of men's lost immortality, or they are human stories of heroes which bewail the tragic mortality of the living being.[9] But these productions have an unambiguously collective character and, in this respect, are definitely not out of keeping with the primitive art-ideology. Nor do we know the individual writers of these myths and epics, and this is not merely for lack of historical data, but because oral tradition admits of no such individual authorship. And whether the man who later wrote down any such song—even with additions and embellishments of his own—can really be described as its author, even if we could trace him, is a question which the Greeks tried in vain to solve in their research on Homer.[1] Today we are certainly too ready to regard offhand the recorder of ideas as their author—a technical way of looking at it which has already gone far beyond the pure idea of creativity.

But the question as to wherein the collective element of mythic and epic poetry consists has become a central problem in scientific literary criticism ever since the Romantic period. It is probable that various individuals—even, perhaps, races and nations—participated in the beginning and particularly in the oral handing-down of these poems. And equally we may suppose that this collective genesis also corresponds to a collective *content* of that which was transmitted. A race or a nation appears as the victorious hero of the story, mostly in the figure of an individual champion as representative and carrier of the race's interests.[2] In every case the hero and his fate are the main thing, and not the poet, in whom we should take little interest if we did know him. For the motive of his song and saga was, at this stage, certainly not individual, but collective or, as we should call it today, "national." The individual author of modern times differs from the collec-

[9] See, further, the chapter "*Traum und Wirklichkeit*" in my *Seelenglaube und Psychologie* (1930), and expositions in the following chapters of *Art and Artist:* "Myth and Metaphor" and "The Poetic Art."

[1] Cf. my preliminary studies on the folk-epic in *Imago,* V (1917).

[2] This point of view is emphasized in the *Psychoanalyse de l'art* (Paris, 1929) by Professor Charles Baudouin of Geneva.

tive creators of folk-epic, not only through the personal nature of his theme, but also because he himself, his individual ego, is the real hero of his story. In lyric poetry, with its reflection of fleeting moods, this is plainly and admittedly the case, but it also applies to a great extent to novels and even to dramas. It is as if the personal artist-ideology, which we have taken as the foundation of modern art, comes in the individual poet to consciousness of itself. Hence the favored position, the high cultural significance indeed, of the author as censor of morals, philosopher of life, and educator of mankind in our world of today. In attaining this position of general responsibility he has, however, left the sphere of pure creativity, which, from now on, he represents only in his ideology. He is now himself the work of art, but as such he can represent either a good or a bad one, according to whether and how he succeeds in shaping his life. Goethe remains, in this regard also, the unparalleled model of a universal genius of the modern age; for he was able to balance the destructive elements in him creatively, by absorbing them into his poetry and his various other constructive activities, and thus to shape his life as an artistic-constructive whole. Other great writers have failed to achieve so complete a harmony, either ruining the artistic build of their lives by Romanticism or leading a philistine existence in order to have enough vitality left over for creation.

This fact confronts us again when we come to deal with the problem of the individual artist-personality as expressed in the relation between experience and creativity. No single causal relation appears to exist between the two phenomena—certainly not the one favored by psychography, which purports to explain creativity by experience in general or by special experiences. It seems likely that the reverse is more possible, since the creative will which underlies them both manifests itself more clearly in the created work than in experience. On the other hand, creativity itself is, of course, a special form of experience and one peculiar to the artist, and all depends in the last resort upon whether the individual is capable of restoring harmony, or at least a temporary balance, between the two forms of experience—artistic and vital—and to what extent he succeeds. This does not by any means signify that the person who better adapts himself to, or succeeds in, life must needs be the better artist. In this respect Goethe forms a signal exception in the whole long line of really great men whose lives have been swallowed whole by their work. Croce maintains that this was the case even with Goethe, but in reality the *man* Goethe has come to be more important to us than his work, which we are inclined to regard as more interesting from a psycho-biographical than from a purely artistic standpoint. Goethe himself looked upon his works as "fragments of one great confession," as "life's traces," and it looks as if this had been more or less consciously the artist's general attitude toward his work. His work is not only his particular expression of life: it both serves him and helps him to live, and his worth as an artist comes second—or even plays no special part at all. A mediocre work, acceptable only to a small circle, may yet satisfy the artist more and mean more to him than the undying world fame of a poem that has grown into a folk song, the author of which most people are quite at a loss to name.

Again, we must admit that the psychology of a productive personality gives no clue to the understanding and appreciation of art. The Romantic who, having adopted the attitude that I once called "artist-mania" and now call art-ideology, neglects or sacrifices or even destroys his life, has often achieved more in art than the genius who allows the human being in him to come to fruition also. What makes Goethe the highest type of artist in our eyes is not really his work, any more than it is his civic life—which served rather to protect him from his own genius than to enhance it. Where he is great is in his attitude to art and life, his conception of their relation to each other, which he only bought—and dearly enough—after long wrestling. As Bahr so excellently puts it, his achievement lay in having "put down the revolution by which he had risen" and "in recognizing that art's freedom lay in its submission to the law." This explains his aversion from all Romanticism, which meant, at bottom, from the Romantic within himself; for the Romantic stands at the other end of the scale of artistic development as the pioneer and earliest specimen of the individual artist-type, whose art-ideology is the cult of personality with its idea of liberty. Not only is he an individual-revolutionary in creation, but he confuses life with art: he *is* dramatic or lyrical, he acts the piece instead of objectifying it, or rather he is obliged to act it as well as merely objectify it. His art is as chaotic as his life, whereas the pure art-ideology is based on order, law, and form—in fact, on traditional and therefore collective ideologies. Now, Goethe wished to re-establish this pure art epistemologically, and therein lies his greatness as an *artist-type*. First, however, he had to curb the individual Romantic in himself, and this he succeeded in doing, though only at the expense of his productive power, which exhausted itself in the conscious and deliberate transformation of the Romantic type represented by him into a Classical artist-type, and which nevertheless he never completely achieved in his work.

If Goethe's importance lies rather in his representing the purely Classical ideal, as against the personal artist-ideology of Romanticism, then in his actual creative work, he is perhaps the first example—and at the same time the highest possible type—of the poet who becomes a universal genius. Also, in our own day, such a type could express himself as an essayist, a cultural critic, or a first-class journalist. As we have already pointed out, our modern author has become conscious of the personal art-ideology that is within him; but the first result of the process has been to project this intuitively recognized artist-ideology on to the history of art and to misinterpret the whole of its development in the light of its latest phase. We have seen how the establishment of a will-to-form (originally impersonal) as the real creative element had an essentially progressive and deepening effect on the study of art as a problem, and we shall find that the extended application of this theory to the genius's personal, and the modern artist's conscious, will-to-art has thrown new light on the whole question of art and artist. At the end of our first section we left it an open question whether an understanding of the individual artist-type with its personal will-ideology—working itself out primarily in the artist's ego—might not clear up certain methodological ambiguities in Worringer's aesthetics. However abstract we imagine the primitive will-to-art that is supposed to produce simple art-forms of crystalline structure, it still retains a tinge of anthropomorphism—even in Schopenhauer's philosophical interpretation of it. For the will is a human phenomenon, and we cannot assume offhand that Nature and all her creatures possess it, even in the form of "unconscious willing." Certainly, in our view, the individual will is a derivative of the biological life-impulse, but it is a purely human derivative, though, again, it is in a prime mover of Nature that we find the biological premise; this differentiation between life-impulse and expression of will, which psychoanalysis has ignored, seems to me to be the basic human problem par excellence since it comprises both the dualism of ego and species, of mortality and immortality, that is inherent in the individual, and all those creative tendencies that go beyond the mere function of propagation. In any case we can fail to see how the sex-urge, which is designed primarily to preserve the race, should produce even the most primitive ornamentation, still less a higher art-form. The attempt made by psychoanalysis to find such a solution is today recognized to have been a failure, and only left the real problem more acute than before. Not even in cases where the *content* of the representation has a more or less definite relation to the sexual function or its organs—as in the case of certain primitive art-symbols—can we find an intelligible path from the direct to the symbolic or sublimated expression of the sexual instinct unless we build the bridge of the individual will that converts the propagation of the species into a perpetuation of the ego. Even with animals, to whom we cannot ascribe this individuality-consciousness (or at least not in the same degree), the development and variation of species do not appear to be the achievement of a sexual instinct that is focused on reproduction and repetition, but (as first Lamarck was bold enough to postulate) the result of an individual condition of suitability, and it is only a judgment by results—namely, the better adaptation of the individual—that leads us to predicate some sort of deliberate intention in it.

Be that as it may, once we recognize that the modern artist has of himself arrived at a consciousness of the individualness of the creative will that he formerly attributed to his god, we are bound to assume that a similar will-tendency existed in the artist of former epochs, even though he may not, as an individual, have always been conscious of it. One might think, then, that this volitional creative urge came nearer to the sexual instinct in proportion as it was more unconscious—that is, in proportion as we come nearer to primitive art. But this hasty conclusion as to the predominantly sexual character of primitive art has been refuted by objective observation[3] and cannot be used to support the thesis of the sexual character of creative art, just as we may not, on the other hand, refer the self-consciousness of the modern artist back to the genesis of artistic development. For despite this closer relationship of the unconscious will to the instinctive, never, at even the lowest stage of any creative production, do the two come together. The will, conscious or unconscious, will always be the expression of the individual, the indivisible single being, while sexuality represents something shared, something generic that is harmonious with the individually-willed only in the human love-experience[4] and is otherwise in perpetual conflict with it. In art this conflict is won in a different way; though closely akin to the individual conquest in love and the collective conquest in religion, it is differentiated from both by a specific element we may broadly call the aesthetic. We shall deal with the peculiar qualities of which this consists in our next section.[5] In closing this chapter we need only say, without particularizing, that the artistic solution of this original dualism is not merely psychological, but appears, as regards its evolutionary history, to lie between the

[3] See, for instance, Emil Stephan's important work on art in the South Sea Islands (*Südsee Kunst: Beiträge zur Kunst des Bismarck-Archipels und zur Urgeschicht der Kunst überhaupt;* Berlin, 1907).

[4] See my *Technik der Psychoanalyse,* Vol. II, p. 77.

[5] Chapter iv of *Art and Artist.*

religious and the erotic solutions. The religious solution is at bottom collective; that is, the individual is delivered from his isolation and becomes part of a greater and higher whole—not in the biological-generic sense, but through his spiritual ideology, by becoming one with God. In the love-experience, which becomes possible only at a stage of fully developed individualism, we see this spiritual process objectified: God, as representing the idealized self, is found in the beloved, and, with the sense of union, the individuality seems to be exalted and intensified, lost, and yet enriched. Finally, in art, which has developed out of the collective consolation-ideology of religion and at whose further limit we find the Romantic artist striving after the complete love-experience, the individuality-conflict is solved in that the ego, seeking at once isolation and union, creates, as it were, a private religion for itself, which not only expresses the collective spirit of the epoch, but produces a new ideology—the artistic—which for the bulk of them takes the place of religion. True, this happens only at the summit of individual "artist's art," where there is deification of the genius-concept and an adoration of works of art that is comparable only to the worship of statues of gods, though they already represent mere men. Before this, art is still—particularly in its Classical period —an individual working-out of the forces of which religions are made. These forces then become concentrated in the single creative individual, whereas before they animated a whole community. The works of these peak periods of artistic production manifest in their development the individualized religion-forming forces that finally return, by way of Romantic love-experience, to their origin, which is the personal craving for immortality of the ego. All three ideologies, however—the collective-religious, the social-artistic, and the individual-erotic—lift the individual above the biological life-plane of reality—in which only the sexual immortality of propagation counteracts the individual isolation—on a higher, supernatural, super-real, or superindividual sphere wherein reigns an ideal collectivity that is created by individual intention and may at any time be altered at will.

V *The Artist's Fight with Art*

THESE last folk-psychological chapters,[1] in which we have dealt with those cultural ideologies of the various nations and epochs that underly artistic production, have brought us back to our initial problem—the relation of the artist to the art-ideology of his time. We began by approaching the problem from the side of the psychology of the artist and there said that the creative personality makes use of the art-ideology his culture supplies; but the subsequent discussion of cultural questions led to another and almost contrary view. For, from that point of view, the individual, however powerfully his personality may develop, appeared more as an instrument, which the community uses for the expression of its own cultural ideology. This is not by any means a new conception, for it played the chief rôle in the so-called "environment" theories of genius; but the fresh problem that we wish to discuss here is the double attitude of the personal artist to the prevailing art-ideology, which, on the one hand, he uses for the justification of his individual creativity, but, on the other, opposes with all the vigor of his personality. This conflict between artist and art is quite as important for the understanding of the creative process as is the positive influence of the cultural art-ideology on the individual work; it has its social analogue in the defensive reaction of the individual to collective influences of every sort, and its biological basis in the conflict between individuation and generation, from which the individual can only to a limited extent escape.

Thus the ideological art-will of form and the human art-willing of the artist stand in opposition, and the work

[1] Chapters x–xi of *Art and Artist.*

of art, which results from this conflict, differs in the different epochs of cultural development according to the strength of the personal or that of the collective will. Let us take an example of a general ideology that is not only a strong one but also a pretty rigid one. The art of Egypt, as Miss Margaret Murray has well shown,[2] left almost no freedom of artistic invention. But this does not imply that an Egyptian sculptor was not an artist: he was just as much an artist as the Gothic stonemason who could obtain the most extraordinary aesthetic effects from his single figure. Yet Egyptian art is the outstanding instance of a rigid art-ideology in which all rules of proportion and representation were fixed once and for all. As Diodorus explained, Egyptian forms were not settled, like the Greek, by external appearance, and consequently Egyptian artists are not classified according to their artistic ideas, but according to the material in which they worked. Nor indeed was the sculptor's work valued as such, but only as part of a whole building, in which it fulfilled a definite purpose. And Miss Murray regards just this external lack of freedom as the very thing that aroused an individual ambition, in creating within the limits of a rigid and obligatory framework. But this conflict between outward and inward freedom is just what we mean by the conflict between art and the artist; indeed, we have been led to conclude, from far more general considerations, that this is one of the essential dynamisms of all artistic creation.

If we take Greek art as a second example, we have here the same conflict between art and the artist—not so much individually as nationally. The classic period of Greek art, from the Persian Wars to the time of Alexander, shows us the highest and purest expression of Hellenism, freed from every cinder of Oriental influence. In other words, here it was not an individual but a whole people that in self-dependent unity completely mastered an art-form taken from without, and impressed upon it the stamp of their own national peculiarity. Greek art, moreover, stands so high, not only because it is so greatly art, so beautiful, but because it is so Greek. Further, if we look at the

[2] *Egyptian Sculpture* (London, 1929).

Renaissance, we find there, in the individualism that worked counter to the communal ideology of Christianity, a victory not only over the Nordic Gothic, but equally over the Classical (that is, Greek) art-style—a victory wrested by the strong personality of Renaissance man, who infused his individual dynamism into both the Greek ideal of beauty and the abstract forms of Gothic. Renaissance art does not owe its special place to the fact that it brought back the Classical form into use. What we admire in it is the life that was put into it by a dynamic personality—for instance, by Michelangelo, who represents in his work an inner conflict between pagan and Christian tendencies, and in whom the Renaissance not only was completed, but also finished.[3] Then comes Baroque, arising out of the victory of a Church become worldly over the Nordic Reformation; and in the rebuilding of Italian churches, as in other things, the Spanish Jesuits are credited with playing the leading part.[4] In Baroque, pagan Renaissance and Christian Gothic are both suffocated under the dominant splendor of the temporal Church. Rococo, finally, is the defeat of Church Baroque by the French spirit, and so on.

Thus the great collective ideologies of art, which we call styles, also show us the conflict between a newborn ideology (religious, national, or individual—that is, of genius) and an old one—ending in the defeat of the latter—as the principle of development. This struggle of world-views, which is represented microcosmically by the conflict of the artist against art, is undoubtedly powerfully forwarded by the strong artistic individualities, and leads to the triumph of a new style. But the beginning of the movement is cultural and not individual, collective and not personal—only, through his inner conflict, the artist gains the courage, the vigor, and the foresight to grasp the impending change of attitude before others do so, to feel

[3] E. Lucka describes this conflict between Renaissance and Gothic in his *Michelangelo: Ein Buch über den Genius* (Berlin, 1930).

[4] Cf. the latest account in L. Collison-Morley: *Italy after the Renaissance: Decadence and Display in the Seventeenth Century* (London, 1930). Cf. also the earlier accounts of this period, which is so important for the history of art, in W. Weisbach: *Der Barock und die Kunst der Gegenreformation* (Berlin, 1921), and Wölfflin: *Renaissance und Barock.*

it more intensely, and to shape it formally. But he must do something more than gradually liberate himself from the earlier ideologies that he has hitherto taken as his pattern; in the course of his life (generally at its climax) he must undergo a much harder conflict and achieve a much more fateful emancipation: he must escape as well from the ruling ideology of the present, which he has himself strengthened by his own growth and development, if his individuality is not to be wholly smothered by it. This, however, is only so in the case of artists in individualistic ages, and even there only great artists, whose greatness consists precisely in this reaching out beyond themselves, beyond the ideology which they have themselves fostered. They must ultimately, so to say, carve their own individuality out of the collective ideology that prevails and that they themselves have accepted, like the sculptor who carves his figures out of the raw stone. In this self-representation he seeks, indeed, to make himself individually eternal, but the immediate cause is the impulse to self-preservation from complete absorption of the ego in the collective or of the individual in the genus. This battle for liberation from art, which has to be fought out again and again by every artist, received *cultural* expression in the Renaissance, in which the individualist artist-type saved himself, by the concept of genius, from threatened suffocation by Gothic and Classical. He had, indeed, to accept and employ the ideal forms that are born of the primal human conflict, if only that he might assert himself positively as artist; but the cultural significance of the much-admired Renaissance lies not in the Classical form —which was developed to a higher level in Greece—but in this individual winning through, which equally raises it above the anonymous Gothic.

The further this assertion of the individualist type—as man or as artist—goes, and the less capable the collective ideologies are of carrying it (especially in the case of religion), the more internal the struggle of the cultures becomes, and the great artist finally has to carry it personally, in artistic development and in human suffering. The essence of the artistic type lies therefore in this, that he can pass through his individual struggle, the conflict between individual and genus, between personal and collective immortality, in an *ideological* form, and that the peculiar quality of this conflict compels him, or enables him, to use an *artistic* ideology for the purpose. For, as we have seen, the same fundamental conflict may, with a different attitude, lead to the individual's resolving the inner dualism by means of a scientific or a political ideology. If we ask what particular cast in the individual settles whether the personal conflict shall be fought in terms of this ideology or that, we can only find the answer by continuing to use the comparative method that we have followed hitherto. In other words, the artist, like art, is not to be comprehended through a specialized study of creative personality or of the aesthetic standards of art-ideology, but only by a combination of the two and by other comparative methods. That is, we cannot understand the artist by a purely individual psychology—without taking account of the collective art-ideology—nor the development and changes of the latter without the psychology of the artist and the primal conflict that lies at its root and that is the cause equally of art and of artists. Nor can we understand the development of this general human conflict and particularly of artistic creation without noting how, and why, the same basic struggle is passed through in other cases in terms of scientific, political, or other ideologies.

To understand this ideologizing of personal conflicts—which in a greater or lesser degree affects all choice of and all practice of a calling[5]—we must return to the most general principles of the development of personality, various other aspects of which I have discussed elsewhere.[6] The human individual must have at his disposal from the start some sort of ideology, even if of the most primitive kind (such as the notion of good and evil), not only that he may find his place in the society that is built up on these ideas, but also that he may find relief from the inner

[5] See the chapter on "Vocation and Talent," in my *Modern Education*.

[6] *Gestalung und Ausdruck der Persönlichkeit* (1928), and also the chapter on "Self and Ideal" in *Truth and Reality* (1929). [The latter is reprinted on pp. 280 ff. of this collection.]

conflicts that would otherwise compel him to create for himself some ideology for the objectification of his psychic tensions. This ideologization of inner conflicts manifests itself in the individual in a form psychoanalysis has called "identification"—with parents, teachers, and other ideal patterns—without being able to explain the process thereby. I have shown in another place that the motive of these identifications is the individual's root fear of isolation, and that their result is that the individual masters his conflict himself, independently of the persons who mediate and represent these ideologies. But this inward independence of teachers and educators as such, which is gained in the first instance by accepting the collective ideology that they offer, turns—usually about the time of puberty—against these collective ideologies themselves, under which the growing individual feels just as dependent and as restricted as he had previously been vis-à-vis their individual representatives.

This liberation of the ego, as we should expect, occurs in the artist also, but with the difference that in his case no time is lost in taking up the *artistic* ideology, in preference to the general social. But this brings us back to the question, What is it that favors such a preference for the artistic ideologies in particular individuals and not in others? To make any progress on this question, we must state the problem more narrowly, for we must remember that the general social ideology is made a specific in other people besides the artist, by their choice and practice of professions, so that the turn from general to special ideology is not a specifically artistic problem, but one of vocational psychology. As to this, I will refer the reader to what I have said in other works already mentioned, and only emphasize, in the present context, the formulation there proposed, which is that, compared with the average professional man, the artist has, so to say, a hundred-percent vocational psychology. That is (as I have said earlier in an introductory fashion), the creative type nominates itself at once as an artist (or, in certain circumstances, as scientist or otherwise)—a periphrasis we are now in a position to replace by the formula that in the artist-type the creative urge is constantly related, ideologically, to his own ego, or at any rate that this is so in a higher degree and fuller measure than in the average man, so that one can say of the artist that he does not practice his calling, but *is* it, himself, represents it ideologically. For whereas the average man uses his calling chiefly as a means to material existence, and psychically only so far as to enable him to feel himself a useful member of human society—more or less irrespective of what his calling is—the artist needs his calling for his spiritual existence, just as the early cultures of mankind could not have existed and developed without art.

For the artist, therefore, his calling is not a means of livelihood, but life itself; and this explains not only the difficulties of his existence, since his main object cannot be the earning of money, but his struggles in love and life, which in the productive type spring from the impulse to create, and not vice versa. This conflict arises from an intensification in him of the general human dualism, but it is soon transformed from the purely dynamic conflict between impulse and will into an ideological conflict between art and the artist. The first stage in the growth of an artist is that which we have described as his "nomination" and which marks the subordination of the individual to one of the prevailing art-ideologies, this usually showing itself in the choice of some recognized master as the ideal pattern. In doing so, he becomes the representative of an ideology, and at first his individuality vanishes, until, later, at the height of his achievement, he strives once more to liberate his personality, now a mature personality, from the bonds of an ideology he has himself accepted and helped to form. This whole process of liberation from a personal or ideal identification is so particularly intense and therefore difficult in the artist (and the productive type generally), not only because he has a stronger personality, but because this needs stronger identification for its artistic ideologizing; the process of liberation being thus particularly complex, and exposing the artist to those dangerous crises which threaten his artistic development and his whole life. These conflicts, which the "madness" theory of Lombroso and the pathological literature based on it try to explain rationalistically as neurosis, can only be understood ideologically; and when we so regard them, our insight into them is the deeper. In this creative conflict, it is not only the positive tendency to individual self-liberation from ideologies once accepted and now being overcome that plays a great part. There is also the creative guilt-feeling, and this opposes their abandonment and seeks to tie down the individual in loyalty to his past. This loyalty again is itself opposed by a demand for loyalty to his own self-development, which drives him onward, even to strive beyond his own ego and artistic personality. So the struggle of the artist against art is really only an ideologized continuation of the individual struggle against the collective; and yet it is this very fact of the ideologization of purely psychical conflicts that marks the difference between the productive and the unproductive types, the artist and the neurotic; for the neurotic's creative power, like the most primitive artist's, is always tied to his own self and exhausts itself in it, whereas the productive type succeeds in changing this purely subjective creative process into an objective one, which means that through ideologizing it he transfers it from his own self to his work. The artist is helped, moreover, by another dynamic difference which not only enables him to construct a valuable ideology but to transform it into actual artistic achievement.

A deep study of neurosis has shown me that a characteristic quality of both the productive and the thwarted, marking off these excess and deficiency types from the average, is an overstrong tendency toward totality of experience. The so-called adaptability of the average man consists in a capacity for an extensive partial experience such as is demanded by our everyday life, with its many and varied problems. The nonconforming type tends to concentrate its whole personality, its whole self, on each detail of experience, however trivial or insignificant; but as this is not only practically impossible but psychically painful (because its effect is to bring our fear), this type protects itself from a complete self-exhaustion by powerful inner restraints. Now, the neurotic stops at this point in the process, thus cutting himself off from both the world and experience, and thus faced with the proposition "All or nothing," chooses the nothing. The artist, however, here also, in spite of many difficulties and struggles, finds a constructive, a middle way; he avoids the complete loss of himself in life, not by remaining in the negative attitude, but by living himself out entirely in creative work. This fact is so obvious that, when we intuitively admire some great work of art, we say the whole artist is in it and expresses himself in it.

This, however, holds good for different kinds of artists in different degrees—a point to which we shall return later. Some artists persistently partialize themselves and thus leave a greater complete work unaccomplished; others pour themselves out wholly in every partial work. The same seems to be true of whole periods, or rather epochs, of style, which are, after all, only the expression of psychical and spiritual ideologies. The best example of a complete style seems to me to be Gothic, but only since it strives after an all-embracing whole, but because, more perhaps than any other style-tendency, it expresses, and insists on expressing, the spiritual-in-itself. This, however, is no longer the purely abstract spirituality of primitive art, but a world-embracing "pantheistic" dynamic of the spiritual. Hence, as Worringer rightly saw, it is not merely "a phenomenon of its age, but the great irreconcilable antithesis to the Classical, which is not limited to a single period of style, but reveals itself in ever new clothing throughout the centuries." [7] Now, wherever one manages to find this opposition of Classical and Gothic, it seems to me to correspond to that eternal dualism that lies at the root of all art and all artistic creation, and precisely because it is something inherent in the individual. I believe that I have found one of the fundamental aspects of this primary individual dualism in the total-partial conflict, and in this sense Gothic would be the total and Classical

[7] *Formprobleme der Gothik,* which lays even more stress on the racial influence than Worringer's latest work, *Griechentum und Gotik* (Munich, 1928).

the partial—a partial, it is true, that always gives the whole in the detail, the psychic dynamism expressing itself aesthetically as the beauty of proportion that was the Classical ideal. Gothic, on the other hand, does not try to symbolize the whole in a part, but rather aims at a dynamic picture of the whole in its actual totality.

In what we call Classical or Gothic, then, these two spiritual principles have been aesthetically objectified, and each presents itself to the individual artist as an external compulsion of form that he must accept as artist but fight against as individual. But we have also gained some further insight into the inner processes of the creative artist, which make it possible for him fully to express his own personality at the same time that it yields precedence to the art-ideology of the work. We must, further, return to the difference between a total and a partial experience, which is basic for the attitude of all such individuals. In the ceaseless struggle for liberation of the self from the moral, social, and aesthetic ideologies and the people who represent them, the individual goes through a disjunctive process of which I have regarded the process of birth as the prototype. But the process, though similar in principle, is not a simple repetition of the trauma of birth; it is, broadly, the attempt of the individual to gain a freedom from dependence of any sort upon a state from which it has grown. According to the stage of development, this separation will take the most varied forms and symbols, whereas the basic conflict is always the same: the overcoming of previous supporting egos and ideologies from which the individual has to free himself according to the measure and speed of his own growth, a separation that is so hard, not only because it involves persons and ideas one reveres, but because the victory is always, at bottom and in some form, won over a part of one's own ego. We may remark here that every production of a significant artist, in whatever form, and of whatever content, always reflects more or less clearly this process of self-liberation and reveals the battle of the artist against the art that expresses a now-surmounted phase of the development of his ego. In some artists the representation of a process of personal development seems to be the chief aim of their work, by which I do not mean the accidental biographical material, though this is itself (as we said above) an objective expression of the same inner conflict. Finally, there are artists, especially among the poets, for whom not only is this self-representation the essence of their work, but who are conscious to a very considerable extent of the process and have studied it "philosophically." Goethe and Nietzsche are perhaps the most conspicuous examples of this type, which is becoming more and more common nowadays and in which we can notice an ever-increasing preponderance of the psychologically disintegrating over the artistically formative ego. This process of the increasing extension of consciousness in humanity, which psychoanalysis has fostered so enormously in the last decades—but not entirely to the advantage of mankind as a whole—was prophesied by me in my *Künstler* in 1905 (at the time of my first acquaintance with Freud) as likely to be the beginning of a decay of art. In this early work I not only foretold the collapse of art through the increasing consciousness of the artist, but observed and established the manner of it in the nascent state.

My observations of those days seem to me to have been very emphatically confirmed by the later development of the problem of art and the artist; but I can now give it a better psychological foundation, and so perhaps a more hopeful future. The question of how it is that the great artist can express his whole personality in his work and yet subordinate it to his art-ideology is only to be understood, as I remarked, where the conflict of the partial and the total has come out at a particularly happy issue. I spoke of the constant detaching of the artist from earlier ideologies, which on the one side correspond to a separation of the individual from a great whole, and on the other to the extrusion of worn-out parts of the ego. This double separation of the ego from the collectivity and of part of the ego from its totality includes the two fundamental life-processes: individuation on the one hand, and procreation or generation on the other. Now, these fundamental processes, as is well known, are not sexual, but occur at a very low biological level, before the differentiation of the sexes, as cell-division. They survive, however, in rudimentary form even in the highly differentiated sex-life of humanity and thus continue to bulk large and to matter deeply in such highly complicated processes as the development of personality and the creative impulse that rises from it. At the highest level of human personality we have a process that psychoanalysis calls (without explaining its deeper biological and human aspects) "identification." This identification is the echo of an original identity, not merely of child and mother, but of everything living—witness the reverence of the primitive for animals. In man, identification aims at re-establishing a lost identity: not an identity which was lost once and for all, phylogenetically through the differentiation of the sexes, or ontologically in birth, but an identity with the cosmic process, which has to be continually surrendered and continually re-established in the course of self-development. In the attempt at this re-establishment, the two types with which we are dealing, the "totalist" and the "partialist," diverge fundamentally. The average type of a well-adapted "partial" being can feel himself as part of a greater whole—in religious communion, social and vocational grouping, or family feeling—and thus find his identity with the world. The "total" type, on the other hand, is set on maintaining himself as a whole and on absorbing the world as part of himself. In so far the artist and the neurotic are alike, that in contrast to the average man they have a far wider, more "magic" feeling of the world, which is gained, however, at the cost of an ego-centric attitude toward it. The neurotic stops at the point where he includes the world within himself and uses this as a protection against the real claims of life, though a price is paid for this protection in the feeling of world-sorrow which has to be taken in with the rest. The artist, too, has this feeling of *Weltschmerz* in common with the handicapped neurotic; but here the paths diverge, since the artist can use this introverted world not only as a protection but as a material; he is thus never wholly oppressed by it—though often enough profoundly depressed

—but can penetrate it by and with his own personality and then again thrust it from him and re-create it from himself. This extrusion is a process both of begetting and of bearing, not at the level of sexual differentiation of male and female, but at a deeper and more fundamental level: the liberation of the individual from the burden of generation by repulsion of part of the ego, which is felt as a relief and not as a loss.

The primitive process of biological propagation by fission of a part from the whole is thus ideologically "macrocosmized" in the artist, and he puts forth into his work not only a personal part of his ego but also a part that includes either the whole world or at least an important portion of it. This representation of a part of the world or of nature in his work is not the result of an aesthetic impulse to imitate or of technical capacity, but the precondition of all creation. If the artist had not already absorbed the world within himself on account of his emotional needs, he would not have the urge to throw this cosmic self off in creation and so save himself again as an individual. In this super-individual, almost cosmic, creative process, all the purely human factors—love, sexual relations, social duties—throng in to hinder or help, so that a psychological cast is given to the conflict (though this is by no means as important as artists themselves feel and as biographers and analytical psychographers still would have us believe).

Particularly, the relation of the creative artist to women has been, ever since Homer invoked the Greek Muse to help him, a favorite theme of rather superficial essays. For the artist to project on to the beloved woman his bisexual creative urge—of begetting and of bearing, or of self-begetting, and self-rebirth, which he has fused into one —is not only his perfect right but a necessity of life for him. And that the biographer who confines himself to describing the external life-course of his hero is forced to give the Muse the position she had in the life and consciousness of the artist is also quite natural. But for psychologists to believe that they have therefore understood anything about the creative process or even about a work of art is a presumption that has prevented a right view of very complex facts. This does not touch psychoanalysis directly, but it does so indirectly; for though it does not regard the Muse of whom the poet sings as the real source of creation, yet in the so-called "deep" psychological substitution of the mother for her it postulates an equally external and less credible motivation in place of the inner motive, which is beyond its reach. I am, of course, the last person to deny the influence of birth or of the mother, after my works on incest and on the trauma of birth, but the point is whether we take a concrete view as psychoanalysts still do (and many poets perhaps with them), or regard it only as typical and ideological, making the mother the symbol of the external separation and rebirth which is ever repeated in the development of personality.[8] When once it has become such a symbol, the idea may be easily transferred in the course of life to another person, especially if the latter is identified with the ideological ego of the artist, in the same way as the mother was identified with the biological. In this sense the artist is both practically and theoretically justified vis-à-vis the psychologist when he ascribes more influence on his creativity to his master or his later Muse than to his mother or father, to whom he owes his existence, but not his artistic development.

For we owe our artistic development, as we do every other form of personality-development, to none other than ourselves and the conditions of our time, though we always tend, and sometimes are driven, to ascribe to other people not only the development and further growth of ourselves, but of our work and creativity. This is because of the creative guilt-feeling, which is a problem I have dealt with elsewhere in its psychological significance.[9] At present we are more interested in the artistic consequences and the biographical precipitates, which are inextricably connected. One of the radical mistakes made by most ordinary biographies and by psychography is the notion of a parallelism

[8] C. G. Jung, in his *Wandlungen und Symbole der Libido* (1912), has insisted, against Freud, on the symbolic significance of the mother, though one-sidedly, with emphasis on passive rebirth and without recognition of the active self-creative force.

[9] *Truth and Reality* (chapter on "Creation and Guilt").

between experience and creation. This certainly exists, if not causally, at least phenomenally connected. Quite as important, however, or even more so, is the opposition of life and creation, which has been emphasized, but not understood, since this is impossible without taking account of the creative feeling of guilt. It is significant that many of the greatest artists (though by no means all) have a strong bourgeois tinge, and Kretschmer, in his study of men of genius, declared that genius needs a strong touch of conventionality. Many whose work is of the highest value and who live wholly in their art lead a very simple, ordinary life, and this purely human side often comes to the surface in their work, in contrast to the divine quality of genius. The Muse, too, whose idealization by the poet himself and whose apotheosis in the mother-principle by the psychographer look so fine, often comes off badly enough in real life. She not only has to endure, even enjoy, the moods of the divinely inspired master, but she very often becomes for the artist a symbol of an ideology that is no longer adequate, which she may have helped him to create, but which he has now to overcome and throw overboard. In that case we have that conflict in the artist, with which the psychoanalyst so often deals—since the artist is both unable to create without her and prevented by her presence from any further creation. His inclination may be to let her go, along with the earlier ideology, but his guilt-feeling will not allow it. This feeling is, however, not only ethical and concerned with the loved companion, but inner and psychical, since it concerns his own development and his loyalty to himself.

Not only will the artist who finds a creative issue from this conflict show its traces in his work, but his work will often enough be purely the expression of the conflict itself, whose solution has to be justified as much as the failure to reach a solution would have to be. As the artist, during this process of liberation from the ideology, has to include in what he surrenders the person or persons who were connected with it, he has to justify this action, which is usually done by magnification. That is, he will either really create something greater, in order to justify his action, or in the effort to create this greater he will be impeded by a still more enhanced feeling of guilt. In the first case he will use the guilt-feeling directly for creation; in the second even his previous creative power will be impeded. But if the artist takes the step forward in a purely ideological sense, without the need of concrete figures for the resolution of his creative conflict, his tendency will be to *lessen* his work, even if in fact is has become greater. This minimizing tendency also is due to the feeling of guilt, but, on the other hand, this has already worked itself out creatively in the artist, and it is only humbler second thoughts that are obliged to lessen the splendor of creation. A splendid instance of this is Rodin's lifework; no outsider, regarding it uncritically, would imagine that, in masterpieces like the "Thinker" or even the mythological groups, he sees only fragments of a never-completed work, called by Rodin himself the "*Porte d' Enfer.*" Even though the artist was convinced and permeated by the greatness of his work, and expressed it directly in works like the "Hand of God" or the "Thinker," the aim which he set up and never attained of a vast and ideal achievement (on a par with the whole creation) represents a minimizing of the actually achieved, only intelligible by the creative feeling of guilt. This type—of which Goethe also is an instance, with his *Faust* trailing ever in his hands as his *magnum opus* by the side of which everything else was meant but as "fragments" of one great confession—has its opposite in another type of artist, who not only gives and fulfills himself in every work, but whose whole production is one vast justification of his impulse to create. Of this type Shakespeare seems to me to be the best instance—and precisely because we know so little of his actual life and even doubt his authorship. Shakespeare's work and the biographical material that has been gathered about the Stratford butcher's son have just as much psychological connection as have the Homeric poems and our scanty information about the blind Ionian singer. Even if we did discover that neither Shakespeare nor Homer[1] were re-

[1] It is worth mentioning that a life of Shakespeare by Nicholas Rowe (1709) is the first modern poet-biography, and also characteristic that

sponsible for the work assigned to them, yet the psychological types thus designated are just as much masterpieces of a people's creation as are the poems and dramas that bear their name. I mean that Shakespeare's work requires an author who because of his creative impulse would give up home and family and all the life of an ordinary citizen in order to justify a foolish and irrational migration to the metropolis by brilliant achievement there. His success is the measure of his greatness. But even if an English noble or gentleman were the author of the dramas, I am sure that folk-fantasy would have been compelled to invent such antecedents for him—which means, would have invented a Shakespeare who happened to exist in Stratford or was transplanted there. The same has happened with greater world-historical ideas, such as Christianity, which certainly needed a Jesus from Nazareth, and it can hardly be chance that the greatest creations of the human spirit, such as the New Testament, the Homeric poems, and Shakespeare's plays, should, on the one hand, have been centers of academic disputes as to authorship and, on the other, should have inspired the imagination of whole centuries in favor of one author. Even Goethe, who could hardly dispute his own authorship, felt himself compelled to describe his whole creation as a collective work which only happened to bear his name. This feeling of the poet that he is the mouthpiece of his age or, for that matter, of all humanity, explains not only why he has to ascribe his work to a Muse and thus connect it with his personal life and give it concrete form; it also throws a light on the fact that, and the degree to which, the art-ideology affects the poet's life. There is thus an influence of personal experience on creation and a reciprocal influence of creation on experience, which not only drives the artist externally to a Bohemian existence, but makes his inner life characterologically a picture of his art-ideology and thus once more calls forth the individual self in protest against this domination by that ideology.

---

a life of Homer (probably the pseudo-Hesiodic life) provided the pattern. Thus fictitious biography, which essentially constructs the life from the work, is the real ancestor of all biographical literature.

Let us take the case of Shakespeare once more. His life may just as well have been invented to suit his work as it may have been lived by the poet in a deeper sense to suit his ideology. Paradoxical as this sounds, yet we quite habitually in simpler circumstances take this adaptation of a man to his profession as self-evident. Between a night watchman who has to adapt his external life very differently from that of his fellows and the poet whose personal life is an ideological expression of his artistic production, there is a difference only of degree, not of quality. When modern biography and psychography attempt to explain a man's work and production from his personal experience, the effort must remain not only incomplete, but also superficial, as long as the influence of the art-ideology on life and experience is not included. But this is not as simple as it is with the night watchman and will not fit the same stereotyped formulae, as most psychographers, even analytical ones, try to make it do. For the impulse to create puts itself into life and into work alike, and the great artist will in himself experience his own creation at the same time as, in his work, he will shape what he has experienced: for here too form and content are once more one, as they were in primitive art.

This brings us to the real problem of biography. Biography is as little an objective science as history is, even when it endeavors to be so, and would never fulfill its purpose if it were. The *formative* process of the biography begins long before the actual attempt to picture the life of the artist; after all, the main purpose is the picture of the creative personality and not merely of the man of actuality, and the two portraits can naturally never be wholly identical. The effort to make them so is, however, the avowed or unavowed tendency not only of the biographer but of the artist himself and of his public, present and future. If there is plenty of biographical material, as in the case of Goethe, we do look in his life for the experience that would explain his work. But we never find it; though masses of material are accumulated in a futile attempt to find an experience that can explain the creative work, it cannot as a matter of principle be intelligible on that basis alone. In other cases, of which we have cited Shakespeare as the type, creative biography has an easier task in constructing a life to fit the work. But always the starting point in the formation of a biography is the individual's ideologizing of himself to be an artist, because thenceforward he must live that ideology, so far as reality allows him to do so; and so far as it does not, the artist makes for himself the experiences that he needs, searches for them and gives them forms in the sense of his ideology. Nowadays we quite naturally give the lives of certain types of poet a definite dramatic and novelistic form,[2] since this is the only form adapted to the shaping of a biographical legend. That in every age the poet's life should be revalued and re-edited to suit the ideology of that age is only natural, though this does not exactly lessen the complexity of the problem.

Before we deal with this process of biographical legend-formation, which is set going by the artist's own ideologizing experience, in terms of its effect on success and permanent reputation, we must see how the process bears on our immediate question, that of the artist versus his art. With the partial experience of his own artistic ideology, the artist is in conflict a priori, fighting for his life, and in the event (as we have shown) he achieves the compromise in his ideological experience that allows him to enjoy both his life and his productivity, instead of having to attain the one at the cost of the other. On the other hand, we must never forget that creation is itself an experience of the artist's, perhaps the most intense possible for him or for mankind in general. Nor is this true only of the unique instant and act of creation; for during the creation itself the work becomes experience and as such has to be surmounted by new actuality of extension and formation. This cumulative dynamic character of creativity, which marks it as an experience, can as a rule be

[2] For the predecessors of this modern mania, see Helene Goldschmidt: *Das deutsche Künstlerdrama von Goethe bis R. Wagner* (Weimar, 1925); Erna Levy: *Die Gestalt des Künstlers im deutschen Drama* (Berlin, 1929); Kate Laserstein: *Die Gestalt des bildenden Künstlers in der Dichtung* (Berlin, 1930). For Ibsen, who pictured the modern artist-type, see later.

reconstructed only genetically, since it is rarely the object of direct observation. Hence it is more easily observed in the arts of time and rhythm like poetry and music, which in their temporal succession and extension often show the development of this vehement dynamism during the process of creation, while we cannot see it in the fine arts except in sketches and studies. But it is almost typical for great artists that at the beginning of a work they are not quite clear about its formation, working-out, and completion; even in spite of a clear original conception, the work turns during production into something other than the artist had originally planned. This process also is only intelligible through a realization of the specific dynamism of creativity, which must operate on the *potential* life plane if it is to liberate his energy and not consume it, as we have explained in the case of play.[3]

We have said above that the artist-type, with his tendency to totality of experience, has an instinct to flee from life into creation, since there to a certain extent he can be sure of matters remaining under his own control; but this totality-tendency itself, which is characteristic of the really productive type, in the end takes hold of his creation also, and this totality of creation then threatens to master the creative artist as effectually as the totality of experience. In short, the "totality function" of the artist-type in the end makes all productivity, whether in itself or in a particular work, as much a danger for the creative ego as was the totality of experience from which he took refuge in his art. Here the conflict of the artist versus art becomes a struggle of the artist against his own creation, against the vehement dynamism of this totality-tendency that forces him to complete self-surrender in his work. How the artist escapes this new danger, after he had previously avoided that of the total experience, is one of the obscurest and most interesting problems of the psychology of creative artists. There will of course be special modes of escape for each artist or artist-type, which are decided for him by his personality and circumstances. But I think that certain ways are universally accessible, of

[3] See "Play and Pleasure," Chapter iv of *Art and Artist.*

which I will mention a few that are typical. One means of salvation from this total absorption in creation is, as in ordinary life, the division of attention among two or more simultaneous activities; and it is interesting in this connection to note that work on the activity is begun during work on the first just at the moment when the latter threatens to become all-absorbing. The second work is then often an antithesis in style and character to the first, though it may be a continuation at another level. This can, of course, only happen with artists who have various interests and capacities; thus Goethe indulged his scientific, and Schiller his philosophical, studies at periods apparently of weakness in poetic creativity, but really, according to our view, of danger to the poet when he had to find respite from that creativity. If a second sphere of interest of this sort—which is frequently a second form of artistic achievement—is lacking, periods of disappointment, depression, and even illness are likely to occur, which are then not so much a consequence of exhaustion as a flight from it.

This brings us to a second means of escape for the artist from his own creation, which in this case is not put onto another level, but simply set aside for the time being. The creative process, with its object of totality, always contains in any case a time conflict, which expresses itself in the difficulty the artist finds both in beginning and in finishing his work. Just as he can escape from threatened domination in the midst of his creation, so he can hold back instinctively as long as possible from the beginning of it; but this so overstrains the inner dynamism that delays of various sorts must be intercalated later, so that he may not be carried off by the violence of the productive experience. The inhibitions, then, of which most artists complain, both during creation and in its intervals, are the ego's necessary protections against being swallowed by creativity, as is the case, for that matter, with the inhibitions of normal or neurotic types. This form of protection may naturally in some cases have a disturbing (pathogenic) effect. But the retardation of or refusal to complete, some work may have another, deeper reason. The restraint that holds the totality-tendency in check is basically fear, fear of life and of death, for it is precisely this that determines the urge to eternalize one's self in one's work. Not only, however, has the completed work the value of an eternity symbol, but the particular creative process, if it involves an exhaustive output, is by the same token a symbol of death, so that the artist is both driven on by the impulse to eternalization and checked by the fear of death. I have elsewhere shown that this restriction between the two poles of fear—fear of life and fear of death—is one of the fundamental processes of life; the artist seems to experience it in a similar intensified fashion to the neurotic, but with the difference that in the neurotic the fear of life predominates and so checks all expression in life, while the artist-type *can* overcome this fear in his creation and is driven by the fear of death to immortalize himself.

This conflict of the artist, first against his art and then against the dynamism of his own work and finally against its actual accomplishment, finds a peculiar expression in modern artists—clearest perhaps in the poets, but unmistakable also in plastic and pictorial artists. This is the diversion of creation into knowledge, of shaping of art into science and, above all, psychology. Naturally, spiritual self-representation in the work is always one essential element in artistic creativity and in art, but it is only in modern artists that it becomes a conscious, introspective, psychological self-analysis. But we are not concerned with those artists of the day whose work claims to represent a psychological confession as such and no more—though in point of fact it *is* something more. Here we are discussing the far more interesting halfway type, which, whether in the course of an ensemble of creation or even within the compass of a single work, passes suddenly from the formative artist into the scientist, who wishes—really he cannot help himself—to establish, or, rather, cannot help trying to establish, psychological laws of creation or aesthetic effect. This diversion of artistic creation from a formative into a cognitive process seems to me to be another of the artist's protections against his complete exhaustion in the creative process. We have here the ideological conflict of beauty and truth, which we have already studied from the general cultural point of view,[4] reappearing as a personal conflict in the creative artist. But we also better understand how far the artistic form is in itself a necessary protection of the artist against the dynamism of a conflict that would destroy him if he failed to put it into form. In this sense, in the need, forced on him by that dynamism, for putting order, meaning, and control into the psychic chaos into which his totality-urge drives him, the artist, even if he is never conscious of the fact, is always a bit of a scientist. Conscious reflection about creativity and its conditions and about all the aesthetic laws of artistic effect is only a continuation at a fully conscious level of the process that ensues whenever the artistic formative power is inadequate to control the chaos—that is, when, instead of being a protection, it becomes a danger to the survival of the ego.

Seen thus, the development of modern art and the modern artist is a manifestation of the same general development of Western art-ideology, as this resulted from the Greek conflict between the notions of beauty and truth. There is a rescue of the immortal soul by the aesthetic idea of beauty, and a controlling of the psychic chaos by the artistic form, with its eternal material. This was followed by the disruption of the form by individuality in the modern genius-art, the overflow of the ego beyond the form in a romantic *Sturm und Drang*, and finally the flight from that loss of the ego which would be involved in a total creation or a total experience, into psychology. This cultural development-struggle between art and the ideologies of art has to be gone through by modern artists—burdened as they are with the whole weight of Western culture, both in their personal development and in their individual growth as artists—in themselves and with themselves. And if one of the leading art-historians of the day, Worringer, some ten years ago delivered before the Munich Goethe Society a funeral oration over modern Expressionism, contrasting our generation's will-to-art with its formative capacity, we must balance this view with some under-

[4] See "Beauty and Truth," Chapter xi of *Art and Artist*.

standing of the artists' struggle if we are to avoid passing prematurely from the establishment of a fact to its valuation. Worringer is certainly right[5] in his warning to modern artists to be satisfied with the last flicker and echo on the fringes of our culture and to avoid the great mistake of promising us, because we possess an increased insight into the essence of what art was at creative periods, an equal increase in the decaying vigor of our own uncreative epoch. That is easier said than done; not because real resignation is always harder than a struggle, but because the problem that is touched is the deepest problem of artistic creation, and it can never be solved by conscious deliberation and decision, however correct and sincere. As long as there is in man an impulse to create, he seeks and finds artistic expression in the most varied ideologies, and yet these have always been in some way traditional and collective. Nietzsche was therefore quite right when, long ago, in *Human, All Too Human*, he warned us against "revolution" in art and saw in its break with tradition its end. For unless it has some collective or social basis—for instance, in religion or, later, the "genius-religion"—artistic creation is impossible, and the last hopeless effort to base it on a psychological ideology not only leads away from art into science but, even so, fails on points of principle. Education or art can no more be supported on psychological ideologies than religion can be replaced by psychology. For psychology is the individual ideology par excellence and cannot become collective, even if it is generally accepted or recognized. But modern humanity, through its increasing individuation, has fallen ever deeper into psychology and the ideologies thereof, precisely because they justify its individuality and its consciousness of it. But this individual ideology—as I declared in my first book in 1905 and have since sought to prove from the examination of world-outlooks[6]—is an impossibility for art and has brought us to our present pass, which we may regret, but cannot alter by comparative studies of culture. So that Worringer's "funeral oration" really applies to

[5] *Künstlerische Zeitfragen* (Munich, 1921).
[5] *Seelenglaube und Psychologie* (1930); *Modern Education* (1931).

art as a whole and not its present form of Expressionism.
If, however, we regard the whole culture of a people or of an age as being not merely a means for the production of art, but as the expression of a particular form of life, within which a particular art-form plays a part, great or small, we may reach a less pessimistic position. As I have already hinted in my *Künstler*, we shall perhaps have to be content with cutting down the claims made for art and further, shall have to sacrifice the artist-type as it has hitherto existed. Modern art, as Worringer complained, does suffer from the claims of modern artists to be put on a level with creative artists of other ages, and the artist-type suffers also, since he has to put this modern ideology of art-for-art's-sake in the place of every other. The modern artist attempted to maintain the vanished art-ideologies of earlier ages at least in his personal ideologies, even if he could not transform them into productivity. But this draping of the modern individual in the ideologies of earlier ages was bound to lead, in such individuals, to a conflict between their real selves and the self adopted as an ideal—like the fundamental struggle of the neurotic. The conflict between the idealistic and realistic aspects of all art, which we have described as the struggle of the notion of beauty against that of truth, is duplicated in the modern artist as a conflict between his true self and an ideal self, in which he tries to conserve the art-ideologies of past ages. But it is not only modern art that (as opposed to Classical) is realistic, but the modern artist also, which means that he is oriented toward truth and not beauty, and this not only in his pseudo-naturalistic art-ideology, but in his whole psychological attitude toward himself and his art. His aim is not to express himself in his work, but to get to know himself by it; in fact, by reason of his purely individualistic ideology, he cannot express himself without confessing, and therefore knowing, himself, because he simply lacks the collective or social ideology that might make the expression of his personality artistic in the sense of earlier epochs. This individual realism, however, which reveals itself as a search for truth in art and life, only intensifies the conflict in the

person of the artist. The more successful his discovery of truth about himself, the less can he create or even live, since illusions are necessary for both. The clearest representative of the modern artist-type seems to me to be Ibsen, who was still just capable of an artistic elaboration of this destructive problem—and he too sometimes came suspiciously near didactic, doctrinaire phychologism.

Thenceforward nothing was possible but a frank breach of all artistic forms and restraints, and the door was opened to a purely personal psychology of self-confessing and self-knowing in art, especially in poetry. Poets at first seemed to find some support in psychoanalysis, which they hoped to be able to transform into a new artistic ideology. But, for the reasons mentioned, this proved impossible, and, further, psychoanalysis has used the modern artist as an object of study rather than helped him to a psychological ideology of art. Thus from both alike, from the side of art and that of science, the way seems to be prepared for the decisive crisis, in the midst of which we stand—but also for its solution, which I foresee in a new structure of personality. This will be able to use in a constructive form the psychological insight that is so destructive when it exists as introspection, and the individual impulse to creation will turn positively toward the formation of its own personality, as indeed it did, and actively, in the earliest phases of primitive art. This is the goal that has hitherto been vainly sought by the so-called neurotic; in earlier ages he was occasionally able to achieve creatively, thanks to some collective art-ideology, but today all collective means fail and the artist is thrown back on to an individual psychotherapy. But this can only be successful if it sees its individual problem as one conditioned both by time and by culture, whereas the modern artist is driven by the unattainability of his ideology into that neurosis out of which the neurotic vainly seeks a creative escape—vainly, because the social ideologies are lacking that could fulfill and justify his personal conflict. Both will be achieved in a new formation of personality, which can, however, be neither a therapy of neuroses nor a new psychological art-ideology, but must be a constructive process of acceptance and development of one's individual personality as a new type of humanity, and in order to create the new it will have to give up much that has been received from tradition and become dear to it. This new must first of all be a new personality-type, which may thereafter perhaps find a new art-form suited to it, but in any case will not feel any compulsion to justify its personal impulse to create by starting from the ideology of long-surmounted art-forms.

VI Success and Fame

Not in that he leaves something behind him, but in that he works and enjoys and stirs others to work and enjoyment, does man's importance lie.

—GOETHE

THE struggle of the artist against the art-ideology, against the creative impulse, and even against his own work shows itself also in his attitude toward success and fame; indeed, these two phenomena are but an extension, socially, of the process we saw beginning in subjective form with the vocation and creation of the personal ego to be an artist. In this entire creative process, which begins with this self-nomination to be an artist and concludes in the fame of posterity, two fundamental tendencies—one might almost say, two personalities of the individual—are throughout in continual conflict: the one that wishes to eternalize itself in artistic creation, the other that wants to spend itself in ordinary life—in a word, the mortal man and the immortal soul of man. This universal human conflict, which was resolved through many thousands of years by religion and the art which rested upon its ideology, has become more and more acute and difficult with the growth of individual art, until with modern artists it has taken on a form very like that of a neurosis. The conflict was always particularly intense in the artist, and this of course is one of the reasons why he was obliged to seize hold of ideological means for its settlement. For because of its "totality-tendency," the creative type is inclined, in this struggle between life and creation, to give up the one wholly in favor of the other, and this naturally intensifies the conflict rather than solves it.

We have already discussed in detail how this conflict spreads itself over experience and production. I should like to add, in outline at least, how the same fundamental conflict is reflected in that most remarkable relation between achievement and success, which are often indeed in the harshest opposition. This problem falls within the bounds of our present investigation in point of subject—seeing that concerns the artist and his creativity—but even in method it does not go *beyond* them, since we are once again concerned with interaction of individual and society. Nevertheless, I can only deal with it in outline because, whereas the history of religion and art provided a basis for the arguments in our earlier chapters, in this case the collective phenomenon that stands opposed to the individual—namely, the group or community—has been very inadequately studied hitherto. There is in fact no really useful social psychology that deals with the relation of the individual to the group, and vice versa, in a way we could draw upon for the study of the special relation of the artist to his public and of the attitude of posterity to his work. We should therefore have ourselves to lay the foundations of a social psychology before we could apply it to our special problem; and this is obviously far beyond the scope of this investigation, which is, indeed, only a preliminary toward a social psychology.

The problems of a group, of the crowd and its leader, with which we are here concerned, have been so inadequately treated hitherto that even Lange-Eichbaum, who, so far as I know, has provided the best collection of material, complains equally that he can find no basis of social psychology for his chapters on the effect of works of art and on the fame of the artist. Independently, in my book *Modern Education,* I had found myself compelled to give a sketch of a psychology of leadership, because in the very little literature existing I found nothing of use. In fact, there is a complete lack of a fundamental study of social psychology, which has always been one-sidedly treated as art has, either by the psychologists in terms of the individual or by the ethnologists and sociologists in terms of the group; and there is no real common ground. Even these one-sided studies are of course useful as preliminaries, but they cannot be turned to account here, since they are merely peripheral and we have to study the particular relation of the artist to the world around and after him—though this study itself may of course provide another stone for the edifice of a future social psychology, which will have to take the relation of the individual to the group as its basic principle.

We shall therefore begin by trying to show, in the light of our own study and without any regard for the ordinary views of social psychology, what seems to be the relation of the artist to his public and to posterity, and their attitude to him and his work. It seems to be quite certain that primitive art, in contrast to modern, was collectivist—though doubt begins immediately with the conclusion that Hirn draws, that the driving power of primitive artistic creation was not individual but social—namely, the imparting of pleasure. We are the less in a position to say this in that we know nothing of the individuality of primitive artists; while it does appear on the contrary that primitive body-ornament, which is the preliminary to art and artistic creation, indicates strong subjective motives and forces. Probably both tendencies, the individual and the social, have always been at work, though naturally in different measure and with different emphasis. For just as primitive body-ornament indicates subjective tendencies in the otherwise collective view of primitive man, so also we find in the most subjective and egocentric modern artist a need to communicate himself, to rouse applause or at least to make an impression on others—in a word, to win success. This very rough schematization of the development-history has further to be toned down by the fact that artists emphasize the one or the other aspect, according to the times, from personal motives; and we must not be misled by the fashionable generalizations and slogans of the day concerning the artist's exhibitionism and the like into forgetting that almost every productive type is also possessed of an opposite tendency to secrecy, which can in some cases be just as pathological a tendency as exhibitionism is in others. Even in judging this exhibitionism, we must be careful not to take it at its face value, for what the artist exhibits in this apparently frank way is not his real, certainly not his whole, self, of which he only gives away part that he may keep the rest the more secretly for himself. Nor is it even simply that the artist always shows us his best side, in order to conceal his weakness and deficiencies. Experience has shown that man often has the opposite tendency to show his worst side and keep the best for himself.

Without going here into the deeper individual-psychological reason for this attitude (for it is far from being explained by the concept of "self-punishment"[1]) I should like to show here how this parsimony of one's self may affect actual creation and influence both success and fame. We can naturally study only the one side, that tendency in the artist we have called the struggle of the artist against art, his work and success, and must ignore for the present the opposite tendency to want effect and success. From this one-sided standpoint, the artist obviously creates for himself; we do not mean this in a narrow egoistic sense, but as primitive art was part of collective life, so modern artistic creation is an expression of individual life. The artist creates in the same way as he eats and breathes; that is one of his forms of life-expression, which—by chance, one might almost say—results in a work that happens to be of significance for others. But here begins in the history of the work a sort of second chapter, which we might call the discovery of the work of art—not by patrons or dealers, but by the artist himself, who discovers to his surprise that what he is producing has aesthetic qualities and artistic value. The attitude of the artist toward this discovery is of course determined by his personality, but in its turn it decides, to a considerable extent, the destiny of the work and therefore that of its creator also. For the creation was a liberating process of life, a bringing to light—a birth, if one likes—which, though of great, is not of final signifi-

[1] See my latest technical work: *Die Analyse des Analytikers* (1931).

cance for the future of the child. The next problem which confronts the artist is that of giving on his part, and of accepting on that of the public. Obviously I do not mean supply and demand in the market, but a purely spiritual problem, which is one of the deepest there is—the problem, that is, of how far the artist is willing and capable of "weaning" this work he created by and for himself, and how far he tends to keep it for himself, or at least refuse to impart it to others.

We must leave aside here the important economic and practical motives that force the artist to overcome his opposition to public demand, though they may often be so strong or so emphasized that they overshadow all others. Indeed, many artists feel in this regard that they only produce for the public. This of course is true in part of successful artists; but psychologically what they do is to use the fact to justify their own need to create. But however the artist may settle this problem of publishing his work, the decision, coupled with other motives, affects his future creation. Whatever the admitted or hidden incentive, one motive for further creation is certainly the need to keep something for himself which others do not yet possess. That this work is meant to be something better is due not only to obvious artistic ambition, but to the already mentioned egoistic tendency to keep something better for one's self alone, to keep it away from others. For from the moment when the work is taken over and recognized by the public, or even merely offered to the public, it ceases to be the possession of the artist, not only economically but spiritually. Just as the artist created it from his own needs, the public accepts it to alleviate its own wants, and whatever they may make of it, it never remains what it was originally; it ceases to be the personal achievement of the individual and becomes a symbol for others and *their* spiritual demands. This "misunderstanding," which the artist *feels,* is inevitable and the price at which fame is bought.

While we have here an important motive of the struggle against fame, which is to him almost a depersonalization, we can trace in the artist an opposition to success that is perhaps still stranger. The artist or his circle may complain unceasingly of lack of success, and yet they will often reveal motives that impede or delay that success. We have already mentioned one such in what we said above about fame: the retention of individuality, which is meant here not only ideologically, but personally. Achievement and success are seen to be psychologically representative of the two basic tendencies that struggle against each other in the artist, the individual and the social. Achievement is ideological, success is personal; and the more the artist achieves in idea, the less disposed will he be to follow this up by personal success; we might say, indeed, the less need also, since the great achievement finally transforms itself into success without the help of the artist. Our interest here is in the psychological attitude of the artist-type that has diverted the creative impulse away from its own person into art and its ideology. Here we come upon the same antagonism that lies at the root of life and creativity; for success, even when it is won by artistic means, implies a personal success in life and is thus that very life from which the artist had originally fled to art as a refuge. Gustav Ichheiser therefore is quite right to distinguish, in his subtle study, *Kritik des Erfolges* (Leipzig, 1930), between "achievement-competence" and "success-competence," though he does not go far enough beyond the social phenomena. He comments tellingly on the fact that with many individuals social success is automatically ascribed to personal achievement, whereas it implies rather that a man is skillful at "putting a thing across" than a really productive activity.[2]

In artistic success or fame the process at work is indeed

[2] Of the earlier literature on this subject I would mention here: Norbert Einstein: *Der Erfolg: Ein Beitrag zur Frage der Vergesellschaftung* (1919); Julian Hirsch: *Die Genesis des Ruhmes* (Leipzig, 1914); and the literary essays of Remy de Gourmont: "*La Gloire et l'idée d'immortalité*" and "*Le Succès et l'idée de beauté*" (1901), both in *Le Chemin de velours;* the last work particularly has a very modern analysis of the social rôle of art. Philosophic thoughts on the greatness of historical persons, as well as of artists, may be found in Burckhardt's *Weltgeschichtliche Betrachtungen* (see the special edition under the title *Grösse, Glück und Unglück in der Weltgeschichte* (Insel-Bücherei, No. 126). I would mention also that Max Dessoir's *Ästhetik und Allgemeine Kunstwissenschaft* differentiates the type of man who accomplishes and the type who creates.

usually the reverse; for the artist's competence is credited with, or directly associated with, his "deserved" success. In other words, the gaining of fame does for the artist what he cannot or will not do for himself: it hands back creative power from the ideological work to the individual, who can indeed nominate himself to be an artist, and even ideologically make himself one, but whose power of achievement does not include that of imposing himself. In this, the artist, with all his opposition to pushing and publicity, is dependent on critics and dealers, who usually represent the complementary type of success-competence without exhibiting any particular achievement-competence. This successful type, which is usually centered on personal effectiveness, is in other ways too the psychological counterpart to the artist, whose only desire, indeed, is to achieve indirectly through his work. It differs from the artist particularly in the fact that his "identification" faculty remains concentrated on persons and does not extend to ideologies, as it does with the creative type; it is thus from this point of view much more personal than the artist-type, just as it is more personal, direct, and immediate in the assertion of its own ego.

This brings us, however, to an essential quality of the public in general that is also decisive for its attitude to the creative artist and his work. The average man has great difficulty in dealing with ideologies; he needs concrete personifications—in religion, for instance, or myths or leadership—and his preference for a definite concrete person is something that even such spiritual movements as Christianity cannot evade. It is here, and not merely in a curiosity and sensationalism, that the origin of the public's interest in the person of the artist lies. This interest, moreover, cannot be satisfied with the usually dull facts of the artist's external life, for his personality is inquired into, not for human or psychological reasons, but in order that he may be made the concrete representation of his work. In this, also, the public completes the process of artistic self-creation that the artist alone cannot achieve and would not if he could. For the residue of human nature that lies between his person and his work is his life in actuality, and it disturbs the harmonious unitary picture of work and creator that the hero-worshipping public demands. And we see at once the similarity between this and the creation of a god, a process that has been so magnificently successful because the god could be abstracted from the creation without even a cinder being left.

But though the artist, at least at the summit of his ideological development, is far less dependent on concrete personalities than the masses, yet he cannot wholly dispense with them and is therefore dependent on men for a link between his artistic creations, however vital, and real life. In this need to make real and actual, humanly and through the public, the unreality of his creation and of the immortality impulse that is its symbol lies the deepest root of his striving after success and fame—since it is they that give his individual and ideal creation a completion in accord with reality and the truth of life—and it is this necessity that enables him to overcome the individual resistances, of which we have spoken, to the fame that collectivizes him. Here again we have the two root tendencies, individual and collective immortality, of which the second is seen to be the only permanent form and to which the first must be surrendered. But such a collective immortality is no longer religious, but social, however many religious elements may infiltrate into the psychology of fame and success.

We must now deal with the relation of achievement and success, but particularly that of success and fame. Without committing ourselves to definitions of these very vague terms, I should like to refer success to the living and fame to the dead, or, more loosely, to understand by success something which means something actual to the creative artist—I do not mean merely material gain—whereas fame, like work itself, has a more ideological significance and concerns the work rather than the artist. No matter how far this distinction is justified, it at least opens up the possibility of approach to the actual psychological problem, which is what chiefly interests us here. Fame, which we have taken as a collective continuation of the artistic creative process, is not always, certainly not necessarily, connected with the greatness of a work; it often attaches to an achievement whose chief merit is not its high quality but some imposing characteristic, sensational either in itself or in its topical circumstances. Putting it roughly, we might say that an achievement marked by supreme quality tends to bring success, and one marked by something other than this quality to bring rather fame, both then and thereafter; not only because the masses are probably inaccessible to the supreme quality and can only be gradually educated up to it, but because the qualitatively supreme achievement leaves nothing for the public to do—at most, to imagine another equally perfect creator. The one-sided or (psychologically speaking) compensatory work is more amenable to the catch phrases of a fashion or movement, but to attain to such importance it needs certain favorable circumstances, whereas the supreme work can wait in peace, since the valuation it awaits will always supervene. In the other case, what the work lacks to make it complete is added to it by the social acquisition of fame. After all, society and posterity are far more concerned in this than in the original creator and his work, which is only more or less annexed by some collective need, as a means of giving concrete expression to some general trend, and at the same time to invest it with the sanction of genius.

Seen thus, fame not only is a hollow thing, because it is almost a depersonalization, but is transistory, since it is dependent on definite circumstances that give it birth and with which it often perishes, even though later ages may give it a new life for other purposes.[3] Fame seems to at-

[3] Well-known instances are the revival of Aristotle in the Middle Ages and of Plato in the present as the expression and justification of similar ideologies. Shakespeare was unheeded for nearly a century and a half after his death, till the Romantics made him their ideal of the poetic genius. Goethe's influence originally, in *Götz* and *Werther*, worked over wide areas quite anonymously; later in Weimar he was only admired as a poet by a small group of friends. It was only later still that he became the national hero of Germany, symbolized especially in *Faust*. Lange-Eichbaum has referred to the transformation in the poet in the growth of his fame. Luther, being pathological, becomes a hero type, the melancholy Mozart a lively contemporary of Rococo. One of the most interesting examples of this kind in the history of art is Virgil, who appears in the Middle Ages as a magician, a true precedessor of the black magician Doctor Faustus, whom Goethe again transformed into the type of the struggling poet's soul.

tach itself to men and achievements that we call "epoch-making," but when a creation of the moment is recognized and rewarded with fame, it is really conditioned by an epoch already in course of growth. Again, fame seems to come to men and achievements that do in some sense make history (or help to make it), or exercise (or are subject to) some practical influence—in a word, to those men who act on life immediately and more directly than the higher artist-type who creates purely ideologically—whereas the epoch-making artist is something that the masses can develop further themselves, since this type stands nearer to life and practical success. I do not mean necessarily actual practical success, but the ultimately practical success of a whole movement, to represent which he has been summoned by the masses. For there would appear to be another contradiction here, between actual personal success and the renown attaching to epoch-making, just as a man who is personally very successful is often ideologically higher and draws no practical advantage from being recognized. Men whose work has been epoch-making and who have later become famous, whose work has had great practical influence, have often been dreamers and phantasts—and all the better material for the formation of legends (Columbus). It almost seems as though there were an economic law that only *one* party can extract something from a great achievement, either the man himself or others, either his contemporaries or posterity. From this it is clear that the chances for the creator to get something for his work are one out of three, and that even the first possibility is never perfectly fulfilled, because he must in any case share his success and fame with others, and thus has to give up a share not only in his work but of his own self, for collective valuation in terms of success and fame.

These last remarks lead us once more to the actual problem of *artistic* success, which we have unwillingly lost sight of in this discussion of success and fame as social phenomena. Artistic success, concerned with essentially ideal values—which indeed are ultimately the only epoch-making values, or at least used to be—is less disputed than success in other social spheres, and the person of the artist, in spite of all the public interest, vanishes to a very large extent behind his work. The building up of fame is a collective creation of the community, and thus the artist, with his work, becomes the material for a new creative achievement of the community. In the course of this process the individual work is incorporated socially in a particular community-group, which may in some cases extend to the whole of humanity, and in any case is oriented toward a common assertion of the immortality of the individual artist. When contemporaries or posterity grant an artist immortality, they participate in that immortality, just as burial in a royal tomb or a similar-intentioned burial in the church (as the grave of Christ) gives the ordinary mortal a share in divine immortality.

The artist, therefore, not merely creates collective values from his individual need, but is himself finally collectivized, since out of the totality of his existence the community makes a new collective work, which survives as posthumous fame. From this point of view art is unintelligible without a consideration of its effect on its contemporaries and posterity—meaning thereby not its aesthetic but its social and cultural effect.[4] The continued existence of art through successive generations shows that the individual creative process, even its actual product in work, is no more than the precondition of collective creation, which selects and transforms whatever in individual work can maintain itself as an expression of the contemporary general ideology. The artist in himself provides in his work the raw material the community uses in the creation of biographies and fame as an expression of its own eternalization. This partially explains the mysterious agreement between the great achievement and the prevailing general ideology—especially when we consider that this process always begins in the lifetime of the artist, who often anticipates this collective transformation by adapting his creation to a great extent to the needs of the community. This

[4] As Du Prel effectively remarks, the co-operation of the recipient begins even with the aesthetic pleasure, in which the individual annexes the work just as the community does in the creation of fame.

obviously does not mean in the case of great artists a concession to the masses, but something of a deeper kind, a strong sympathy with the spiritual ideals of his public.

On the other hand, there is always a distinct reaction of the artist, not only against every kind of collectivization, but against the changing of his own person, his work, and his ideology into an eternalization-symbol for a particular epoch. This resistance of the artist to his absorption into the community will show itself in more than his objection to success and fame; it will also influence his further activity so far as the assertion of his own individuality is concerned, and become a strong stimulus to further creativity in general. Certainly this will be the case with the great artist, who always tries to escape this collectivizing influence by deliberate new creations, whereas the weaker talent succumbs to a conscious concession to the masses or becomes mere raw material for the collective perpetuation-instinct. These diverse outcomes of the struggle of the artist against success and fame explain, too, why many of the greatest geniuses only attained fame after their own time, and, on the other hand, why mediocre gifts enjoy a seemingly undeserved success. A strong-willed creator lends himself far less to collective influence than a merely talented artist, whose work may easily be made the material for a mass creation that genius opposes.

But we see too in this matter of success and fame that the struggle of the artist against the art-ideology and his own creative dynamism is objectified and becomes a struggle of the artist against the community of living men and against posterity. The struggle is carried on on both sides and is so obstinate because it is at bottom again that opposition of individual and community that was the original source of all artistic productivity. The individual artist wants to free himself by his own creativity from the spiritual immortality-idea of the community, while the recognition of his achievement, manifested as fame, amounts to an incorporation of his own personality in that of the community. Thus general recognition of the artist and his work is the spiritual counterpart to his own asserted claim to be an artist; the latter is a gesture of independence, whereas fame, which is something granted to him, again makes him dependent.

Success stands, in a sense, halfway, since it is both deserved and won by the self, but leads easily to the fame that must be bestowed by others. This brings us also to the positive side of the whole problem, which we have hitherto kept in the background, because it could only be understood after considering the artist's disinclination to fame. The assumption that the artist seeks only success and fame originates with the unproductive type, who may not only be eager for it himself, but also be actuated by a belief that the artist wants to become famous, whereas really he himself wants to make him famous so as to participate in his immortality. It would be an exaggeration, of course, to deny that the artist is attracted by success and fame, but his motives are other than the motives of those who grant it to him. For the artist, success is a way of returning to life when the work is completed, and fame is a sort of collective after-existence that even the greatest cannot dispense with, since there is no more individual after-existence. The tragedy lies in the fact that the collective continuation of existence, which every individual aims at, extends in the artist's case to a complete depersonalization in his work, or at least to its radical transformation into a collective product; in any case, it leads far beyond the goal that the artist himself aimed at. Success gives him both, the individual justification of his work and its collective recognition, whereas fame stamps both himself and his work as a creature of the community.

These observations indicate that the desire for success and fame may at first act as a stimulus to the creative impulse, but that later, when the artist approaches success or has attained it, other social ideologies must take its place. In any case, this change in the social relation of the artist decisively affects his art-ideology, and the success-fame motif turns from a stimulus to creation into the material of creation and may thereafter as such determine the artist's life as well. It would be fascinating to follow out in art—and especially in literary history—the relations between the personal success of the artist and the representation of success as a theme in his work, as well as the effect the success attained has, not only on his creation, but on his life. The successful artist will evolve a quite different personal and artistic ideology from that of those who are not a success during their own lives. Many artists return, artistically or at least spiritually, to an earlier period of their struggle for success, as we can see from the well-known dreams of great poets and other successful artists, in which they seem to be set back in their modest beginnings. Here there is obviously a rejuvenation-wish,[5] for fame has a flavor of death, and immortality is only distinguished by two small letters from the arch-evil they dread.

But fame not only threatens the personal immortality of the artist by making it collective; it is moreover directly hostile to life, since it forces the artist to stay officially in the groove that he has chosen for himself. This is seen in success, of which we said above that it was a sort of "return of the artist to life." It is a return that disappoints the artist because it does not give him freedom of experience, but compels him to further *artistic creation.* Success is therefore a stimulus to creativity only so long as it is not attained—which means, as long as the artist believes he can regain life by his success and so free himself from the bondage of creating. Bitterly, then, he finds out that success only strengthens the need for creating, and that fame, which is the end of it, leads to depersonalization during his lifetime and is of no use for life if it comes after death. The artist does not create, in the first place, for fame or immortality; his production is to be a means to achieve actual life, since it helps him to overcome fear. But he cannot get out of the bypath he has once trodden, which was to lead him back by means of his work for life. He is thus more and more deeply entangled in his creative dynamism, which receives its seal in success and fame.

But along with all these expressions of the opposition of the artist to art-ideology, to the dynamism of creation and the final absorption of his individual immortality by

[5] In this context belongs Goethe's remark about his repeated adolescences.

the community, there must exist other, and even stronger, tendencies of surrender, self-renunciation, and self-sacrifice. These seem to be just as necessary for the artist as the tendencies of self-assertion and self-eternalization; and, indeed, we have had to assume that what is perhaps the most decisive part of creative dynamism originates in this conflict of opposing tendencies and their settlement in the harmony of the work. This conflict between self-assertion and self-surrender is a normal phenomenon in human psychical life, which in the artist is extraordinarily intensified and reaches gigantic, one might say macrocosmic heights. As the strong creative personality is driven to destroy a pre-existing ideology, instead of a mere individual, as his "building-sacrifice," before he may eternalize himself in a new one, the conflict between surrender and assertion, which otherwise takes place in relation to a person, is here manifested with society and its whole order as the player on the other side.

The individual may, by his nomination to be an artist, have asserted his independence of the human community and rooted himself in self-sufficient isolation; but ultimately he is driven by the work he has autonomously produced to surrender again to that community. This creative self-sufficingness that generates the work out of one's self alone has misled us into thinking of the artist, at least spiritually, as a bisexual combination of the male and female principles, which create the work, as it were, hermaphroditically. But this view, which the artist himself often shares, is contradicted not only by the existence of definitely masculine or feminine types among artists, but by the complete lack of creative power in many hermaphroditic or homosexual types. In any case, this explanation seems to me to be rather a metaphorical illustration of a much more complicated fact. I believe that we have here a deliberate denial of all dependence—in other words, a primary expression of an antisexual creative impulse that seeks to bring forth the world and itself from itself and without help. This tendency toward a self-sufficing independence brings the individual into conflict with sexual life, of which the very essence is creation or generation by the help of another. But even the autonomously functioning artist, who may produce his work himself, is ultimately dependent on others for recognition, success, and fame, and even more so than the average man is dependent on his sexual partner. The artist therefore has to give himself the more and the more intensively and exhaustively in his work because he has created it the more independently of others.

This seems almost a compensative justice, but is really only the result of a violent dynamism that willfully alters a natural dependence of the individual into an apparent freedom in creation. Success and fame then supervene to assure the artist that for all his lordliness he is still dependent on the collective forces that he seeks to escape by autonomous creation. From our point of view, according to which an artist is made by the individual's raising himself above nature and making himself eternal in his work, we might put it in this way: that success and fame make him once more a collective being, take him from his divine creative rôle and make him human again—in a word, make him mortal. However much he may like to return to earth and become human, he cannot do it at the price of his own immortality; and the paradox of the thing consists in the fact that success and fame, which make him collectively immortal, make him personally human once more and restore him to mortality. His work is taken from him by the community, as the child is taken from its parents, and in place of it he receives his title to fame, rewarded like a mother by a state hungry for soldiers. The artist, too, looks for this reward, but he hopes to return by his success to life, whereas fame condemns him often enough to spiritual death.

If success is the result of an irresistible dynamism which gives success to that artist who achieves it, fame is in the same way the result of an irresistible dynamism in a community always hungry for material for its own eternalization. Every group, however small or great, has, as such, an "individual" impulse for eternalization, which manifests itself in the creation of and care for national, religious, and artistic heroes. Yet this is impossible without the productive achievement of outstanding individuals, who then become the pioneers and victims of this collective immortality, whether they will it or not. In this sense success is a measure of the extent to which the individual paves the way for this collective eternity-impulse; and fame might then be taken as an expression of regret on the part of the community which has annexed this man and his work as its own.[6] In spite of this guilt-feeling, however, the community really takes back only what genius, by using collective ideology, had previously taken from it—magnified, it is true, by the personal achievement of the creator. And this is the more important since the community annexes the man and his work, depersonalizes him, and thus really robs him of the fruit of his work—in return for which he is offered the distinction of fame. Success and fame thus complete not only the work of the artist, but, far more than that, a vast circle in the eternal conflict between individual and group. The individual tries, by taking over a collective ideology that he creates anew in the personal sense, to assure his own immortality, and this is manifested in success; but the community, by the bestowing of fame, annexes for itself the immortality that had really been won by an individual, makes itself eternal in the work, and offers the artist in return its collective glory.

[6] Lange-Eichbaum has expressed a similar idea.

VII *Deprivation and Renunciation*

The individual becomes conscious of himself as being this particular individual with particular gifts, tendencies, impulses, passions, under the influence of a particular environment, as a particular product of his milieu. He who becomes thus conscious of himself assumes all this as part of his own responsibility. At the moment of choice he is thus in complete isolation, for he withdraws from his surroundings; and yet he is in complete continuity, for he chooses himself as product; and this choice is a free choice, so that we might even say, when he chooses himself as product, that he is producing himself.

—KIERKEGAARD

THE last chapters have brought us back to the narrower problem with which we started, the relation of the artist to art; but permit us now to formulate it from the standpoint of the artist, whereas at first we had to do so from that of art. We started with the primitive art-forms of ornament and noted that their abstractness yet contained an element of the concrete that alone really made them works of art. For if they were nothing but abstraction, we should value philosophical ideas more highly than art and so return to the position of Greek thinkers, who identified beauty and truth and saw their ideal in the wise man and not in the inspired artist. The essence of art, however, lies precisely in the concrete representation of the abstract; and we tried to show why such a representation was thought beautiful and roused aesthetic pleasure. In order to understand primitive ornament, we adduced, in addition to the personal and social motives of the "artist," the general ideology within which these forms were necessary or possible, and thence we found the first deduction of the concept of beauty from the concept of the soul. The primitive world-outlook rests on a collective ideology of the soul, which must in its nature be abstract to attain its object of supporting the belief in immortality. Primitive art is abstract, because it wants to, or must, represent this abstract idea of the soul as like as possible, in order that its actual existence may be proved by concretization. Whereas, then, primitive (and even later) religion supports the belief in immortality by a collective soul-ideology, art proves the existence of this abstract conception of the soul by its concretization in symbolical form.

We traced the development of art from its primitive beginnings to the personal masterpieces of Classical, Renaissance, and modern times, until we finally found in the individual artist himself a representative of the same ideology of immortality. Not only does his work become the most concrete proof that the individual can live on in spirit for centuries, but the last chapters have shown us how the artist is under a sort of organic compulsion to transform his art-ideology into experience. In this he makes reality of the unreal to just the extent that it represents the concretization of the soul-concept in the work. In other words, the artist must live his ideology so that he, as well as others, may believe in it as true; on the other hand, this ideological experience acts both as a means to make artistic productivity possible and as a means to live a real life. For we have seen that the basic conflict of the creative personality is that between his desire to live a natural life in an ordinary sense and the need to produce ideologically—which corresponds socially to that between individuality and collectivity, and biologically to that between the ego and the genus. Whereas the average man largely subordinates himself, both socially and biologically, to the collective, and the neurotic shuts himself deliberately off from both, the productive type finds a middle way, which is expressed in ideological experience and personal creativity. But since the artist must live as a human being and yet feels compelled to make this transitory life eternal in an intransient work, a compromise is set up between ideologized life and an individualized creativity—a balance that is difficult, impermanent, and in all circumstances painful, since creation tends to experience, and experience again cries out for artistic form.

In this sense, the general problem of the artist—not only in its psychological, but in its human aspect—is contained in the two notions of deprivation and renunciation. The psychological point of view, as it culminates in psychoanalysis, always emphasizes only the deprivation, from which artists seem to suffer most in themselves; the philosophical view, to which a few artists like Goethe or Ibsen attained at the height of their achievement, emphasizes renunciation. But the two aspects are complementary, like outer and inner, society and ego, collectivity and individuality. The great artist and great work are only born from the reconciliation of the two—the victory of a philosophy of renunciation over an ideology of deprivation.

From this point of view, discussions about life and creativity, the conflict of various modes of life and ideas of creativity, seem superficial. An artist who feels that he is driven into creating by an external deprivation, and who is then again obstructed by a longing for life, can rise above these conflicts to a renunciant view of life that recognizes that it is not only impossible but perilous to live out life to the full and can, willingly and affirmatively, accept the limitations that appear in the form of moral conventions and artistic standards, not merely as such, but as protective measures against a premature and complete exhaustion of the individual. This means the end of all doubt as to whether he is to dedicate his whole life to art or send art to perdition and simply live; also of the question whether he is to live a Bohemian life in accordance with his ideology or live an ordinary life in despite of his art; and in the end his creativity is not only made richer and deeper by this renunciatory attitude, but is freed from the need to justify one or the other mode of life—in other words, from the need for compensation.

But this justifies a question as to whether such a human solution of the creative conflict may not have an unfavorable influence either on the urge to create or at least on the quality of the work. A study, psychological and ideological, of the artist and the history of art certainly gives the impression that, as we said above, the great artist and his work are due to a forced justification or a strained overcompensation; but also that only the greatest artists at the end of this struggle reach a renunciatory philosophy. The "at the end" is important, for it would indicate that their chief work dated from the period before this achievement and therefore came into being out of the still unresolved conflict of life and creation. It is certainly clear that a thoroughly satisfied bourgeois existence would give no stimulus for creation; it is equally clear on the other hand that the creative genius must approximate to such a life if he is not to sacrifice the one to the other and so possibly land himself again in sterility. We often see the artist, and the neurotic, who vacillates in a similar conflict, manufacturing the conflict (or intensifying it if it already exists) just so that he may resolve it. For the neurotic, this is a test which he fails; he remains neurotic and proves to himself that he must do so. For the artist, these self-created conflicts are also ultimately tests, but, in contradiction to the neurotic, they prove his capacity to create, since he masters the conflict, in form and content, by giving it aesthetic shape. This tendency, which is especially marked in the Romantic, to dramatize this experience does not, then, come from a mere wish to make one's self interesting, but is deeply connected with the general problem of artistry. On the whole, we may say that the great artist —and most admirably in the Classical type—can free himself from the parallelism between his life and work, while the Romantic is more dependent on the dramatization of his experience on the lines of his ideology, since his creativity has definitely a compensatory character.

Here too we must pass, in the case of the individual artist and his work, if we are to judge it rightly, beyond this classification, since the same artist may in the course of his life develop from Romantic to Classic. It seems, indeed, from our previous observations, that the mature artist can only be born from victory over the Romantic in himself, irrespective of whether this Romanticism has come out in actual work at an early period, as with Goethe, or whether the artist only emerges at the fullness of life, as a complete Classic, as did K. F. Meyer. Here, too, as in an ordinary professional career, the spadework will find its reward in magnificent masterpieces. This view of the development of the artistic personality and his work is only now beginning to appear in the study of art and has so far no solid principles on which to build. I will mention as characteristic, and as far as I know as the best, examples two works which deal respectively with the work of maturity and of youth. The one is A. E. Brinckmann's lucid work on the *Spätwerke grosser Meister* (Frankfurt, 1925), the ripe humanity of which work is manifestly and admittedly conditioned by the author's entry into his fifth decade; the other is the contrary: *Die Frühvollendeten; ein Beitrag zur Literaturgeschichte*—a study of artists who reached maturity young, in which the author, Guido Brand, puts before us a series of poets of the seventeenth to twentieth centuries who died prematurely, so that he may find the typical connection between early maturity and early death. He can naturally not avoid touching, at least in an introductory way, on the borderland problem between masterpieces produced in youth and mature works of age; and rightly feels that "works of youth and of age should be regarded as a new theme which should explain to us by the help of psychology and phenomenology the psycho-spiritual attitude of youthful and the older creative types and thus describe the spheres within which the one grows up through the intuition of origin, the other from the experience of long life. Critique of language and philosophy of style would reveal the hallmarks of a creativity that is, inwardly, fundamentally different in the two cases."

In my book on incest (1912), which was conceived essentially as a basis for the psychology of poetic creation, I included, together with some remarks on the decisive periods of change in great poets (for example, Schiller), a chapter on the psychology of youthful poetry, and attempted a psychological valuation of the "fragments and outlines" (Chapter vii) of greater and uncompleted works. In many cases, the youth has nothing in common with the old man except the name; sometimes also, though not always, he has a favorite theme, which he uses at various periods in such different ways that it might be the work of more than one artist with more than one ideological attitude. In the sphere of this study come the works of pupils, which—especially in painting—are hardly to be distinguished from the masters', and the whole problem of schools of art, both plastic and poetic. Schiller's *Räuber* is as much a poem of the *Sturm und Drang* as it is an individual work, and several of its motifs can only be grasped ideologically and not psychologically. I had once intended to deal with this problem under the title of "Schiller's Brother" and to point out, in connection with the ideas already treated in relation to the incest theme, that the motif of fraternal hate, which in Schiller lasts right up to the *Braut von Messina,* might lead a biographer—supposing he had to construct the picture of his author from the pattern of his work and had lived in a less exact philological age—to assume a quarrel between brothers in Schiller's family, which, as is well known, contained no brother. But I did show, in my incest book, how Schiller, thanks to his *Sturm und Drang* ideology, made a brother out of his brother-in-law, called him so, and used him so. This same motif of fraternal hatred, which is one of the typical requisites of dramatic poetry from the time of Greek tragedy (see Chapter xv in that book), is to be found very often in Shakespeare, of whose family life we are less well informed, but of whom we do know that he (or the author of his plays) lived during the reign of Queen Elizabeth; and she was regarded on many sides as a usurper of the English throne, which she ruthlessly withheld from the rightful heir, her "sister" Mary Stuart. If an English court poet wanted for some reason or other to refer to this idea, which was afloat among the people, he would not only have to use a historical or mythological dress,[1] but would be well advised, in view of the proximity of the Tower, to make the feminine rivals into masculine rivals of two royal families—which indeed is the case in the main plot of *Hamlet* and is the chief motif in many other plays. Whether he had really quarreled in childhood with a brother about his toys or for his mother's love or a father's notice is of very little importance when we remember how common such things are and how often they are absent in the childhood of other poets. Indeed, the facts which are so well known in Schiller's case, and may be assumed with probability in Shakespeare's, should warn us against drawing overhasty conclusions on the strength of some superficial relation in the biographical material. For the artist is either born as such, in which case his attitude to his family involves almost a priori a sort of Hamlet tragedy, or else his experiences make him an artist, in which case again we cannot be concerned with those universal childhood impressions that are in no way different in his case from those of others.

This does not mean, of course, that such childhood influences are not among the important ones in the work of great artists, nor that psychoanalysis has not done a service in definitely emphasizing them; the question is simply that of the value to be ascribed to them, and their importance for the understanding of the artist and particularly of his work. The undoubted overemphasis that psychoanalysis lays on this fact of artistic biographical

[1] Similar ideas, though carried to excess in their application to detail, I saw later in Lilian Winstanley: *Hamlet and the Scottish Succession. Being an Examination of the Relations of the Play of Hamlet to the Scottish Succession and the Essex Conspiracy* (Cambridge, 1921). Miss Winstanley identifies Claudius and Gertrude with Bothwell and Mary, who also occur later as Lord and Lady Macbeth (cf. her book: *Macbeth, King Lear and Contemporary History*), Polonius as Lord Burleigh, etc. Cf. also Percy Allen: *Shakespeare and Chapman as Topical Dramatists,* and E. Stucken's novel: *Im Schatten Shakespeares* (Berlin, 1929).

method has various reasons, and these will lead us in their discussion back to our proper theme. First there is a confusion, or at least a certain want of distinction, between the development of personality in general and that of the artist in particular; but even in the former case, in which infantile influences are undeniable, psychoanalysis overestimated their effect and neglected the individual will, which interprets these influences in its own way. This is still more the case if the personality is one in which the will is strong and shows itself not only as dominant but as creative. Childhood influences therefore do not build up the personality by themselves, and decidedly not the artistic type, which, after all, distinguishes itself very largely by its surmounting of everything traditional. A second reason takes us deeper into the psychology of the development of personality in general and of that of the artist in particular. The aim of psychoanalysis, indeed, in its interpretation of childhood influences was to emphasize, not the rôle of these as such, but that of the unconscious in general in artistic creativity. This was not new—what analysis did contribute to the subject was the scientific proof of this influence in some particular childhood impressions that the individual had repressed, yet which forced their way upward and manifested themselves later in his work.

On the other hand, there are two points to be taken into consideration. Firstly, childhood impressions are not so unconscious, in either the artist or the neurotic, as is so eagerly assumed. Indeed, most neurotics suffer from conscious recollections of their childhood—of which, try as they may, they cannot rid themselves—and we have very complete childhood memories in the case of poets particularly, who provide more, and more interesting, material than we can ever get from the analysis of neuroses (Goethe, Rousseau, Tolstoy, etc.).[2] Secondly, exacter observation has shown us that artistic creation is far less unconscious than the psychoanalyst, or even the artist

[2] See the comprehensive study of H. Reichardt: *Die Früherinnerung als Trägerin kindlicher Selbstbeobachtungen in den ersten Lebensjahren* (Halle, 1926).

himself, believes. From Schiller, who was both artistically productive and psychologically interested, down to the modern aesthetics, such as Oscar Wilde, there is a long series of facts that prove the part played by consciousness in artistic and especially in poetical creation, which I traced in its main stages in my incest book, though I then put the unconscious too much in the foreground. The part played by the latter is undeniable; but ever since the time of the Greek poets it has been so much emphasized, especially by the productive artist, that it was necessary to give its due to the consciousness or, as I prefer to say, to the conscious artistic will. The question, too, of the greater or lesser part played by the unconscious or conscious cannot be taken as a problem only of the individual artist, though there are certainly types in which one or the other predominates. How could it be possible otherwise that, in spite of all individual differences, two poets like Goethe and Schiller, subject to the same contemporary ideology, could express such contrary views on this question? We can understand, too, that the difference of ideologies would account for the fact that the aesthetic philosopher, who is somewhat akin to the scientist, would as a rule agree with the poet here, but—from Aristotle to Baumgarten—regards the poetic art as teachable and learnable. But how can we understand that the singer of the Homeric poems calls to the Muse for inspiration and then produces a masterpiece of political history, in the logical development of which his memory failed him far less than it did in his incidental digressions—which also were perhaps intentional?

This example, which is possibly too far away from our theme, is meant to show that the invocation of the Muse, the demand by the poet himself for unconscious inspiration, is perhaps not infrequently a pretext—a poetic license even—for a more unrestrained expression of himself. If he is inspired by poetic frenzy, he is less responsible for what he says; and, remembering our previous remarks about Shakespeare, it seems to me not improbable that the inspired poet portrayed himself in the Danish prince, so that he might with impunity utter high treason.

It does not seem to me improbable, for example, that the participation of Hamlet in his entrapping play might be explained from the fact that powerful opponents of Elizabeth did really use the poet as a means to attack her and stir her conscience. In this case, we should have a reflection, in Hamlet's editing of the "play," of the part important friends of the poet actually had in his work. Anyhow the invocation of the Muse, which we have seen to be the effect of the guilt-feeling, and the emphasis by the poet himself on the unconscious impulse to create must not blind us to the part played by the conscious in creation; the reference of creation to the unconscious, if nothing else, is a conscious act. If, then, for example, Goethe and Schiller were different artist-types, it might well be that for that very reason the one worked more unconsciously than the other, but also that one exaggerated the part played by the conscious, and the other that played by the unconscious, in his own observation of himself. The overvaluation of the unconscious would then be explained by a more or less strong feeling of guilt, such as is felt by every productive type; and the overvaluation of the conscious would be due to a desire to magnify and exalt one's self—as the other is due to the already mentioned tendency to minimize.

From these observations we arrive at a similar view of the value of artistic psychology as we did previously in the case of aesthetic as a science. We came to regard aesthetic as a scientific ideology that changes with the contemporary art-ideology so that it justifies, positively or negatively, the dominant art-ideology, as we explained in the illustrative instance of the nature-imitation. Similarly, the psychology of the artist that is fashionable at the moment, though naturally more individually conditioned, represents an ideological justification of the creative artist. In our account—which penetrates to the roots, in cultural history and in individual psychology, of the creative feeling of guilt—there was no room for an aesthetic that laid down laws for art, nor for an artist's psychology in the ordinary sense, which would always have to resort to values, whether like Lombroso's mania theory or the psychoanalytical justification of creative lordliness in the unconscious. We tried to understand all these phenomena, included under the label of "art," in their psychical and historical genesis, as the expression of the individual's impulse to create, and to understand this in turn from the ineradicable belief of man in immortality. This impulse, however, produces both the work and the artist, and ultimately the ideologies necessary for artistic creation and for the artist's psychology (which are neither true nor false—that is, have no eternal validity) but change with the development of collective and individual ideas and thus fulfill their real purpose, their extension to infinity.

But the more conscious the creative process becomes in the artist, the more the creative tendency is imperceptibly and unnoticed being pushed back from the work to the artist himself from whom it originated. Only, primitively this self-creative tendency showed itself, as we saw, corporeally in *body-ornament,* whereas in the modern artist it ends with the psychical will-to-experience, his own art-ideology in full. This is, of course, impossible and brings the artist into all the conflicts—which we may describe as neurotic, but which are not any the more intelligible for being so called. For these difficulties of the creative type show also that his true tendency is always toward actual life; as is shown also in the so-called realism or verism of modern art. This, therefore, discloses itself as the counterpart to the tendency, which has been mentioned earlier, to mold life in accordance with an artistic ideology, since the idea is now that art is to be made wholly true to life. But in this wise the boundaries between art and life are obliterated; each is to replace the other, whereas formerly each complemented the other. In both spheres the movement from art to life is clear; but the creative men of our time are not capable of going the whole way and accepting the development of their personality as the truly creative problem. What hinders them is the same individual feeling of guilt that in earlier times was able, owing to the counterforce of religious submissiveness, to work itself out creatively, but nowadays limits both complete artistic creation and complete personality-development.

For artistic creation has, in the course of its development, changed from a means for the furtherance of the culture of the community into a means for the construction of personality. But the more successful this is, the greater is the urge of this personality away from art toward life, which yet cannot be fully grasped. Our Western art has thus lost its old function in proportion as this movement (beginning perhaps with the Renaissance) from the collective to the individual increased. But similarly it has had to give up its new function as soon as its purpose of personality-development was attained. This historical process, which we can trace from the Renaissance through the *Sturm und Drang* into Romanticism, has become an individual process that runs its course in the modern artist's life. The productive individual of today tackles artistic production under the influence, which still operates, of the original art-ideology, which promised immortality to the individual in the form of success and fame, but he does not possess, socally or spiritually, the attitude inherent in that old ideology. In this sense, the "art for art's sake" movement was justified at least psychologically, for art had lost its old collective function and had not yet discovered the new one of personality-development.

Now, however, this last function of art having worked itself out as far as is psychologically possible, the problem of the individual is to put his creative force directly into the service of this formation of personality, without the assistance of art. The more an individual is driven toward real life, the less will traditional art-forms help him—indeed, they have for the most part already been shattered individualistically. Especially in poetry, which of course represents in general this conscious level of artistic creation, this permeation by the personal psychology of the poet and the psychological ideology of our age is almost completed. Even the last element of art that poetry retains, language, is becoming more and more an echo of realistic talk or a psychological expression of intellectual thought, instead of being a creative expression of the spiritual. But the reality that modern art seeks to reproduce cannot be represented in language, and other traditional forms are suited only to the creative form of the spiritual and not to a realistic expression of the actual. That is why the film and talking film have become the most popular art, because this art reproduces the real faithfully, and the more so, the more it progresses.

I would not deny, however, that there are still great artists in all spheres of artistic activity, who have succeeded either in preserving the old art tradition and ideology a while longer into our times or have breathed a new spirit into old forms. But in both cases I feel that the modern artist has to buy his success too dearly, since he feels either like a believer among unbelievers or like the founder of a new religion who is persecuted and scorned by the members of the old religion. This comparison with religious conflicts comes naturally to us; for just as there is a continuous increase in the number of the irreligious and at the same time an enhanced need for substitutes for the old belief in the gods, so the art-manias of modern society, with their overvaluing of the artist, indicate a decline of real artistic vigor, which is only speciously covered over by the last flicker of a snobbish enthusiasm. It is certain that artists nowadays do not create for the people, but for a few exclusive groups, particularly of intellectuals who feel themselves artists. With an increasing individualization, art-forms also must become more individual so that they suit the ideology of a few small groups, and no attempt to exalt artists into national heroes can conceal the fact that there are ever fewer artists of really national importance and still fewer of international.

On the other hand, this individualization of art-forms and art-creation leads not only to the breakup of the collective function of art, but to its democratization, which is the direct opposite of the aristocratic religion of genius that constituted the last effective art-ideology. From the Renaissance on, a man felt himself driven to, but also chosen for, artistic expression; nowadays, with individualism so common, art is looked upon as a means to develop personality. Every strong individuality feels nowadays that a potential artist lies somewhere within him, which is prevented from growth and expression only by the external decay of a materialistic and mechanistic environment. And though it is true that a strong personality is necessary for the creative artist, it is a fatal confusion to assume that every strong personality must express itself artistically if it is to develop. Furthermore, as we have seen, artistic creativity does not, after a point, favor the personality, but impedes it, since it forces on the artist a professional ideology that more and more penetrates the human self and finally absorbs it.

It is certainly not, however, merely the outward deprivation (that is, the pressure of a mechanical age) that obstructs the artistic development of modern individuals, but the strong impulse toward life which goes hand in hand with personality-development and makes the creative will of the individual feel that artistic creation is an *unsatisfactory substitute* for real life. In other words, the conflict between life and creation, the basic problem of all productive work, has nowadays become a social instead of a psychic conflict. A harmonious reconciliation of an art-ideology with an ideology of practical life is more and more difficult as life becomes more technical and the members of a community become separate individuals. The two masters whom the artist has to serve at the same time, a self-confident productivity and a life of sacrifice, are less and less reconcilable, so that art and life are both dissatisfying, or, rather, the individual attains neither, because he is not satisfied with one and cannot attain both. This is characteristic of the so-called neurotic type, in which I had long ago seen an *artiste manqué* rather than an undeveloped normal type. The neurotic is himself a symptom of the modern conflict between the individual and society, a conflict that might in other ages have been productively surmounted in artistic creation. Nowadays the old art-ideology is no longer, and the new personality-idea not yet, strong enough to admit of either solution for the individual impulse to create. Everyone suffers—individual, community, and not least, art as an ideological expression of their interrelation.

Everything seems to drive us to the conclusion that we are at one of those crises in human history in which once again we must sacrifice one thing if we want the full enjoyment of another. If we look back at the modern artist-type as we know it, even in biographical form, since Renaissance days, there can be no doubt that the great works of art were bought at the cost of ordinary living. Whatever our attitude toward this fact and interpretation of this fact, it is at least certain that the modern individualist must give up this kind of artistic creation if he is to live as vigorously as is apparently necessary. Not only are the two things incompatible, in terms of soul and of energy, but there seems to be a spiritual law whereby nothing can be wholly won or enjoyed without something being given up or sacrificed for it. From the fabulous ring of Polycrates, who tried to buy his good fortune from heaven, down to the neurotic feeling of guilt, with its apparent self-punishment, we see this compensatory principle operating in the relation of individual to society. The individual, it seems, cannot permanently endure one sort of condition—even if it be happiness—because he immediately loses a part of the full humanity needed for his real personality. Where happiness and misery are concerned, the individual is clearly controlling his own destiny by meeting good and ill fortune halfway ere it can surprise him.

If there are really these two incommensurable magnitudes, such as supreme art and full experience seem to be, the conflict can only end with the surrender of the one to the other. But as long as this involves a feeling of sacrifice, there is no real solution, rather an intensification of the conflict, for the responsibility is always laid on an external deprivation that is to be fought against. Only a full renunciation, such as a few great artists have achieved despite their natural inclinations, can overcome this feeling of sacrifice so that surrender means, not an imposed necessity, but a freely chosen decision. This turning-point in the life of the individual artist has also become a secular crisis of our age, in which we have to see that the surrender of traditional forms no longer means a loss to us, but a liberation of creative force from the chains of old ideologies. Now, our previous conclusions show that this creative impulse can be set free from artistic ideologies, because it is not irrevocably bound thereto as an art-ideology is obliged to assume. We have seen that the impulse was originally directed toward the body and only gradually was objectified in collective art-forms. On the other hand, we see modern individuals, particularly the neurotic, striving once more to direct this creative instinct toward the ego in order to make it more useful and efficient for life. The fact that the neurotic at present fails in face of his problem cannot diminish his pioneer achievement—if he seeks his salvation in artistic creation instead of in the development of his own personality, it is because he is still in the toils of old art-ideologies. The many forms of psychotherapy, psychoanalysis included, cannot free him from the dilemma, since they either try to restore him to the normal or force him to a false artistry instead of allowing to develop a true form of himself.

The new type of humanity will only become possible when we have passed beyond this psychotherapeutic transitional stage, and must grow out of those artists themselves who have achieved a renunciant attitude toward artistic production. A man with creative power who can give up artistic expression in favor of the formation of personality—since he can no longer use art as an expression of an already developed personality—will remold the self-creative type and will be able to put his creative impulse *directly* in the service of his own personality. In him the wheel will have turned full circle, from primitive art, which sought to raise the physical ego out of nature, to the voluntaristic art of life, which can accept the psychical ego as a part of the universe. But the condition of this is the conquest of the fear of life, for that fear has led to the substitution of artistic production for life, and to the eternalization of the all-too-mortal ego in a work of art. For the artistic individual has lived in art-creation instead of actual life, letting his work live or die on its own account, and has never wholly surrendered himself to life. In place of his own self, the artist puts his objectified ego into his work, but though he does not save his subjective mortal ego from death, he yet withdraws himself from real life. And the creative type who can renounce this protection by art and can devote his whole creative force to life and the formation of life will be the first representative of the new human type, and in return for this renunciation will enjoy, in personality-creation and expression, a greater happiness.

VIII *Sexual Enlightenment and the Sexual Impulse*

> *I consider it a most significant advance in the science of education, that in France, in place of the catechism, the State should have introduced a primer which gives the child the first instruction in his position as a citizen and in the ethical obligations which will be his in time to come. The elementary instruction provided there, however, is seriously deficient in that it includes no reference to sexual matters.*
>
> —FREUD

WITH regard to the much discussed problem of sexual education, we must first separate two aspects of it; the education of sexuality or the training of the sexual impulse, and the education through sexuality or by means of love. Although the two sides are practically inseparable, yet it seems to me necessary to separate them theoretically and to consider each in regard to its own significance before considering their mutual relationship. The educational systems of primitive peoples somehow seem to reconcile sexuality and education in that they defer the education of the boy to man's estate, to the time of puberty. Whether it is only a matter of a forced sublimation of the sexual impulse (threat) as inferred by psychoanalysis, or of a deeper mystical, symbolic act, we shall not discuss here. Obviously through the ceremonial of the boys' initiation, as already mentioned, the second adult or mature phase of the individual is ushered in. This initiation withdraws the child from the influence of maternal training and "drums" into him (in the true sense of the word) the community ideology represented by the fathers (elders), not *the* father. I should like to formulate this process that is still operative in all our systems of education, thus: At a given period in individual development the rôle of educator is transferred from one person (mother) to the community; more precisely expressed, *in place of a human being as a pattern of education*, a collective *ideology* appears *as the educational ideal*. One might almost say that instead of an education using emotional means (love) there appears the intellectual (compulsory) education, if one did not know to what extent all collective ideologies have to be emotionally based in order to be capable of becoming an educational ideal. The primitive initiation ceremonies of the boys show this quite clearly, their emotional impetus being so much greater than their intellectual significance. Indeed, it seems just as if these ceremonies had to remain unintelligible in order to exercise more surely their emotional and affective value.

There is no doubt that the intellectual part in education has continually increased in the course of time, yet it is also evident that there can be no effective education at all without strong emotional influences. Here is to be found another difficulty inherent in every system of education—a difficulty that we shall consider more closely in dealing with the emotional development, but perhaps also one that will throw a first ray of light on the significance of the sexual problem in the present psychological educational ideology. By increasingly intellectualizing education and making it more technical, new and stronger emotional forces had to be mobilized for its achievement, and also to give it balance. This emotional force psychoanalysis believes it has found in its appeal to the strongest factor of the emotional life, namely, the sexual impulse. Whether we entirely approve this or not, it has been, perhaps, a necessary step in the utilization of the last emotional resources that an exaggerated rationalization of our education has left us. It is naturally always precarious to call to one's aid the last relief forces, above all, because only a desperate crisis compels one to such a step, on whose success life or death depends. But we can only take cognizance of the fact that this step is forced upon us, and try to understand what advantage and disadvantage may be derived from it.

If we compare this last phase of psychological sexual education, at the commencement of which we are now, with the earliest known to us, namely, that of the primitive initiation of boys, two essential differences strike us immediately. Psychoanalysis shifts the beginning of sexual education from puberty to childhood and makes the incision between family and community approximately there where it had already been made by the state (compulsory education). Secondly, psychoanalysis raises this sexual education from the purely emotional sphere to the intellectual level of our community ideology, in that it proclaims sexuality—as mentioned—not only a means of education, but—in the form of sexual enlightenment—also the subject of education. But for both these a prerequisite—or rather a consequence—would be an earlier maturity, not to say prematurity, of the child in an emotional as well as in an intellectual respect. Again we may regret this, but we may perhaps have to be resigned to an earlier maturing of our children since they have to achieve a greater development to reach our present-day level of civilization. As life apparently cannot be prolonged at the one end, it must indeed commence earlier since we have more to assimilate. In so far as this is the case, it is valid only for the child of a definite cultural period, namely, our present Western civilization, and it scarcely has the universal significance for mankind which psychoanalysis would obviously like to claim for it.

However, we must investigate how far this is correct even for the present-day child; in other words, how far the current psychoanalytic ideology that is an objective comprehension and correct description of existing conditions, and how far it comprises on the one hand an interpretation of the same and, on the other hand, an ideological preparation for new conditions. This is not meant to be critical, and could only be taken as criticism from one narrow viewpoint that would accept the whole Freudian ideology at its face value, as an objective description and explanation of facts. If the Freudian ideology were only that, it would be nothing at all; but its influence alone proves that it is much more than that. It is what every influential ideology always was and, according to its nature, must be, namely, a genetic explanation of existing conditions, but at the same time a psychological interpretation of the same and an ideological indication as to their future reorganization.[1]

In relation to the problem we are considering here, that of modern sexual education, this would mean, speaking simply: Is the present-day child already actually mature (or premature) for sexual enlightenment? If so, to what extent and what are the reasons for it, and in what way shall sexual enlightenment take place? If the child is not ready, then it is a matter of an interpretation, which projects into the child our own problem, and hence it must at least throw some light on the psychology of the interpreters—that is, ourselves. Probably both possibilities are correct to a certain extent, and they suggest a third question: To what extent is it a matter of a correct perception of a commencing process of development that psychoanalysis has interpreted in the meaning of its scientific ideology and that will work itself out only in the near future? In the following pages we shall mainly consider the interpretative aspect, because it is by far the most interesting, the most important, and also the most characteristic for the psychoanalyic ideology. Psychology, and particularly psychoanalysis, is a predominantly interpretative science, and what specifically concerns the problem of education has been gained only indirectly through the analysis of adult neurotics. The actual observation of children was undertaken with the ideology already accepted, and according to the reaction of educators and experience

[1] Eduard Spranger finds the same factors at work in the far more objective science of history and estimates it from a philosophic point of view (*Das deutsche Bildungsideal der Gegenwart in geschichtsphilosophischer Beleuchtung;* Leipzig, 1929, second edition).

hitherto, the future prospects of its universal application seem for the time being too few to be taken into consideration.

It is well known that psychoanalysis became aware of the educational problem when in the therapeutic influencing of adults it was able to trace their difficulties back to early childhood. These difficulties seemed in the adult to be of a sexual nature, whereupon Freud drew the conclusion that they must also have been so in the child. This course of reasoning has already been manifoldly contested with reference to the fundamental difference between the child and the adult, and also it has not been justified by the non-convincing psychoanalytic observations of children. But there are graver doubts than this purely methodological one, since it is recognized that also in the adult the difficulties are not always of a sexual nature. This became obvious through closer investigation on the one hand, and through the failure of a purely sexually oriented therapy on the other hand. The concept of the sexual etiology of the neuroses thus proved to be an interpretation even with regard to adults. Not only was the child's mental and emotional life interpreted in the meaning of the adult theory of neuroses, but the adult neurotic already had been interpreted according to an ideology that we here designate "materialistic" because it tried to explain all difficulties in biological terminology and tried to influence these therapeutically by means of practical measures. Indeed, the whole concept of the reducibility of the adult's difficulties to the faults and influences of education could only arise on the ground of a "behavioristic" psychology such as would conform to the modern scientific world-concept. The interpretation of which we speak thus consists not only of the application to the child of what has been observed in the adult, but also of a genetic connection which states reversely that the adult has difficulties (obviously of a sexual nature) because the child had the same difficulties that were not opportunely recognized and corrected by education. In other words, the adult neurotic is "infantile" *also* with regard to his sexual difficulties or indeed *only* in relation to these. The remedy that psychoanalysis had to offer for this was twofold: therapeutically to make the infantile neurotic grow up, but prophylactically and pedagogically to liberate the child from this "infantility" because the danger seemed to be that it would be dragged along into later life. We already see here that the child's maturity of which we spoke earlier is really a "prematurity" artificially produced or hastened from the desire to prepare the individual better therapeutically and prophylactically, for actual maturity. But we also recognize that the concept of maturity corresponds to a natural process of development that, when artificially produced or influenced, would be out of place in any kind of educational ideology. The sexual education and enlightenment of the child, as advocated by psychoanalysis, might be considered with regard to its rational character a kind of immunization of the individual against later sexual difficulties by an early inoculation with a dangerous serum. Expressed in psychological terminology, it would be a matter of the avoidance of a later sexual shock by a timely and gradual preparation.

So far this sounds quite plausible, but apart from the technical question of improving this prophylactic measure, there is the doubt as to whether and how far physiological viewpoints, especially of a medical nature, are applicable to the psychical sphere. Sexuality of course is without doubt a biological factor of first importance, but even psychoanalysis could not overlook the psychical significance it has among individuals, and has taken this into account in its concept of "psychosexuality." But if the mental significance of sexuality for mankind could be questioned, yet the influencing of it educationally is a purely psychical affair and the antitoxin of sexual enlightenment may have as its consequence undesirable reactions in the whole psychical establishment that may paralyze the desired effect in the purely sexual sphere. To this may be added further reflections if we follow the comparison to its final consequences. Serum therapy ought to prevent disease, sexual enlightenment ought to promote progress. We do not want to suppress the sexual impulse but only to emancipate it. This desired result, however, is supposed to take place only at a later period. The question of *how* sexuality is to be discussed and explained, and at the same time its activity restricted, seems to me not yet solved. The explanation, for example, concerning masturbation, treating it as something harmless and not dangerous, is supposed to have a calming effect and not a threatening one; but I should say there are few parents, even among the pioneers of modern education, who would be inclined to draw from this enlightenment the conclusion to let their children masturbate. But when they do not allow it, they place themselves in a new difficulty of having to give a reason for it. The whole movement of sexual enlightenment is doubtless praiseworthy in its tendency to consider sexuality as something harmless and not as something sinful and forbidden, an attitude that can only poison the entire later life of the individual. But this inoffensiveness tacitly comprises the release of sexual activity, for it cannot be comprehended—especially by the child—why one should not do something when it is not "bad." In its extreme consequences, then, sexual education would not result in an education of the sexual impulse (in the sense of training it), but in a release of it, and this would lead us back to the level of the primitives, who have no sexual problem and no sexual education because they give free rein to sexual expression at least up to the time of puberty (or marriage).

Fortunately the child himself vigorously upsets all our psychological calculations by carrying on his sexual activity independently of our attitude toward it. But that means that the child not only gives in to his sexual impulse in spite of our prohibitions, but also that he experiences it as something forbidden, bad, and something to conceal even when we permit and release it. This is the first momentous discovery we have made with our sexual propaganda for children. This experience points to the fact that it is not the external prohibition or the influence of education that connects sexuality with the idea of sin and guilt, but something inherent in it that is experienced by the individual as dangerous and, perhaps, rightly so. But this also shows that the hitherto prevailing education of the child was not—as our radical psychologists maintain—false and unreasonable and based only on ignorance so that it needed merely the focusing of our better knowledge on it, in order to wipe out with one blow all evils of education.[2] Certainly the child has always asked questions, wanted explanations, and above all wanted to be understood. But the answers that religious education gave to these questions were not false but only adequate if we understand them correctly; as the child has in any case a guilt-feeling in reference to sexual matters, religion, then, has only sanctioned it for him, although sometimes in too drastic a manner. On the other hand, however, also our sexual enlightenment does not have the desired effect of taking this guilt-feeling away from the child because the child then seeks elsewhere to have this guilt-feeling corroborated if the parents do not do it. Whether for this the child goes back to religious and mythological ideas, or gets false information from companions or unenlightened people is irrelevant in comparison to the undeniable fact that the child refuses the correct scientific explanation including the release of sex implicitly implied in it.

What is apparently manifest in the conflict between school and church is that sex education is on the point of replacing the religious training, and it is now also psychologically evident that the religious education has been a legitimate precursor of the psychological education and not merely a hindrance to it. This is clearly shown in the different answers given to the famous question of the child as to where we come from; the religious training answers it by pointing to God as the creator of mankind, modern education answers it by giving a biological explanation. But still no child has been satisfied with this sexual explanation, even not when the rôle of the father was explained with it. The statement of psychoanalysis that most of the child's questions really aim at something other than their pretext would have been much more meritorious if it

[2] Such naïve radical tendencies appear in the symposium brought out by V. P. Calverton and S. Schmalhausen (New York, 1930), *The New Generation: The Intimate Problems of Modern Parents and Children,* although a minority of contributors (like Havelock Ellis and Bronislaw Malinowski) represent a sober and scientifically sound objectivity.

had not obstinately kept to the preconceived opinion that this did not hold good for overt sexual questions. I call it a prejudice, for the experience that children are not satisfied with the biological answer to their sexual questions seems strongly to contradict this assumption. I believe that most of the child's questions concern philosophical and religious problems that also occupy the minds of adults even today, and are still unsolved and perhaps even are insoluble. I am convinced, however, that particularly the sexual questions of children have this enigmatic background and that we answer these eternal problems of humanity concerning our origin, our future, and the meaning of our whole existence at the time only in the natural scientific terminology of our sexual-biology and materialistic psychology. But this answer does not satisfy the child in the least, and if we want to be honest we have to admit also that it does not satisfy ourselves; it only seems to satisfy because we know we have no other reply. Perhaps this explains why the adult seems to suffer from the sexual problem as much as the child, because the biological solution of the problem of humanity is as ungratifying and inadequate for the adult as for the child. The religious solution was and still is so much the more gratifying because it admits *the Unknown,* indeed, recognizes it as the chief factor instead of pretending an omniscience that we do not possess. Besides, religion is also more consoling —I should like to say more therapeutic—because, with the admission of the unknown and unknowable it also leaves room for all kinds of hope that it still may not be as hopeless as it seems. The feeling of inferiority, from which apparently our children now seem to suffer, is certainly increased by the impression they get of the godlike omniscience of their parents and their own ignorance in sexual matters. But the sexual instruction of children, that is, putting them on an equality with adults in *this* matter, does not help much if the parents' valuation of the sexual problem excludes their religious belief, or in other words, if the parental knowledge of sexual matters has the appearance of being a knowledge of all the mysteries of life, a knowledge that the child does not and never will possess even as the adults do not possess it. Religion, from the very beginning, here places children and adults on one level in so far as their inability to know ultimate things is concerned.

If we compare the idea of sexual education with the religious education hitherto prevailing, we shall find that in sexual training there is an element of wishful thinking carried over by the adult into the childish ideology. It has indeed thus arisen that the therapeutist has wished that the adult neurotic might have been sufficiently experienced as a child to be able to avoid all later difficulties. It is primitive wishful thinking projected back in this form, and in this respect sexual educaton differs in no way from other ideologies of education that want to spare the child the adult's harmful experiences or at least to give the child a taste of them in the form of education. But since sexual education differs from other educational ideologies in early childhood neither in this respect nor in relation to its disappointing answer to life's riddle, we must concentrate our attention on the one point in which it does clearly differ—that is, *its content*. Before we go into the psychological significance of this difference of content, I should first like to emphasize its intellectual quality. This new content is not only different from earlier contents, but it differs in this respect, that it is supposed to be the "truth." This truth, however, is here confused with reality. We might give the correct biological answer to the child's concrete question as to the arrival of a little brother or sister, but we do not thereby touch the child's fear of life that is behind this question and that cannot be explained causally because it is rooted in the fear of the Unknown and Unknowable. The new educational ideology thus seems to be enforced by a fanaticism for the truth, which has found its clearest expression in the demand for sexual enlightenment, but which extends beyond this to the whole attitude of the modern educator. This may be, among other things, also a protest against the existing opportunism in education that at the same time has not always coincided with the truth. But this craving for the truth is a fanaticism for reality rather than a real love of the truth and hence stops short before the admission of the truth concerning our lack of knowledge. This is predominantly expressed in education in a negative way, namely, by avoiding what we consider "untruth," the true value of which we no longer understand, such as for example, religion. Thus, also, this ideal of overvaluing reality, a characteristic of our natural scientific world-concept, originates from adults and is carried over into education by them. The child, like primitive man, tends more to the unreal; he does not want logical, causal explanations, but emotional consolation, and he denies reality in favor of consoling illusions that therefore seem to him to be "truer." These are apparently necessary in order to live, and the child has the right instinct for it just as did man of the primitive and religious ages.

But again, we must bear in mind that the present-day child sooner or later has to recognize these illusions as disappointing, and it might be better to prepare the child for this at an early age. But it seems that adults also still need illusions and always know how to create them anew as soon as earlier ones disappoint. Precisely the sphere of sexuality has formerly been an essential promoter of illusion, and it has already been brought as an objection against sexual enlightenment, that by it, one might possibly be damming up this fertile source of illusion. It seems as if the child feels like the many disappointed adults who react to the first sexual experience with the exclamation "Is that all!" For one actually has the impression that most children react in the same way to sexual enlightenment. And rightly so! For it is not all! But the rest, which is the most important for so many, seems to be based on illusion, as, for example, the quite general idea of romantic love. The question that we approach here leads us back again to our starting point, namely, education of sexuality or education by means of sexuality. From its own sphere, the therapeutic situation, where education through love besides being the greatest furtherance to education became also its greatest hindrance, psychoanalysis has drawn the pedagogic conclusion that naturally the chief thing to do is to give sexual education or, more correctly, to train the sexual impulse. But at the same time it is believed that in the sexual impulse itself there is to be found the real agent of educational sublimation. Now perhaps one can use sexuality *consciously* as a *means* of education as it always has been used *instinctively*, and get good results from it; the question is only, What happens thereby to the sexual impulse itself? Might not the result be similar to that in our colleges where the students are compelled to study the Greek verbs in Homer? The student may indeed in this way learn the conjugations, but his taste for the beauty of the poems is thereby spoiled.

Whatever one's attitude to sex is, it cannot be denied that a great part of its attraction arises from curiosity, from its being kept secret and forbidden. The purely physical sensations of pleasure would scarcely be strong enough alone to overcome the resistances that apparently oppose the sexual activity in the individual himself. This resistance to sexuality inherent in the individual is the real problem therapeutically as well as pedagogically. The answer of psychoanalysis to this question has proved to be inadequate, because it is only a rational paraphrase of the old biblical explanation. We are supposed to have sexual difficulties because our religious education teaches that sexuality is "bad," that is, it has made it a moral problem, whereas originally it was a natural source of pleasure. But, as the study of primitive races shows, this is not so obvious as it seems from purely biological considerations. Indeed, the primitives furnish us with a grand example of the fact that even unrestricted sexuality becomes a moral problem, exactly as we can observe it in our enlightened children. The primitives certainly do not separate, in our meaning, the function of pleasure and the function of procreation, but they act as if the latter did not exist at all for the individual, which is true to their group-ideology. This group-ideology arises, however, from the belief in the soul, according to the original concept of which the individual is immortal and hence procreation in one's own children is looked upon as a danger that threatens personal immortality. I believe that the deepest resistance to sexuality arises from the claim of the species that directly threatens individual integrity. The child, who, as it were, begins at birth to sunder itself from the species and to develop its individuality, feels sexuality first of all to be an inner claim of the species hostile to individuality and hence resists it. This leads, as I have already stated elsewhere,[3] to an inner strife in the individual against sexuality, a conflict that arises necessarily and independently of external influences. This strife within is carried out by the individual in the same manner as in external strife, by means of *the will*. For the will represents the individual energetically; it is psychologically synonymous with individual will. *Sexuality* is a kind of racial will forced upon the individual, the final acceptance of which is made possible through the individual love choice, against which, however, the individual and the individual will are continually striving. *In this strife between the individual will and the biologically given community-ideology of the species we have before us the prototype of the educational problem* with all its conflicts and difficulties.

This means to say that the sexual problem necessarily provokes in the child itself the conflict inherent in all education between the individual will and the community-ideology, and indeed it presents this conflict in its most human form, because the sexual conflict is universal and independent of the particular educational ideology characteristic of definite systems of civilization. Certainly also the specific ideology of any particular civilization is influenced by the attitude taken toward the sexual problem. This is not only on account of the fundamental significance of the sexual life in itself, but because in the individual's attitude to it there is implied the mutual interplay of individual and collective ideology. In this sense the sexual education would be the educational problem par excellence. The application of this knowledge to pedagogic practice is, however, not so simple as it is imagined to be by the psychoanalytic educator, who has in mind chiefly the therapeutic and prophylactic effect of sexual enlightenment. In relation to the positive constructive side that

[3] *Seelenglaube und Psychologie*. See also "Self and Ideal," [pp. 280 ff. of this collection].

forms the real task of education, the sexual education signifies a radical attack on the fundamentals of all pedagogy and this, not prudery, explains the resistance against it. But first we must be clear as to whence this "resistance" arises, and for this we must understand what the very nature of sexual education signifies.

These considerations are necessary not only for practical reasons but so that we may be able to lay the foundation stone for a new educational ideology. This can only gradually be crystallized out of and following on the revolutionary advance of the psychoanalytic theory and its precipitate application to radical pedagogic reforms. For the construction of ideologies consists not in revolutionizing, but in the conscious elaboration of the dangerous as well as the useful elements, which latter are naturally overrated by the radicals. So the idea of sexual education gives the appearance of emancipating the individual and his impulse-life from the chains of a religious and conventional morality; whereas its practical application in educational reforms is in fact not at all radical but conservative, because it is not individual but collective. In that sexuality is first consciously and then officially made the subject of education, the idea of sexual enlightenment loses its individual-revolutionary character and necessarily becomes—like every educational ideology—a representative of the collective community will. This regular and necessary *transformation of an individual's revolutionary ideas into the conservative ideology of the community* encounters in the sexual problem quite peculiar difficulties. Not, perhaps, because sexuality is too individual, too personal, to be made into a community-ideology, but just the reverse, because in essence sexuality is a collective phenomenon that the individual at all stages of civilization wants to individualize, that is, control. This explains all sexual conflicts in the individual, from masturbation to the most varied perversions and perversities, above all the keeping secret of everything sexual by individuals as an expression of a personal tendency to individualize as much as possible collective elements in it. On the other hand, we see the community at all times and under all circumstances endeavoring to deprive the individual as far as possible through convention, law, and custom, of the arbitrary practice of sexuality. But the community's every step in the direction of making the sexual life collective leads to new attempts at individualization that again bring forth community reactions.

This everlasting armament of the individual against society, and vice versa, has hitherto been carried out chiefly in religious, social, economic, and lastly in educational ideologies. In other words, it has been a fight for belief, for race, for class, a conflict between the older and younger generations, certainly also a fight of the sexes against each other—in which each group wants to assert its individuality as against a bigger or stronger group, ultimately against humanity. What is most characteristic of the present educational struggle is that it seems to concentrate more and more around the sexual problem that contains in it the two irreconcilable antitheses of individual and species. One might express this figuratively thus: Formerly the solution of this difficult problem had been attempted in algebraic formula, and now one attempts to solve it in terms of its real value. But it might easily happen that the calculation did not turn out as one expected, because one cannot correctly estimate the value of sexuality. Psychoanalysis also is not free from this error, since from its medical standpoint and by reason of its therapeutic attitude it has overestimated the individual pleasurable factor of sexuality rather than another, more important factor. This other is the collective factor, which Freud valued only as a social inhibition (moral training), not, however, as an element inherent in sexuality itself and characteristic of it. From this racial claim, inherent in sexuality, arise all the individual's resistances that psychoanalysis has simply understood as the result of intimidation.

However, if we consider the collective nature of sexuality and assign to it the position due, we recognize that the modern sexual education that seems to be so individualistic is really aspiring to exploit this collective character of sexuality in order to combat increasing individualization of it. Sex teaching, as a subject of education with the admitted purpose of introducing sexual enlightenment into the curriculum of the schools, would thus prove to be a grave interference with the individual's personal freedom. As I have already stated in an earlier work,[4] there seems to be a peculiar inner connection between the personality-development and the development of sexuality, and indeed, I believe chiefly because the sexual sphere had hitherto been exempt from educational influences. It remained the only domain that was surrendered to the individual, as it were, for self-education and self-development, and the child reacts with open protest or with secret resistance to insure that this remaining sphere shall not be withdrawn from self-administration and be "socialized" like everything else. In spite of all infantile sexual curiosity and incessant questions, we cannot overlook the fact that the child does not want sexual education—as he does not want any kind of education—and refuses sexual enlightenment as unsatisfying. The more positive the enlightenment, the more is the child compelled to create his own private sexual ideology and sexual sphere where he can do as he likes in individual freedom, unhindered and uninfluenced by adult educational tendencies.

Even if sexual education were necessary as the last resort of the community from increasing individualism, we should not pretend that it is in the child's interest; it is in the interest of the community represented by the educator. It seems to me that this threatening socialization of sexuality—indeed, one might say communization of sexuality—as implied in modern enlightenment, is a necessary reaction of the community in its struggle for self-preservation against increasing individualization. On the other hand, I believe that the individual's stronger inclination for sexual freedom manifested in the increase of divorce, promiscuity, and perversions, is nothing but an individual reaction against the threatening invasion of the uprising sexual socialization implied in the modern ideology of education.

[4] *Gestaltung und Ausdruck der Persönlichkeit* (1928).

Another symptom of the same deserves to be brought forward. Education actually begins at adolescence, not only among the primitives but also with the higher-standing civilized races such as the Greeks and Romans, so that time and room are given for individual development and unfolding before the direct intervention of collective forces takes place. Modern psychologists would like education to begin as early as possible, which has been the case only in the religious systems of education of the Jews and Christians. In these systems, the individual is trained from the beginning to carry on and transmit a religious ideology that had been created for a self-protection only at a definite period and can fulfill this aim also only temporarily. Since man always needs and wants collective ideologies, the possibility for creating new ones must be permitted him when previous ones wear out. The earlier they are inoculated in the individual, the earlier will they also lose their value, and the more difficult will it be for man to replace these deeply rooted ideas with others. The sexual ideology of education, as it may appear from the therapeutic and prophylactic viewpoint, thus signifies an enrichment and necessary improvement of the present system of education, and contains at the same time a completely new ideology of education altogether, which is marked by the systematic communizing of the individual sex-impulse. In this sense, the modern sex education is conservative—that is, however, anti-individualistic—and hence it may provoke a revolutionary protest from the individual, a protest that one cannot explain as a moral resistance alone. The fact that the demand for sexual enlightenment appears to be revolutionary is to be explained from the emphasis laid on the *individual* aspect of the sexual impulse by psychoanalysis, which valued it therapeutically only as the individual's source of pleasure. But the individual's struggle against the collective force of sexuality is as old as humanity and is repeated in every child in the well-known sexual conflicts that can be avoided by no kind of education or explanation because they are inherent in the dualistic nature of the sexual impulse and of man himself as an ego and as part of the species. And the more parents and educators advocate from their collective attitude the sexual enlightenment of their children, the more (so experience has taught us) will the children themselves oppose this interference of society in their private lives.

IX *Life Fear and Death Fear*

Cowards die many times before their deaths;
The valiant never taste of death but once.

—SHAKESPEARE
(*Julius Caesar*)

HAVING broached the metaphysical question as to whether there is a cosmic death instinct or not, we can now proceed from the indubitable psychological fact of the fear of death as it manifests itself in human consciousness. Regarding death fear in the actual meaning of the words, however, we can speak only in terms of the knowledge of death, that is, on a level of consciousness, which the infant at the time of the first development of fear certainly cannot yet have. On the other hand, we know that the child experiences his first feeling of fear in the act of birth—not fear of death, however, but fear in the face of life. It seems, therefore, as if fear were bound up somehow with the purely biological life process and receives a certain content only with the knowledge of death. Whether this contentual tie-up, which so frequently increases to a pathological fear of dying or of being dead, represents the rationalization of another more fundamental fear, we will discuss later in detail; at all events, this primary fear cannot be castration fear, for this also presupposes a certain development of consciousness that we could not assume for the infant. Moreover, the point of view I have maintained regarding the historical and genetic primacy of the birth fear as compared with castration fear, in spite of all the arguments of psychoanalysts to the contrary, seems undeniable. Since I was concerned first of all in *The Trauma of Birth* (1923) with an explanation of the fears of the infant, I did not evaluate the death fear sufficiently, as it belonged to a later level, although it can appear astonishingly early in childhood; on the other hand, I confess that at that time I had not advanced far enough beyond the birth symbolism, which here as elsewhere covered the death theme therapeutically. When for example, P. Schilder doubts the existence of a death instinct and asks "whether the impulse to death may not be a covering for erotic strivings, the wish for a rebirth," [1] it is certainly to the point in many cases, especially of neurosis or psychosis, but no argument against the death instinct, as little as are all the other erotic or masochistic disguises of it, which are covered by Freud's assumption of the pleasure principle as a special case of death instinct. This disguise, moreover, Schopenhauer has already seen clearly when he speaks in his *Metaphysics of Sex Love* of the pleasure primacy (*Lustprämie*) with which nature entices men to pay tribute in the sex act.

Responsibility for this erotic disguise of death seems to me to rest not only on the psychic tendency to denial of its terrors, but much more on the polar nature of the life process itself. For otherwise it would not be comprehensible why the death complex appears so much more clearly in religion, mythology, and folklore than in the individual, who apparently can bear the idea of death only collectively, just because this again promises therapeutic consolation. So it happened that I myself brought out the death symbolism first in *The Myth of the Birth of the Hero* (1909) and still more clearly in the related *Lohengrin Sage* (1911); also in my further *"Mythologischen Beiträgen."* [2] I finally undertook a decided advance in this direction with the investigation of the problem of the "double" in folklore (1914), which I then continued in my book *Seelenglaube und Psychologie* (1930) even to

[1] *Psychiatrie auf psychoanalytischer Grundlage* (1925).

[2] *Psychoanalytische Beiträge zur Mythenforsschung* . . . 1912–14, collected edition, 1919.

the theme of religious belief in immortality and its scientific presentation in the modern doctrine of the psychic. In terms of individual psychology, I have never lost sight of the problem of fear since *The Trauma of Birth,* although therapeutic interests forced me to build up my conception first in the direction of a constructive theory of will. This, however, had become clear to me, that we have before us in the individual neurotic, as it were, the opposite of collective belief in the soul and immortality ideology—that is, instead of the more or less naïvely expressed wish for eternal life, as it appears today in collective ideologies, we find an apparent desire to die, one might almost say a wish for eternal death. From the analysis of the rôle of the analyst in the therapeutic situation, there came to me finally a direct individual approach to the problem of death, and the idea that one could understand neurosis in general, including its therapy, only from this negative side of the soul life. In this sense, the present essay is the completion of my work on the belief in the soul, and as this finally leads to psychology, so the neurotic opposite of the belief in immortality—the death fear—leads to the need for therapy, as an individual doctrine of faith.

Freud has approached the problem of therapy from the forces of life (the libido) and has finally arrived at the death instinct, that is, at the death problem; for it hardly concerns an "instinct." [3] As I have already pointed out in *The Trauma of Birth,* it seems to me essential for the understanding of the neurotic to go at the human problem from the side of fear, not from the side of instinct; that is, to consider the individual not therapeutically as an instinctive animal but psychologically as a suffering being. It soon becomes evident that, approached from the instinct side, a whole series of problems will be viewed falsely, or will be located incorrectly, which from the death side, are approachable. Again we face the paradox of psychoanalysis, yes, of every ideology in general, which only happens to appear with peculiar clarity in the Freudian teaching today—the therapeutic orientation in the broad-

[3] Even analysts like Bernfeld and Westerman-Holstijn find the term "death instinct" inappropriate.

est sense, which despite its scientific nature aims not at knowledge but at consolation, and always emphasizes in its facts just that side that affords help for human need. Freud's emphasis on the instinctual was therapeutic in this human sense, but he used it theoretically for a specific etiology of the neuroses that it was intended not only to heal but at the same time to explain. His pragmatic presupposition was, as is also the case with other practical sciences, that what helps must also be true. So his teaching from the beginning was directed toward consolation in the sense of a therapeutic ideology, and even when he finally stumbled upon the inescapable death problem, he sought to give it a new meaning also in harmony with the wish, since he spoke of death instinct instead of death fear. The fear itself he had meantime disposed of elsewhere, where it was not so threatening and was therapeutically more easily accessible. That the instinctual is repressed in the neurotic, certainly seems clear and equally that it is fear, from which the repression arises. Since Freud conceived of the instinct life sexually, however, he had a double therapeutic advantage: on the one hand, of having made the general fear into a special sexual fear (castration fear), and on the other, of being able to cure this fear through the freeing of sexuality.

This therapeutic ideology rests on the presupposition that man is purely instinctual and that fear is brought in from the outside (hence the concept of castration fear). It has for a second presupposition the displacement of general fear to a partial field, a therapeutic release with which we shall occupy ourselves in the next chapter.[4] The discovery that the freeing or satisfaction of sexuality does not necessarily do away with fear but often even increases it, and the observation that the infant experiences fear at a time when there can be no question of outer threats of any kind, have made the theory of the sexual origin of fear, and its derivation from the outside, untenable. The individual comes to the world with fear, and this inner fear exists independently of outside threats, whether of a sexual or other nature. It is only that it attaches itself easily to

[4] "Total Ego and Partial Ego," Chapter xi in *Will Therapy*.

outer experiences of this kind; but the individual makes use of them therapeutically since they objectify and make partial the general inner fear. Man suffers from a fundamental dualism, however one may formulate it, and not from a conflict created by forces in the environment that might be avoided by a "correct bringing-up" or removed by later re-education (psychoanalysis).

The inner fear, which the child experiences in the birth process (or perhaps even brings with it) has in it already both elements, fear of life and fear of death, since birth on the one hand means the end of life (former life) and on the other carries also the fear of the new life. The stronger emphasis on the one or the other of these two fear components in the birth act itself still seems to me to contain the empirical meaning of the birth trauma for the later fate of the individual. Beyond that, however, for me, the birth trauma was also a symbol of the original suffering nature of man, which, according to the psychoanalytic conception, had been caused in the first place by some guilt of the individual or the environment and could be corrected, therapeutically or prophylactically (educationally.) Here it is again evident that one very soon strikes the boundary of the metaphysical in the discussion of these basic human problems no matter whether one takes it religiously or philosophically. This involves no danger as long as one does not succumb to the attempt to justify the one viewpoint at the cost of the other. I believe that one can never understand the human being purely empirically, as psychoanalysis strives to do; on the other hand, the purely metaphysical conception of man seems to me unsatisfactory also, as soon as it aims at knowledge and fails to consider the purely human.[5]

Birth fear one can only designate as death fear metaphysically, since ideally one should separate it from the

[5] Such a dissatisfaction is presented in the profound book of Werner Achelis, which only came to my attention when I was completing this book: *Principia mundi, Versuch einer Auslegung des Wesens der Welt.* The author who seeks to complete the empiricist Freud with the metaphysician Schopenhauer in a deeper sense, remains thereby as much guilty of empiricism as Freud of metaphysics, since he leaps far beyond the empirically comprehensible directly into the metaphysical, instead of letting himself be led to the boundaries of both spheres.

fear of empirical death, and find in it primarily that undifferentiated feeling of insecurity on the part of the individual, which might then better be called fear of life. The fact is just this, that there is in the individual a primal fear, which manifests itself now as fear of life, another time as fear of death. If birth fear, therefore, has nothing to do empirically with the fear of actual death, one must also test as to its empirical soundness the extreme metaphysical interpretation of Achelis. To call birth fear the first visible condensation of fear of death, that is, fear of the loss of individuality, seems to me open to attack on two grounds: first, the fear of loss of individuality seems to me to underlie fear of (empirical) death; second, I cannot see at all how birth can be viewed as loss or threat of loss of individuality, when it represents exactly the opposite. Such a view would be possible only if one conceives of mother and child as one (which, however, Achelis does not mean), as I have done in the birth trauma theory, and then considers the loss of the mother in terms of an injury to the ego. In this case, however, fear is a reaction to the trauma of separation, which I have comprehended factually as birth fear. Here lies also the connection made by the analysts, including Freud, between birth fear and castration fear, both of which in this sense appear as reaction to the loss of an important part of the ego. Birth fear remains always more universal—cosmic, as it were, loss of connection with a greater whole, in the last analysis with the "all"—while the castration fear is symbolic of the loss of an important part of the ego, which however is less than the whole, that is, is partial. The fear in birth, which we have designated as fear of life, seems to me actually the fear of having to live as an isolated individual, and not the reverse, the fear of the loss of individuality (death fear). That would mean, however, that primary fear corresponds to a fear of separation from the whole, therefore a fear of individuation. On account of this, I should like to call it fear of life, although it may appear later as fear of the loss of this dearly bought individuality, as fear of death, of being dissolved again into the whole.

Between these two fear possibilities, these poles of fear, the individual is thrown back and forth all his life, which accounts for the fact that we have not been able to trace fear back to a single root, or to overcome it therapeutically.

After this theoretical clarification of concepts, I turn to clinical observation and should like first of all to establish the fact that the neurotic, to an even greater degree than the average, suffers from this double fear, yes, that the outbreak of the neurosis actually becomes explicable from the streaming together of these two sources of fear, which even in *The Trauma of Birth* I had designated as the fear both of going forward and of going backward. So there is already included in the fear problem itself a primary ambivalence that must be assumed, and not derived through the opposition of life and death instincts. We have almost come to the point of refusing to man as a suffering being a positive life instinct, and of looking upon that which apparently manifests itself as such as a mere not-wishing-to-die.[6] The opposite of the positive life instinct would be not the death instinct, but fear, whether it be of having to die or of wanting to die. At all events the neurotic gives the impression of a negative instinctual being who continuously strives to delay dying and to ward off death, but who by these efforts only hastens and strengthens the process of destruction because he is not able to overcome it creatively. On the other side, the neurotic illness appears as a constant self-inhibiting of the life instinct, for any expression of which the individual seems to punish himself either before or afterward. Both impressions are surely correct, corresponding to the ambivalent conflict of life fear and death fear; both, however, have been acquired relatively late.

Above all, it is strange that the punishment mechanism of the neurotic illness, which seems so clear today, had not drawn the attention of the analyst much earlier. However, as Freud had attacked the neuroses from the libido

[6] The Chicago biologist, Professor Hayes, allows dying to begin with birth.

problem and not from the fear problem, it was natural first of all to emphasize the pleasure-gain the patient drew from his condition, the so-called "reward of illness," and to consider the suffering bound up with it only as unavoidable evil. The therapy undertook, therefore, to bring him to the giving up of this pleasure-gain through illness, since it held out the prospect of a greater pleasure reward. Thus normal sexual satisfaction became avowedly or tacitly the goal of analytic therapy, a viewpoint many analysts still hold as a standard. As Freud, however, learned to consider the punishment tendencies of the individual not only as hindrances to this goal, but also as the greatest resistances to the analytical process itself, he ascribed to them that genuine meaning, which found theoretical expression in the setting up of a death instinct. The works of Reik and Alexander that followed have pointed out a libidinal goal even in the self-punishment tendencies of the individual, and thus protected the Freudian theory of the neuroses from being stranded in the invincibility of the guilt-feeling.

Before we take this leap into therapeutic ideology, however, we should keep in mind another type of experience that one can understand, not from the study of neurotics alone, but only if one approaches the problem from the development of the creative personality, as I have attempted to do, especially in recent years. Thus I have recognized, not only the constructive meaning of resistances in the analysis, but also the creative side of guilt-feeling, and have attempted simultaneously to utilize these negative manifestations therapeutically. What expresses itself in the individual on the one side as driving force, does not always have to be and certainly is not exclusively "instinct," as little as resistances of different kinds must necessarily work only as hindrances. The self-punishment tendency that operates as inhibition (restraint) is not merely, as Alexander has expressed it, a bribing of the super-ego in the interest of id satisfaction; on the contrary, what manifests itself in this correct observation is a general life principle, on the basis of which no creating is possible without destruction, and no destroying without some kind of new creation.[7] When, accordingly, the neurotic must punish himself so much more severely and strikingly than the average man, this is not merely because he can only grant himself this or that pleasure-satisfaction thus, but because he must bribe life itself, for which, according to Schopenhauer's deep insight, we all pay with death.

The neurotic then is a man whom extreme fear keeps from accepting this payment as a basis of life, and who accordingly seeks in his own way to buy himself free from his guilt. He does this through a constant restriction of life (restraint through fear), that is, he refuses the loan (life) in order thus to escape the payment of the debt (death). The more or less clear self-punishment tendency, which only represents one aspect of this picture, has not so much the intention of granting him life as of escaping death, from which he seeks to buy himself free by daily partial self-destruction; applied to fear, guilt, and inhibition symptomatology, this means that the neurotic gains from all the painful and tormenting self-punishments no positive pleasure, but the economic advantage of avoiding a still more painful punishment, namely fear of death.[8] In this way the lengthening of punishment (drawing-out) is at the same time a drawing-out of life, for as long as he punishes himself—feels pain, as it were—he still lives. This neurotic attitude of the individual toward the problem of death, in the last analysis is comprehensible only from the will psychology, which shows that the human being seeks to subject death, this original symbol of the "must," to his will, and as it were, at his own instigation transforms the death punishment that is placed upon life into a lifelong punishment he imposes upon himself. On the other hand, the ancient idea of the sacrifice plays a part in this, the idea that one could escape the hardest punishment by voluntary assumption of lighter self-punishment. These

[7] As far as I know, Dr. Sabina Spielrein first demonstrated these thoughts analytically and applied them to the explanation of the fear inherent in the sexual instinct. "*Die Destruktion als Ursache des Werdens*," *Jahrbuch für Psychoanalysie*, IV (1912), pp. 465 ff.

[8] The ancient and universally distributed conception of death as punishment I have tried to explain in *Seelenglaube und Psychologie* from the human longing for immortality.

basic remarks are only to characterize the general point of view under which I learned to understand the self-punishment tendency in man. Applied to the neurotic type, it results in a deepened understanding not only of the symptomatology in particular cases but also of neurosis as a whole, showing it to be an individual attempt at healing, against the archenemy of mankind, the death fear, which can no longer be cured by the collective method of earlier ages.

It would be alluring to build up a theory of the neuroses on the basis of the death fear and to show how the particular symptoms, and not merely the neurosis as a whole, can be understood in one way or another as an expression of it, but since we are concerned with the neurotic as a type, as he is opposed to the therapist type, the therapeutic aspects of this concept lie nearer than the theoretical. From the therapeutic standpoint, however, one gets the impression that the overstrong fear of the neurotic is only the necessary defense against an overstrong instinctual basis and a correspondingly strong will, which is prevented by fear from full expression in living, which would be death. For, in spite of the predominance of the death fear in the neurotic, he still stands nearer to the creative type than to the average man, on account of which also he can be understood only as a miscarried artist, not as an incomplete or undeveloped normal type. In this sense, the neurosis is a facing on the part of the individual of the metaphysical problems of human existence; only he faces them not in a constructive way, as does the artist, philosopher, or scientist, but destructively. It is exactly on this account that the neurosis has taught us so much about the nature of man, because it represents the most inexorable form of self-knowledge and self-exposure, than which nothing has less therapeutic value. With his therapeutic ideology, the analyst protects not only the patient from the complete doubt as to the possibility of overcoming fear, but also himself from the destruction of his own illusions. Also the analyst, like the artist, can only overcome this fear creatively, as he is, in a certain sense, a new artist-type, such as has not existed since the Greek period and has not been needed before since the Christian era began. The type of artist who works in living human material, who seeks to create men not like the parents, physically, but spiritually, like God. How far this likeness to God corresponds to a creating of one's self in another, I have worked out elsewhere.[9]

In order to understand the creative, and therewith also the neurotic, expressions of this inhibiting, often destructive, life principle, we must first orient ourselves with regard to its normal forms of expression. The most important is sexuality, whose close relationship to the death principle is not only given biologically but also holds psychologically. Not only in the act of birth but also in the sexual act itself, the resemblance to death, yes, the nearness of death, is unmistakable. The sexual act has a different meaning certainly for the two sexes, a giving up (of an ego part), a surrender, yes, occasionally a complete loss of self; on the other hand it leads to new creation (in the child) and is at the same time perceived by the individual as the high point of the life principle, if the negative ego-destroying aspect does not win the upper hand. Viewed from the individual pleasure-gratification sex affords, it means biologically also a toll from life to death. Sexuality becomes thus the most current coin of this individual guilt to the race. This explains the attractive power which the so-called perversions exercise on the individual, but also why these sexual practices, which lack biological market value or lessen it, are tied up with biological guilt-feeling. On the other hand, we have learned to understand that often enough guilt-feelings coming from other sources are paid in sexual coin, as many a physical surrender, and even masturbation, proves. Of the latter, one could say paradoxically that its shamefulness, actual or acquired, comes just from the fact of its harmlessness to the individual; one has not really paid, and accordingly one feels so guilty.[1]

[9] See the chapter on "Love and Force" in *Will Therapy*, and also Part II of my *Genetische Psychologie*.

[1] The unavoidable nature of the masturbation conflict lies not in a false system of education, but corresponds as most conflicts do to a therapeutic attempt of the individual to overcome fear, which thereby is partially transformed into guilt (sin).

Besides these biological connections between sexuality and death, there are psychological connections which are therapeutically more important. The retrieving of death fear through sexual fear represents an attempt to eroticize the painful as it meets us grossly in masochism today. In this we have a use of sexuality characteristic of man alone, which is only comprehensible on the ground of will psychology. The individual will, as it were, seizes upon sexuality as a means to make suffering and pain, which in the last analysis are symbols of death, into a desired source of pleasure. It is the same ideology that creates from death fear a death instinct. At the basis of this apparently masochistic ideology there lies always the enormous strength of will of the personality, which is able by the eroticization of pain to force the sexual instinct into the service of fear avoidance, and at the same time to strip the primal fear of its dangerous quality. Another means to the same end, which the individual employs in order to escape the fear of sexuality together with the compulsion to it, is love. We can only refer in this connection to one aspect of this perhaps most important of all human phenomena, the significance of which psychoanalysis missed in its identification of sexuality and love. There is just the contrast between love and sexuality that often enough causes love to resist sexuality or to fly before it, just as under certain conditions sexuality can be a flight from love. Naturally everything depends on how one defines or interprets love. In its erotic meaning, it includes at all events the concentration upon a single person, and represents therefore in this sense a turning away from the promiscuity natural to the sexual instinct, which is provided only for the maintenance of the species and not for the satisfaction of the individual. From this theoretical standpoint, which is also confirmed by practical observations, one can conceive of human love as a protection—so to speak, as an economic device—against the waste of the sexual instinct that could impoverish the individual, while he feels himself enriched by love. The much-discussed promiscuity, which may seem to the sexually repressed person like a symbol of freedom, proves from the viewpoint of the individual to be the greatest danger, which he seeks to escape ethically by a definite moral code, and practically through love. That thereby the individual only avoids the Scylla of sexual partial payment to be drawn into the Charybdis of pledging his whole ego, is a problem that is to occupy us again elsewhere.

A further means for defending the ego against death fear, and one just as universal as love, is aggression. One does not need to assume an actual instinct of aggression, as Freud does, in order to justify this primary evil in man, by explaining it as a derivation of the death instinct, which only leads beyond this to speculations as to whether the original aggression turns toward the inside or the original death instinct to the outside. Here also a dynamic conception shows up a more immediate fact one easily overlooks from the metapsychological point of view. The death fear of the ego is lessened by the killing, the sacrifice, of the other; through the death of the other, one buys one's self free from the penalty of dying, of being killed. One recognizes at once that this "criminal" solution represents the opposite of the neurotic, for in both cases we are dealing with anticipation of death punishment, of dying; with the neurotic in the form of self-punishment, with criminals in the form of the punishment or killing of the other, which, however, is followed by the punishment of the ego through society.[2] The neurotic is only a man who cannot allay his own death fear by killing the other, who, in other words, is not capable of aggressive protective behavior, although he experiences the impulse to it strongly enough. By this "killing" of the other for the protection of the self, naturally I do not mean the legal concept of "self-defense" (legitimate), nor the biological concept of self-maintenance, but a purely psychic ideology, which rests upon the primitive feeling of the group (collectivity). According to this conception, which quite naturally values one life equally with the other without considering the individual as such, one death can also take the place of another. To the naïve consciousness of immortality, death must appear

[2] See my comment on the deeper meaning of the death punishment in *Seelenglaube und Psychologie*, p. 95.

as punishment; later it became a self-merited punishment that for the most part followed sexual transgression or more correctly the transgressing of sexuality, because just this in the last analysis leads to death; finally the individual preferred self-punishment coming from the idea of sin, and again turning toward the outside, but as protection, not as aggression, will buy himself free from his own death through the death of another (sacrifice). The impulse to aggression therefore arises from within and has the tendency to transform one's own suffering into the pain of the other, from whom the suffering ostensibly comes. The guilt-feeling ensues then not as a reaction to the aggression, but corresponds to the death fear, not done away with by the projection but only transformed, and thus moralized. Besides, the guilt-feeling is an expression of the identification implied in the sacrifice of the other in the place of one's own ego. In this sense, guilt-feeling and self-punishment appear in the neurotic also as expression of love for the other, for whom one then takes sin and punishment upon one's self instead of blaming him; for somewhere the bad, the arch-evil, must be placated either in the other or in one's own self—a distinction that explains the sadistic or masochistic attitude toward life, and also the close connection of the two.

In this briefly sketched development of the idea of sin, the killing of the other appears as a developmental phase, that is, the sacrifice of a life to death with the neglect of the individual difference. However, this primitive form of the sacrifice that we call murder has undergone a development and therewith a refinement. There are various forms of murder as there are various forms of self-destruction, as for example, in the neurotic symptoms. Ibsen speaks of "soul murder" [3] and means by that a making use of, or exploitation, of the other. The killing does not need to be actual; it can occur symbolically, as for example in the withdrawal of love or in the desertion of a person; it can also ensue partially instead of totally—a slow murder, as

[3] This reminds one of Oscar Wilde's lines in *The Ballad of Reading Goal:* "Yet each man kills the thing he loves . . ./The coward does it with a kiss,/The brave man with a sword!"

it were, through constant tormenting. Always, however, it takes place as a self-protection against one's own death fear, and not as an expression of a primary death wish. The death wish against loved persons shows itself frequently as the expression of strong attachment, which can be resolved only through death and not otherwise. According also in the treatment of many "depressives," the appearance of death wishes against others is not to be interpreted as infantile regression, but as a sign of the inner unburdening and strengthening of the ego.

For the problem of the overcoming of ego phases through the killing of the other, I refer the reader to an earlier work (*Genetische Psychologie*), and here turn to a broader means of defense against death fear, which still falls under normal psychology although it is more closely related to neurosis. This is the borderline case, where the individual neither punishes himself, like the neurotic, nor the other, like the criminal, but lets himself be punished by the other within certain limits. This function of external punishment as a means for inner unburdening is, as it were, the "pedagogical" agent in the therapeutic situation. With the very decision to accept treatment, the patient takes a powerful forward step beyond his neurosis, since he makes the therapist the active agent for self-punishment, a role which the latter cannot avoid however much he may try to protect himself from it. When this punishing agent can also be loved, it represents a further step toward healing, for love presupposes the overcoming of fear. We will follow out these therapeutic meanings later and now turn again to normal punishment situations, which are only crystallized like a paradigm in the therapeutic situation. In every more intimate human relation, whether it be that between parents and child, teacher and pupils, master and subordinate, likewise in the relation of the sexes and particularly in marriage, the punishing element is set up in the other spontaneously and unavoidably, and this is what makes the relationship, as a rule, so hard to understand and often impossible to bear. Even in the child we deal always with a self-punishment displaced outward, which serves as a palliative for fear.

One might object that the conception of self-punishment as a reducer of fear is only another kind of interpretation of a fact which psychoanalysis interpreted libidinally, that is, as sanction for instinct satisfaction. Certainly this phenomenon also, like every other, has two aspects, but this is not only a question of theory, it means that every single individual can emphasize this or that aspect in his general attitude, that is, can interpret life positively or negatively. If one speaks of types, however, it seems to me certain that the neurotic is that type which aims primarily not at pleasure gain but at the reduction of fear, while the application of self-punishment in the service of instinct satisfaction seems rather to correspond to the normal type (for example, to work in order to be able to permit himself pleasure afterward). That the reducing of fear then often leads to the expression of instinct is probably correct, but that must not be misunderstood to mean that punishment serves primarily for instinct freeing, for sanction, which always rests on the presupposition of an original repression of instinct from without. For besides the lightening of fear through punishment, the individual has yet another motive for instinct expression, which complicates still further a process already far from simple. In order to displace the punishing factor to the outside (to let himself be punished), the individual must feel himself guilty, and thus it comes to the paradoxical appearance of instinct expression with punishment as its goal; analytically this can be explained only from masochistic pleasure, which itself by no means represents an original phenomenon. The vicious circle is closed by the realization that the freeing of instinct from repressions causes fear because life and experience increase the fear of death; while, on the other side, renunciation of instinct increases guilt, not because it represents repressed aggression that turns against one's own ego (Freud), but because instinct renunciation is a renunciation of life, and therefore the individual feels himself guilty. The paradox that the lightening of fear (through punishment and instinct freeing) leads to fear, is explained, as was mentioned in the beginning, from the double function of fear, which at one time is life fear, at another, death fear. From the life fear, a direct path leads to consciousness of guilt, or better, to cónscience fear, which can be understood always as regret for the possibility of life that has been neglected, but its full expression, on the other hand, creates death fear.

X *Self and Ideal*

> *"This above all: to thine own self be true."*
> —SHAKESPEARE (*Hamlet*)

WE RETURN now to the presentation of the inner-will conflict, particularly as it is manifested in its effect on the ethical ideal-formation. In the analytic situation we see and feel the will of the patient as "resistance" to our will, just as the child breaks his will on the will of the parents and at the same time strengthens it. But the analysis of the adult gives us this advantage, that we can throw this resistance back upon the individual himself, provided we work constructively; that is, we can show the patient that he actually suffers from a purely inner conflict between will and consciousness, but analysis enables him to project it as an outward one. Now the form and manner in which this inner conflict appears, and what effects it produces within and without, constitute the actual subject matter of the will psychology, which is to be independent of moral, pedagogic, and social viewpoints. The latter we must examine in their turn in judging those situations where we are concerned with the collision of one will with another or with the will of the group. Just now we have to do rather with individual consciousness and particularly with that aspect of it which expresses itself positively and constructively as ideal-formation.

As we are interested here only in the positive, constructive, creative side of the conflict, and indeed only with a specific form of it, it is necessary to remind ourselves that we must ascribe even to the positive will a negative origin with whose genesis we have busied ourselves elsewhere. Long since, especially in the first part of *Genetische Psychologie,* I have pointed out the significance of the mechanism of denial for all thinking and acting. In this denial there is evidenced, as I would like to emphasize now, the original negative nature of will-power, which, as Goethe puts it, "always intends the bad and constantly creates the good." At all events we see man in various situations, but especially in the so-called neurotic reactions, think and act as if he were ruled by two wills that struggle against each other, as formerly his own will struggled against an external, opposing will. These two factors, which lie at the root of all dualistic world views, from the Persian Zoroastrianism to the system of Schopenhauer, were described by Freud in the beginning as the conscious and the unconscious, later with a deepened meaning as the ego and the id. Accordingly unconsciousness was at first identified with sexuality, consciousness with the ego; while Freud later desexualized the id somewhat, or rather made it more cosmic, on the other hand he ascribed to the ego unconscious elements also. This connecting of new terminology with old contents is more confusing than clarifying, especially as the ego plays a relatively slight role with Freud despite its unconscious elements, because it is ruled by the two great powers, the id and the super-ego, the latter of which represents the moral code. I have no occasion to go back to this terminology here, because I would like to describe the phenomena just as they present themselves to me, except to make clear where and in how far my conception differs from the former one.

I see and understand the two opposing powers in the individual as the same forces that are experienced as a conflict of wills in the clash of two individuals, namely, will forces. The one force is that which we experience in impact with the outside world, namely, our conscious will. But what is the other inner force against which it strives, or rather, which strives against it (for this seems to me to be the real situation)? One might say that this is sexuality, as Freud originally assumed, provided one understands it not only in a broader but in the broadest sense of the word.

Accordingly we say in biological terms the generic in contrast to the individual, in which case the question remains open as to whether or not one should include the collective-racial, which in Jung's meaning is a social-ethical concept. At all events we need no external sexual prohibition, no castration trauma, as our daily experience with children shows, to explain the struggle of the individual ego, the conscious will, against sexuality, against generic compulsion. The parents or others in authority may represent to the child powerful wills, but one can oppose them openly or secretly, one can finally overcome them, perhaps can even free one's self from them or escape them. Sexuality, however, as it awakens in the individual about the time of puberty, is an incomparably stronger power than all the external authorities put together. Were it not so, the world would have died out long since.

This generic sexual compulsion which, as sexual attraction, is the root of the Freudian Oedipus complex, when it is actually completely aroused, naturally goes beyond parental boundaries, because generally it goes beyond all bounds. It is so strong and dominates the individual so extremely that soon he begins to defend himself against its domination, just because it is domination, something that interferes dictatorially with his own will as individual, appearing as a new, alien, and more powerful counter-will just as the ego is strengthened by puberty. The reason the individual defends himself so strongly against it is that the biological sex drive would force him again under the rule of a strange will, of the sexual will of the "other," while the ego has only just began at this time to breathe a little freely out from under the pressure of strange authoritative wills. Accordingly he flees of necessity to a mechanism for the satisfaction of urgent sexuality that enables him to maintain the newly won autonomy at least a little while without subjecting himself to an alien sexual will. I speak of the typical masturbation conflict of this and also of later years, which represents nothing but the powerful expression of the conflict between the individual will and generic will, manifesting itself here as sex drive. This struggle always ends with the victory of the individual. Although he must often pay too dearly for it, nevertheless an ego victory it is, since the very appearance of masturbation registers a successful attempt to put the sexual instinct under the control of the individual will.

These individuals, even when they present themselves as weak-willed, falling into vice without resistance, are at bottom people of unusually strong wills who have merely concentrated their wills for the moment in the one direction. They often succeed in becoming master of the sexual urge to such an extent that they can suppress it through conscious effort of will, and can also arouse and satisfy it; that is, when the individual wills it and not when sexuality wills it. Only, as Adler believes, they must continue to prove this will-power of theirs, and that gives the appearance of not being able to get free of the sex drive. This appearance is correct too, in so far as it is based on a denial of will-power that we could here bring into the universal formula: I do not want to will at all, but I must. In contrast to Adler, however, I do not believe that the individual must continuously prove his own strength of will because he feels inferior, and therefore is really weak. I believe much more that he could never prove his strength if he were not actually strong, if he did not have just that powerful a will. Here again the problem is why the individual cannot accept his own will, cannot admit it or affirm it, but is compelled to reject and deny it—in other words, to replace it with a "must." But just this denial tendency brings with it secondarily the guilt and inferiority feeling that really says, "I ought not to have such a strong will, or in general any will at all." In this sense, the powerful compulsion of the biological sexual urge is raised to a representative of the will, whose individual freedom is then justified by the generic compulsion. Herein lies the psychological motive for the tie-up of the conscious individual will with the generic sex drive, as significant as it is fateful, also the origin of the sexual guilt feeling, since the guilt for willing falls into the sexual sphere by displacement and at the same time is denied and justified.

The explanations that psychoanalysis and also the Adlerian doctrine give for these phenomena of guilt and inferiority seem to me unsatisfactory because they do not meet the real problem at all, that is, the denial of will from which secondarily follow guilt and inferiority. The explanation given formerly is that the will of the child has been so broken by the authority of parents that it can no longer trust itself to will; in a word, it experiences anxiety that was added to it from the outside. Not only does every educational experiment contradict this, but also experiences in the psychology of the neuroses and creative personalities testify that the fact is other and deeper. Our conflicts in general go back to much deeper causes than external social restrictions even if we conceive them psychologically with Freud as internal super-ego formation or with Adler as inner inferiority feeling, springing from the externally inferior status of the child. Probably in the beginning we were bound to our milieu, which, however, we are able to outgrow, and just so to a great extent we have remained bound by nature in our sexual life. But what characterizes man or is made to by himself, perhaps unfortunately, is just the fact that his conscious will increases to a power equal to the outer environmental influences and the inner instinctual claims, and this we must take into account in order to understand the individual in all his reactions. Our will is not only able to suppress the sex urge, but is just as able to arouse it through conscious effort, to increase it and to satisfy it. Perhaps our will is able to do this because it, itself, is a descendant, a representative of the biological will-to-live become conscious, creating itself in self-maintenance and reproduction, which in the last analysis is nothing more than supra-individual self-maintenance.[1] When this tendency to perpetual self-maintenance of the species carries over to the individual, there results the powerful will whose manifestations bring with them guilt reactions because they strive for an enrichment of the individual, biologically at the cost of the species, ethically at the expense of the fellow man.

This brings us to the fundamental thought of my whole

[1] See on this point and the following, the beginning of the first chapter in *Der Künstler*—as well as the material on the development of the individual in the introductory chapter of *Genetische Psychologie,* Part II, p. 14.

viewpoint, which I have already expressed in principle in *Der Künstler,* namely, that instinct and inhibition, will and counter-will do not correspond to any original dualism, but in the last analysis always represent a kind of inner self-limitation of one's own power, and therefore, since everything has its roots within, the outer reflects more than it creates the inner. This conception, as was emphasized likewise in *Der Künstler,* relates in particular to all kinds of sexual conflicts which arise not through any kind of outer prohibition but through inner inhibition of one's own will by the counter-will. It explains also the resistance which Freud's sexual theory has met and necessarily must meet since it is an expression of the same conflict, the understanding of which leads us out of all the futile discussions that psychoanalysis has occasioned. Freud said: "Sexuality is the strongest"; the answer was, "No, the will can control it to a great degree." And both sides were right. But each emphasized only one side, instead of recognizing the relationship between them and understanding the conflict in its essential meaning. Freud has gradually yielded, and in his castration and super-ego theory, recognizes the power of the factors that inhibit sexuality. But they are for him external anxiety factors and remain so even later, when he internalizes them in the super-ego, although they establish themselves as the court of morals that evokes the uncontrollable guilt reactions. But guilt-feeling is something other than internalized anxiety, as it is more than fear of itself, of the claim of instinct, just as the ethical judgments are something more than introjected parental authority.

In order to understand what they are and how they arise, we turn back to the struggle of ego-will against race-will represented in sexuality, which actually represents a struggle of the child against any pressure that continues within him. In the so-called latency period, as Freud has it (between early childhood and puberty), the ego of the individual, his own will, is strengthened and has turned, for the most part in revolutionary reactions, against the parents and other authorities that he has not chosen himself. In the struggle against sexuality that breaks in at that point, the ego, as it were, calls to its aid the earlier contested parental inhibitions and takes them as allies against the more powerful sex drive. This introduction of the will motive makes the mysterious process of the introjection of parental authority comprehensible psychologically for the first time. Hitherto it had to be forced upon the child from the outside, and this force must obviously be maintained, because the child opposes the acceptance with his will, his counter-will. Moreover, the child has no occasion to make of these actual outer restrictions an inner censor, and even if he had reasons, his counter-will would resist the acceptance of force. The child obeys because he wins love, avoids punishment and lessens his own inner control. But he does not do these things of his own free will; on the contrary, prohibition strengthens the impulse, as we know, just as permission lessens the desire. In puberty, however, where the individual is awakened on the one side to autonomy of will and on the other defends himself against the pressure of the racial sex urge, he has a strong will motive for making his own these early parental prohibitions and all that he has learned to know meantime in moralistic inhibitions, in order to use them in his encounter with sexuality. Here the individual forms his own super-ego because he needs these moral norms for his own will victory over the sex-impulse. Again it is a victory that many a time is bought at too dear a price and must be paid for by a lifelong dependency on this moral code.

The constructive formation and creative development from what Freud calls super-ego to what I call ideal-formation from the self is a highly complex process that is accomplished in the typical forms of the will conflict and under its pressure. It consists first in the fact that the individual who earlier made his own only externally the limitations accepted of necessity, now affirms them in the service of his own will interests. This affirmation of a condition already established earlier under pressure, is a very important factor psychologically, yes, is *the* essential psychological factor; for the fate of the individual depends on the attitude he takes to the *given* factors, whether these happen to be a part of environment, or the sexual constitution itself. This "I will, because I must," is, as is easily seen, the positive opposite of the denying attitude we formulated in the sentence "I do not will at all, but I obey a force!" The whole difference lies in the fact that this force as external cannot be borne and causes the will to react negatively as denial. But if this outer force becomes inner, then there arise two possibilities, the first of which leads to neurotic reactions, the other to ethical standards. If the force although inner is still perceived as force, the will conflict manifests itself, as already pointed out, in guilt-feeling, which, as it were, represents an inner ethical compulsion resisting the individual's will just like an alien counter-will. But if his own will says "Yes" to this force, this internal "must," then the inner force becomes inner freedom as will and counter-will both affirm the same willing.

The process just described goes beyond the mere affirmation of force, either outer or inner, to its constructive evaluation; that is, positively as ethics in ideal-formation and not merely normatively and regulatively. Therefore the individual only takes over the overcome moral code for a protection, as it were, under the first violence of the sexual impulse. Soon, however, the proud will stirs again and strives to win the battle alone without the help of authoritative morality. Here then begins the ethical ideal-formation in the self, although the individual may turn to external models, ideal figures from life or history. But these ideals he chooses in terms of his own individuality, which, as we know, has nothing to do with infantile authorities, least of all the parents.[2] It does not matter whether the individual succeeds wholly in freeing himself from the traditional moral concepts; probably he never does, especially not as long as he must live with other individuals who more or less depend on this traditional morality. It is important, however, that for everything creative, regardless of how it manifests itself, even in neurosis, we can thank this striving of the individual, of his individual will to free himself from the traditional moral code and to build his

[2] Certainly not with the parents of the hero, the man of strong will, as I explained in *The Myth of the Birth of the Hero.*

own ethical ideals from himself, ideals that are not only normative for his own personality but also include the assurance of creative activity of any kind and the possibility of happiness. For this whole process of inner ideal-formation, which begins with the setting up of one's own moral norms inside, is a mighty and important attempt to transform compulsion into freedom. The broader fate of the individual depends essentially on the success with which this attempt is undertaken, how it is carried through and conducted further, also how far it goes in a particular case and where and how it ends.

Certainly it is no planned and straightforward way, but a continuous struggle against outer forces and a constant conflict with inner ones, in which the individual must live through for himself all stages of his evolution. That cannot be avoided and should not be, for just this living through and fighting through constitute the valuable, the constructive, the creative that does not inhibit the will but strengthens and develops it. The first step in the freeing process is that the individual now wills what he was earlier compelled to, what externally or internally he was forced to do, and the normal, average man perhaps never gets beyond this level that guarantees a relatively harmonious working together of will and counter-will. It corresponds to a willed acceptance of the external compulsion of authority, the moral code and the inner compulsion of the sexual instinct. Accordingly it permits fewer possibilities of conflict but also fewer creative possibilities of any kind. The human being to a large extent is one with himself and with the surrounding world and feels himself to be a part of it. He has the consciousness of individuality but at the same time also the feeling of likeness, of unity, which makes the relation to the outer world pleasant.

The next stage is characterized by the feeling of division in the personality, through the disunity of will and counter-will, which means a struggle (moral) against the compulsion of the outer world as well as an inner conflict between the two wills. The constructive person goes beyond the mere moralistic and instinctual affirmation of the obligatory in his own ideal-formation, which itself having become a new goal-seeking power can work thereafter constructively or inhibitingly. On this level there are possibilities of neurotic or creative development not present on the first level. And again it depends on what position the will takes toward the moral and ethical standards originally called in by it or self-created, after they have once been called into life, or have even achieved power. So the will is always compelled to take attitudes anew, first to the given, then to the self-created, and finally even to the willed. And this taking an attitude can always turn out to be negative or positive, negative even when it concerns something originally self-willed or self-created. This negative attitude in turn can always have one of two results: either it leads to improvement, to a higher level, to a new creativity as with the productive, or it creates itself in self-criticism, guilt, and inferiority feeling, in short, under the neurotic inhibition of will.

The third and highest level of development is characterized by a unified working together of the three fully developed powers, the will, the counter-will, and the ideal-formation born from the conflict between them, which itself has become a goal-setting, goal-seeking force. Here the human being, the genius, is again at one with himself; what he does, he does fully and completely in harmony with all his powers and his ideals. He knows no hesitation; and he knows no doubt as does the divided man of the second level, even though the latter be productive. He is a man of will and deed in accord with himself, although, as distinguished from the type of realistic man, he is not in accord with the world, because he is too different from others. I do not mean that the conflicts of this type would be more of an external nature, played out more in the battle with the hostile environment; I merely wish to emphasize here the creative side of their being, which just through its unlikeness to reality gives to genius its peculiar greatness. This type, in its ideal-formation, in its continuous rebuilding or building anew, has created an autonomous inner world so different and so much its own that it no longer represents merely a substitute for external reality (original morality), but is something for which reality can offer in every case only a feeble substitute, so that the individual must seek satisfaction and release in the creation and projection of a world of his own. In a word, with this type, from all the accepted, the obligatory, from all the wished-for, and the willed, from all the aspirations and the commandments, is formed neither a compromise, nor merely a summation, but a newly created whole—the strong personality with its autonomous will, which represents the highest creation of the integration of will and spirit.

The first level corresponds to the type of duty-conscious, the second to the type of guilt-conscious, and the third level finally to the type of self-conscious individual. We see at once that in these three types, which represent a line of development, the relation to reality and to the fellow man is different. The first level is oriented to the external world, corresponds to the adaptation of the ego to it; in this the individual takes over the social and sexual ideals of the majority for his own, and this is not only a passive identification but an effort of will that certainly ends in a submission of will. On the third ethical level there are no longer the external demands or norms, but the individual's own inner ideals, which were not only created by him out of himself but which the self also willingly affirms as its own commandments. The second neurotic level represents the failure in going from the first to the third stage; the individual perceives the external commands and norms as compulsion he must continually oppose, but cannot affirm the ideals that correspond to his own self. Therefore he has guilt-feeling toward society (or the various representatives of it) and consciousness of guilt toward himself.

In other words, the first type accepts reality with its demands and so adjusts his own individuality that he perceives and can accept himself as part of reality. He removes the painful feeling of difference since he feels himself one with reality. The third type, on the contrary, accepts himself and his inner ideal-formation; he seeks accordingly to adjust the environment and the fellow man to himself. This can take place violently, as with thoughtless men of action, or by way of a reformative ideology, whether it be educational or therapeutic, in the scientific or religious sense of the word. It can, however, also be creative and reaches then its highest level when the individual creates from himself and his own idealized will-power, a world for himself, as the artist or the philosopher does, without wanting to force it on others. Certainly this peculiarly creative type also strives for recognition, but it cannot, as with the therapeutic reformative personality, be through force or violence, but rather must be the expression of a spontaneous movement of the individual who finds in the creator something related to himself. This creative type finds recognition in himself as he also finds in himself motivation and its approbation.

The first, adapted type, therefore, needs the external compulsion; the second, neurotic type defends itself against every kind of external or internal compulsion; the third, creative type has overcome compulsion through freedom. The first type is dependent on reality; the second defends itself against the compulsion of reality; the third creates for itself against the compulsion a reality of its own that makes it independent, but at the same time enables it to live in reality without falling into conflict with it. The second, neurotic type is the most interesting psychologically, because it shows that the whole problem at bottom turns on the acceptance of one's own individuality, on which the attitude toward reality primarily depends. For the neurotic shatters not only on the incapacity to bear external pressure, but he suffers just as much, yes, even more, from the inability to subject himself to any pressure, whether it be inside or out, even the pressure of his own ideal-formation. The essential therapeutic problem is not, therefore, to adjust him to reality, to teach him to bear external pressure, but to adjust him to himself, that is, to enable him to bear and to accept himself instead of constantly defending himself against himself. If one attains this therapeutic goal, that the individual accepts himself—that is, psychologically speaking, that he affirms instead of denies his will—there follows thereupon spontaneously, without further effort, the necessary adaptation to reality.

This, however, cannot form an equally valid scheme for all men, regardless of whether one defines it with the concept of the Oedipus complex like Freud, or again as social feeling like Adler, or as a collective union like Jung. Adaptation ensues with each individual in a different, even in an individual, way, from the three possibilities we have described as types. Psychologically speaking, adaptation on the basis of self-acceptance may be an acceptance of external norms that finally represents a justification of will, but at least a generally recognized one, or the self-acceptance enables the individual to continue his development on the basis of his own ideal-formation and its essential difference. In each case, however, the neurotic self-denial, as it follows from the denial of will, must first be overcome constructively in a therapeutic experience.

How this happens I am describing simultaneously in another book.[3] Here I would only like to point out how, as a matter of fact, the various reactions of the individual only correspond to various attitudes toward the same fundamental problem. The average man adapted to reality finds the justification of his individual will in the similarly adjusted wills of the majority, but accepts therewith also the universal attempts at justification and unburdening, as society itself apparently uses them in its moral norms and religious projections. The neurotic, who in consequence of his stronger individualization feels himself so very different from others, can accept neither the general norms nor the justifications, but neither can he accept his own, because they would be an expression of his own will, which he would therewith have to accept. The creative type, on the other hand, accepts himself and his ideal, that is, his own individual will, at all events in higher degree than any other type. Certainly he also needs all kinds of external justifications, but these work destructively only in the field of intellectual production, like philosophy and science, where they lead to theoretical denial of will and justifications that appear under the guise of truth.

This leads us back from the problem of will to the prob-

[3] See *Will Therapy.*

lem of consciousness and conscious knowledge. Where ideal-formation works constructively and creatively, it is on the basis of acceptance of the self, of the individual will, which is justified in its own ideal, that is, ethically, not morally in terms of the average ideal as with the adapted type. In other words, in its own ideal the originally denied will of the individual manifests itself as ethically justified. The neurotic suffers not only from the fact that he cannot accomplish this, but also from insight regarding it, which, according to the degree of insight, manifests itself as consciousness of guilt or inferiority feeling. He rejects the self because in him the self is expressed on the whole negatively as counter-will and accordingly cannot justify itself ethically, that is, cannot reform and revalue itself in terms of an ideal-formation. Accordingly he strives only this far, to be himself (as so many neurotics express it) instead of striving to live in accordance with his own ideal. Therefore, while the ideal of the average is to be as the others are, the ideal of the neurotic is to be himself, that is, what he himself is and not as others want him to be. The ideal of the creative personality finally is an actual ideal, which leads him to become that which he himself would like to be.

In the sphere of consciousness we see these various levels of development toward ideal-formation comprehended in three formulae which correspond to three different ages, world views, and human types. The first is the Apollonian, *know thyself;* the second the Dionysian, *be thyself;* the third the Kantian, *determine thyself from thyself.* The first rests on likeness to others and leads in the sense of the Greek mentality to the acceptance of the universal ideal; it contains implicitly the morality, consciously worked out by Socrates, which still lies at the basis of psychoanalytic therapy: know thyself, in order to improve thyself (in the terms of universal norms). It is, therefore, not knowledge for the sake of the self, but knowledge for the goal of adaptation. The second principle, in contrast to the first, repudiates likeness and the improvement based on it, as it demands the acceptance of what one is anyway. In contrast to the principle of the Delphic Apollo, I have designated it as Dionysian because, in contrast to adaptation, it leads to ecstatic-orgiastic destruction, as seen in Greek mythology and also as Ibsen shows in Peer Gynt, who on the basis of the same principle landed in a madhouse. The true self, if it is unchained in Dionysian fashion, is not only anti-social but also unethical, and therefore the human being goes to pieces on it. Seen in this sense, the longing of the neurotic to be himself is a form of the affirmation of his neurosis, perhaps the only form in which he can affirm himself. He is, as it were, already himself, at any rate far more than the others, and has only a step to take in order to become wholly himself, that is, insane. Here comes in the Kantian *determine thyself from thyself* in the sense of a true self-knowledge and simultaneously an actual self-creation as the first constructive placing of the problem. Herein lies Kant's historical significance as epistemologist and ethicist. He is indebted to us for the psychology, but also a part of his greatness lies therein, for the avoidance of psychologizing has protected him from falling into all the denials, rationalizations, and interpretations that form the contents of most psychological theories including the Freudian.

An epistemological psychology without flaw, that is, neither moral nor religious as the Freudian system still is, must start at the point where Kant placed the problem. How can the individual determine himself from himself, or better, why does he do this with such difficulty? Here we strike the will-guilt problem, the knowledge of which remains the indisputable psychological contribution of Schopenhauer. But he has denied the will, while Nietzsche sought to deny the guilt-feeling. Freud finally has seen the guilt problem, as the neurotic presented it to him, it is true; but he has tried to solve it by leading it back to a definite content of willing, namely the sexual, while the other analytic schools (Jung, Adler, etc.) differentiate themselves in this, that they have put another content in place of the sexual, and so have hidden the purely psychological will problem itself. The Freudian content disguises itself under the occidental religious morality from which we still suffer, and in its failure to solve his individual problem, the modern man has finally shattered in terms of the neurosis.

XI *Forms of Kinship and the Individual's Rôle in the Family*

Education is love to the off-spring.

—NIETZSCHE

IN THE course of our discussion we have repeatedly touched upon the child's attitude to parents and family,[1] but now we must discuss in greater detail the different relationships within the family. For as long as childhood lasts, the child is very closely, in part exclusively, attached to the home, and modern education has again placed the chief accent on the education of the child in the family. And rightly so! The child is indeed brought into a family of already educated individuals (or, in so far as brothers or sisters are concerned, of partly educated ones), who also have a psychology, whereas the child brings with him neither education nor psychology, and somehow gets both from adults or develops both through them.

In the analysis of adult neurotics, Freud, above all, has studied the influence that the parents exercise on the child partly through their mere existence, partly through their particular psychology or characterology. Under the concept of the "Oedipus complex" he has described the effects engendered by the parents in the child in the form of love, anxiety, hatred, jealousy, obstinacy, etc. But these effects are of different values—they are partly unavoidable, partly avoidable; they partly bring out of the child only what is latent; on the other hand, they partly provoke new reactions to unfamiliar stimulations. A closer study has at any

[1] EDITOR'S NOTE: The reference here is to the preceding six chapters of *Modern Education,* of which only one ("Sexual Enlightenment and the Sexual Impulse") has been selected for reprinting in this collection.

rate taught us to understand that the parents cannot be made responsible for many of the child's reactions, because the child possesses them potentially when he is born into the world. This is particularly so with *anxiety*, which has not the same significance for the child as it has, according to the psychoanalytic theory, for the adult neurotic. The child, at the birth process,[2] seems to bring into the world anxiety, which is then attached to the parents; on the other hand, this anxiety determines from the beginning the dependency of the child on the parents (especially on the mother) and often extends far beyond the time of the child's physical helplessness. The adult may have fear of death or fear of sex, the child has a fear of life itself,[3] which it changes forthwith, even when there is no objective reason for it, into anxiety or fear of certain people or things.

Let us now return to the Oedipus complex, by which a definite phase of the child's relation to his parents, or better, one aspect of this relationship, is circumscribed. The sexual element in it emphasized by Freud, the attraction to the parent of the opposite sex and jealousy of the parent of the same sex, is not to be found in practice so clearly as mythology represents it and as Freud first believed. This purely biological scheme may indeed exist in the child to a certain extent; but it is permeated, indeed, even sometimes completely dominated, by other tendencies emerging from the unfolding ego, so that it was difficult even for psychoanalysis to maintain the original Oedipus concept. The Freudians speak of a reversed Oedipus relationship, of a rudimentary, even negative one, which at least devaluates, not to say contradicts, the purely biological viewpoint. I myself have on one occasion[4] referred to the fact that besides the reverse of the Oedipus complex that contains a greater love to the parents of the same sex, there is also in the child a tendency one might designate

[2] *The Trauma of Birth*, (1929).

[3] EDITOR'S NOTE: "Life Fear and Death Fear," pp. 263 ff. of this collection.

[4] "The Relation of Parental Attitudes to Success and Failure," given at the One-Day Conference on Parental Education, New York, November 2, 1927.

"anti-Oedipoean" because, in contrast to the Oedipus complex, it aims at a bringing together of the parents instead of a separation of them. Certainly this occurs because the child also expects some kind of advantages for himself from it, that is, it gratifies egoistic motives, but this shows that these often enough far outweigh the biological tendencies. The child reacts not only with his innate biological impulses, but also reacts according to the given situation. I found these tendencies of the child to bring the parents together or to hold them together particularly in those marital situations in which the child experiences instability as a dangerous threat to his well-being. This attitude of the child, which can easily be noticed in situations of that kind, was overlooked by psychoanalysis because the attitude mostly does not manifest itself in altruistic ways, but in neurotic reactions, with which the child wants to attain the same result.[5]

But if in a situation where the child experiences the conflicts of the parents with each other as a danger to himself, he can react in a way contrary to our biological presuppositions, then we may assume that he perhaps also reacts with the real Oedipus complex (where this is to be found) only to a situation of better understanding between the parents and not with his innate biological impulses. Actually not only critics of analysis, such as Malinowski by reason of ethnological material,[6] but also practicing child analysts who, unlike Freud, worked with chil-

[5] I wrote in the lecture mentioned, "I surmise that in Freud's 'Analysis of a Phobia in a Five-Year-Old Boy' (1909) the fact of the parental disharmony played a similar part as in those cases observed by me. I do not know whether the obvious conflicts of his parents, who later separated, go back so far into his childhood. But I should suppose from similar experiences that the father's excessive interest in the boy's problems was already an expression of his marital guilt-feeling, to which children, as we know, so react as if they understood it."

The parents had moreover "agreed," as Freud remarks in the introduction to the case history, "to educate their first child with as little compulsion as would be requisite for the maintenance of good manners."

Thus they had apparently also projected the "freedom" which they wished for themselves, on to the child, nevertheless without success—as his neurosis shows, a neurosis that also arose from a wish *for* his absent father and not only as a reaction against his father.

[6] *Sex and Repression in Savage Society* (London and New York, 1927).

dren,[7] have leaned toward this same view; namely that the Oedipus complex may be a reaction acquired by the child in our family organization, and not a biological inheritance brought with him into the world. If this is confirmed, the paradox follows that Freud considers the anxiety present at birth as acquired through later influences (threat) and the Oedipus attitude acquired in the family situation as innate.[8] However that may be, we cannot here go further into this problem and can only refer readers to psychoanalytic literature that deals with the influence of the parents on the child almost exhaustively although one-sidedly and uncritically.[9] At any rate, the therapeutic or psychological aspects of the family situation do not interest us here, but only the pedagogical, and for this, one other side of the problem seems to me of greater significance.

The question is: *What does the child signify for the parents ideologically?* In other words, in what light do the parents see the child, and what do they want the child to be, and for what do they want to use him? But since the ideological attitude of the parents to the child changes in different times and under different conditions, a cultural psychological study of the theme "child" would be necessary for this, similar to that given by Ploss from an ethnological point of view.[1] Such a task would go far beyond the realm of this work, where we are interested for pedagogic reasons only in our *present* parental ideology. Furthermore, the ethnological material is so manifold and so contradictory—especially as more is collected—that one has to borrow psychological concepts from other sources in order to shape it into something more than a mere accumulation of facts. I have already elaborated elsewhere my own essential concept of the child's rôle as a collective soul-bearer,[2] and this can be well brought into

[7] Mary Chadwick: *Difficulties in Child Development* (London, 1929), especially Chapter xii, "Both Sides of the Oedipus Complex."

[8] There are still other fundamental paradoxes in psychoanalysis. See concerning these especially my work, *Truth and Reality*.

[9] J. C. Flügel: *The Psychoanalytic Study of the Family* (London, 1921).

[1] Heinrich Ploss: *Das Kind in Brauch und Sitte der Völker*, third edition (Leipzig, 1911–12).

[2] *Seelenglaube und Psychologie*.

harmony with the ethnological material. The collective significance of the child is expressed in a custom of "child community" preserved relatively late,[3] in which children belong in common to all the mothers and sometimes—not always—when they are bigger are assigned to a father of choice (according to similarity). This primeval custom has practically nothing at all of the fatherhood-ideology, but gives rather the impression of a tutorship, in which the child participates at a definite age for the purpose of further training. This naturally is far from being an education in our sense even today among most primitives. The child among them has not only more collective significance but also more religious significance, that is, the child guarantees the continuation of existence to the community, not only in the social sense but also in the meaning of the original belief in immortality.

The primal family, according to the newer views of sociology, was a kind of herd or group formation, which did not embrace a monogamous form of marriage in our meaning (although it did not make it impossible), nor did it include "promiscuity" in the meaning that we today attach to that concept. For there were definite restrictions (exogamous and others) that were very strictly adhered to. One might best designate this primal family as a kind of "group marriage" in the broadest sense of the word, "in which whole generations of each half of the race lived in community marriage."[4] Regulation of sexual life was closely connected with religious ideas (belief in the soul), and these also determined the prevailing attitude toward children. This development cannot here be followed in detail; only the most important transitional stage to our present ideology of the family can be touched on. The transition from a primitive group-family (kinsfolk) to our present-day small family is characterized by the acceptance of the father's individual rôle of begetter of his children; this rôle was formerly denied him for religious rea-

[3] Ploss, op. cit.

[4] See Alfred Vierkandt's article "Ehe" in the *Handwörterbuch der Sexualwissenschaft,* edited by Max Marcuse, second edition (Bonn, 1926).

sons, the group's desire for immortality. This development changed the child from a collective being into a personal representative of a patriarchal-individual ideology. The transition phase was the matriarchy, with the "heritance from the uncle" (*avunculus*), that is, the mother's brother who was the male head of the family in place of the father; this seems to correspond to a relic of the old group marriage between brothers and sisters. Today with the enfeeblement of the *patrias potestas* and the strengthening of an individualistic tendency, the child is an individual for himself, although he is lawfully the father's successor and is claimed as a collective being by the State. Thus the three chief stages in the ideological development of the child are: a collective being (mother), heir (of the father), private being (self).

We have now to investigate different ideologies in relation to the child, how they have on the one hand influenced educational systems, on the other hand influenced the child himself and, finally, how the child as an individual has reacted to these at different times. For this we shall have to bear in mind the existing antitheses between the ideology of the parents (family), that of the teacher (community), and that of the child (individual). From the history of the family, we know that earlier forms of kinship survive even when the actually existing family organization no longer shows this—indeed, even when their origin is no longer understood. But this does not seem to be merely a useless survival as Lewis Henry Morgan, its discoverer, thought; these earlier forms of wider kinship obviously remain because they correspond to a spiritual need to preserve collective elements that become more and more individualized with an advancing family organization. With the small family and its legal ideology, all earlier forms of kinship finally fall apart. Hence the school replaces within the clan an earlier collective unity wherein the child was the possession of all. Scholastic education springs up, not to replace "the family," but to preserve the rights of the old group community (clan), which is otherwise in process of disappearing.

Here we already see how the school plays a double rôle

for the parents; it takes the place for them of a lost collective religious concept, but robs them at a later stage of their individual claim to the child. So the parents have never fully possessed him, because originally they willingly surrendered the child to the religious beliefs of the clan or tribe and later on they can no longer snatch him from the group's collective claims. In a primitive matriarchal culture, the mother alone had real possession of the child. Later on, when a patriarchal culture established itself with legal and religious sanctions, it was the father alone.[5] In our present small family (with its marriage system), the parents possess the child in common only in so far as the mother trains him in an early period and the father claims him later, when, however, he has to compete for his son with the community (the State). Now the child, especially the son, is trained exclusively in a partriarchal system, as the father's heir and successor. He is also asked to respect a religious ancestral cult. This paternal claim is, however, opposed by the son not only because of his natural attachment to his mother (the psychoanalytic Oedipus complex) but also because of his desire for selfhood or individuality —a double conflict, the climax of which we find presented in Hamlet.[6]

Here is established the third, and for the time being last phase of the parental concept, which, however, springs up neither from the group's nor from the parent's need for immortality. On the contrary, it has been forced, through the child's own individual development, first on the parents, and finally on the community. Today the child is made not only a social but also an individual vindication of marriage, whereas formerly, as long as he belonged to all, he made marriage unnecessary. With this is connected the fact that today many marital conflicts are projected on to the child, a fact which detrimentally influences his collective education, as well as his individual development. One must not forget, however, that this is nothing new, but only one more manifestation of the age-old fact that

[5] The concept and the word *family* is related to the Latin *famulus,* that is, "servant" or "slave."

[6] *Seelenglaube und Psychologie,* pp. 67 ff.

the child has always been used for something, at times by the community, at times by one or both parents. At any rate, primitive civilizations are much more sincere in this utilization of the child than we. For we today psychically misuse and exploit our children under the mask of individualistic education. Indeed, perhaps the acceptance of children as independent individuals, which completely contradicts the whole parental ideology, is a kind of guilt reaction on the part of parents toward exploiting their young. In any case, we can observe that many children are more or less conscious of this guilt-feeling of their parents toward them and take advantage of this situation. A difficult marriage situation may be in this sense a good school for the child to develop individuality and self-reliance early, or it may also be the beginning of a lifelong neurosis, according to the child's disposition and reactions. Experience shows both possibilities, although analysts from their study of the neurotic drew the premature conclusion that it could have only harmful effects, because they never see those children who benefit from a maladjustment between their parents. Such a situation can be for the child a stimulus for thinking, and so promote his intellectual development; it can also develop his emotional life and his will, and he can in this way, if he does not find sufficient *security* in the family, become prematurely self-reliant, just as he can become completely dependent (neurotic).

At any rate it seems that much more depends on what family situation the child finds and how he reacts to it than on inherited biological elements such as are given in libido tendencies and manifestations of anxiety. Analysis has indeed shown, in the neurotic, the harmful aftereffects of parental influence in childhood, but likewise has taught us to see in the analytic situation not only (with Freud) a repetition of the infantile but also a new creation of the ego. The analytic situation makes it obvious that the individual can so easily re-create every situation in his own light because fundamentally he always finds only himself, or better, a part of himself, in the other, or creates it by means of projection. Simultaneously there is also the opposite process of identification, that is, the individual also tries to be like the other and to a certain extent actually becomes like him (psychologically or characterologically). This tendency to "imitate" is so preponderant that the other side has hitherto been neglected. Certainly it must be admitted that in the infantile situation the child identifies at first more than he projects, but at least in the analytic situation projection should have been more valued (by Freud). I have already elsewhere comprehended the so-called Oedipus situation, which is supposed to repeat itself in the analysis, as the child's first clear achievement of projection, in which he re-creates a given situation in the light of his own needs and wishes. The relation to his parents—as we better call the Oedipus situation—is thus in varying degree a creation of the child's, as the transference situation is clearly a creation of the patient's. This creation, however, corresponds not only to the biological tendencies in the sense of the Oedipus complex but to the whole characterological development of the child, who can only identify himself with his parents, in that he simultaneously re-creates them in a varying degree according to his own will or ego-ideal. Paradoxically, one might say, the child has to discover or create the parents as he needs them, which indeed is actually realized in the idea of God, who hence betrays rather our own self than any actual parental characteristics.

But the parents project on to the child as much or even more, that is, they try to re-create the child according to their own wishes. We have briefly described the different stages of this parental attitude and have designated the employment of the child as "heir" as the decisive turning point from the original concept of the child as a collective being to his present position as a free individual. At this stage of patriarchal culture, the child is no longer important as the bearer of the collective soul of the race, but as the individual successor of the personal immortality of the father. Here the child is no longer exclusively a collective being, yet is less of an individual being than earlier, because he has a quite definite and narrowly restricted task to fulfill. Against this designation of being only a son, which robs him of his own individuality, the child has rebelled from the moment when man first accepted fatherhood—although unwillingly—as a means of salvation for his soul. From then on, we see in the history of mankind the imposing duel of these two principles, which is manifested in folklore, myths, and poetic traditions as the duel between father and son.[7] In the strife between Christianity and ancient Rome, there is clearly a conflict between two ideological principles, the patriarchal and the filial. This conflict continues through the whole of the Middle Ages in the strife between the worldly and spiritual spheres (Emperor and Pope), apparently as a struggle for authority, but in truth as a battle for the soul. Modern times alone have brought a temporary solution of the conflict with the discovery of America, which became a new land of democracy formed by fugitives driven from Europe through religious intolerance. In this way they got rid of both Emperor and Pope, although they were gradually forced into an inner bondage. Europe itself needed the [First] World War to overthrow the last external representatives of the father-dominance, who sought and for the moment found in psychoanalysis, appearing at the same time, an ideological solace. But this could be neither lasting nor of constructive value, although it has a transitory therapeutic effect in that it replaces for a while the dying father-ideology that mankind still needs. In this sense, psychoanalysis is as conservative as it appeared revolutionary; for its founder is a rebellious son who defends paternal authority, a revolutionary who, from fear of his own rebellious son-ego, took refuge in the security of the father rôle, which, however, was already ideologically disintegrated.

Having briefly surveyed the collapse of the father-concept under the increasing pressure of the claims of the son, from the time of the world dominance of patriarchal Rome to the last attempt to save it in psychoanalysis, we must remind ourselves of the difficulties that had preceded the erection of the father-dominance. These were not of an external but of an inner nature. As I have elsewhere

[7] See *Das Inzestmotiv*, especially Chapter v.

stated, the patriarchal culture was preceded by a long period of development in which personal fatherhood was not only unknown but was denied, in order to maintain a concept of individual immortality. Following the primitive systems of religion and social organizations that seemed to be created as a protection to individual immortality, we see the protest of man against the rôle of father enforced on him, at its highest in the Greek hero-mythology.[8] Indeed the Oedipus saga itself, which Freud would like to understand simply as an expression of the individual psychology of the son, proves to be from a sociological viewpoint a heroic defence of the man against assuming the rôle of father. The father of Oedipus, Laius, represents the type of man rejecting his sexual rôle, as I have described him in *Seelenglaube und Psychologie*. On account of the prophecy that his son would be his successor, he abstains for years from sexual intercourse with his wife, with whom he cohabited only once in drunkenness or when seduced by her and so accidentally begot Oedipus. The boy was immediately exposed after birth, because the father wanted no successor but wanted to be his own immortal successor, a desire that the myth presents in the incest of Oedipus with his mother. This concept makes Oedipus himself a representative of the father who wants to have no children, yet tries to preserve himself indefinitely. The incest with the mother, from which also children sprang up, proves to be a compromise between the wish to have no children at all (Laius) and the necessity to renounce one's own immortality in favor of children. This compromise to beget oneself as the mother's son and to be reborn from her, must naturally fail tragically.[9] This

[8] The love adventures of Jove in his various animalistic disguises (snake, swan, bull) correspond to the last traces of the totemistic impregnation of the soul, which the father-god of the sexual age had taken over, till gradually he accepted the form of the purely human husband (Amphytryon Saga).

[9] EDITOR'S NOTE: This argument, that Oedipus is seeking to be his own "father" and the author of his own "immortality," is a particular detail of Rank's exposition that may be somewhat difficult for readers to grasp, and comment on it has cautiously been avoided by most critics and expounders of Rank. Perhaps by this act, Oedipus asserts himself in a rôle that is not distinctively that of father or son, but at the same time both and yet neither. He must accept his biological and social

is the veritable guilt of Oedipus, not that he slew his father and took his place with his mother. For as little as the father wants to continue to exist only in his sons, just as little has the son an inclination to play only the part of a successor to the father. In this sense, Oedipus rebels likewise against the rôle of son as against that of father and not as son against his father. This double conflict in the individual himself, who wants to be neither father nor son, but simply self, is portrayed in the myth in all its features that one cannot understand from a personal psychological point of view but only when one regards it as a sediment of sociological development. In this sense, the resistance against the begetting of a son signifies also one's own resistance to come into the world as son; the exposure signifies the son's wish, not to be brought up in the parental home as son, but to grow up a free man in the wilderness. In this sense, finally, the fate or destiny that compels him to slay his father and to marry his mother signifies not only the son's personal wish, as Freud has it, but also the coercion of the species that prescribes marriage and fatherhood against the individual's will.

Thus in the Oedipus myth we see the struggle of the individual represented as a strife between the ego, believing itself immortal, and the racial ego, manifested in a sexual ideology (marriage, children). This inner resistance of man against any kind of racial rôle, whether that of the father or that of the son, is presented in the Oedipus legend as an external strife between father and son. We now also understand why this conflict emerged so relatively late in history; first, the full development of individuality as Hellenism represented it was necessary in order to permit the ego to revolt against every kind of racial compulsion. Hence we shall not concern ourselves

---

compulsions, but he also rebels against them, wishing to be—as Rank states shortly hereafter—solely himself and always his own arbiter. But possibly Rank also intends something else. Quite apart from the ambiguity and complexity of this detail, however, Rank's interpretation of the Oedipus legend, which he sees in its social and historical aspects, as well as the psychological, is arresting and fresh and challenges the now traditional Freudian view. In addition, Rank insists that the meaning of the myth changes—it has a new significance at different times in new cultures—and this point in itself is very pertinent.

with the full historical analysis of the Oedipus tradition and the various interpretations based on it,[1] since we are here interested just in the most recent traditions as portrayed in Greek literature, because only they can show us what the myth signified at the apogee of Hellenism. Now we find the material in its complete human elaboration set forth by the tragic poets, and at its climax in Sophocles' presentation. There the hero is married a long time—according to some sources, nineteen years—before he discovers that he is the husband of his mother. This and similar characteristics do not permit of being disposed of simply as late unessential elaborations, as it might seem from purely psychological interpretations. For a sociological understanding of the legend one must equally evaluate all the manifest details of the whole tradition, since the end product tells more than does its genesis. This statement still holds good for the poetic creation of Sophocles, who perhaps had an Oedipus complex himself,[2] and who in his presentation of the myth was just as much influenced by the old traditions as by the contemporary attitude to it.

With these reservations, I am inclined to recognize in the ultimate form of the legend as it appears in the Greek tragic poets one other application of the Oedipus material. Although this corresponds to the mythological significance set forth, yet it is altered in meaning at a later stage of development. Whereas the mythical Oedipus, as Homer still pictures him, continues to rule in Thebes after the death of his mother-spouse and so—although blinded—somehow saves himself from the catastrophe, in Sophocles' presentation the hero tragically collapses as soon as his deed is revealed. But he provokes this revelation himself in the play, the essential characteristic of which lies just in the obstinate insistence of Oedipus on revealing his crime. Even if this is to be understood as the result of his bad conscience—now spoken of as "self-punishment"—we must ask ourselves why this awakened only after so many years and why just at that particular moment.

[1] See Carl Roberts: *Oedipus; Geschichte eines poetischen Stoffes im Altertum,* (Berlin, 1915), Vol. II.

[2] See my *Inzestmotiv,* 2nd edition, pp. 175 ff.

We cannot be content with the explanation that may be derived from the tradition itself, namely, that originally the discovery directly followed the deed and hence the dramatic author placed the revelation at a later period in the hero's life for mere sensational effect. For as we said, we are not interested here in establishing the original form of the tradition, but only in understanding the form it has ultimately assumed in the poem. And since the revelation in the drama would be just as thrilling if it followed the unconsciously begun deed, the poet could scarcely have had technical reasons for presupposing that Oedipus had been long and happily married and that the marriage had also been blessed by now grown-up children.[3] The age of the Sophoclean hero and the tragic fate of his sons[4] described in *Oedipus at Colonus* suggest that the reason for the displacement of the revelation, which originally followed the deed, to the hero's old age is connected with the growing up of his sons.

In other words, the Oedipus of the tragic poets no longer represents the ego defending its own immortality against the racial rôle (as father and son), but he represents a man already forced into the part of father and into matrimonial laws. In fact, a man at a critical age which is nearer to death than to life, a man who is reminded of his mortal ego and in a crisis that one might call neurotic today, revolts against finding his sexual immortality in his children. In this racial tragedy of the individual, we see a man who is forced against his will into the acceptance of the rôle of father and the matrimonial law. Deprived of his individual immortality, at the approach of age and death, he tries to abandon his fatherhood in order to regain his personal immortality. In the play the hero does this in a "neurotic" way by recalling not only his own childhood (mother) but also the mythical hero Oedipus, whose successful incest with his mother he wants to imitate. At this moment, the hero tries to justify his break with prevailing sexual mores by reference to the

[3] In the ancient epic, the marriage with the mother was childless and the children were ascribed to a second marriage with Euryganeia.

[4] Oedipus expresses the wish (curse) that they might kill each other.

old myth;[5] he becomes *an* Oedipus, not *the* Oedipus of the tradition, whereas before he was anyone, that is, the Greek father wrestling with his conflict.[6] Here also the poet's own psychology may be called in; because Sophocles is supposed to have written this play when he was an old man pursued by his sons—indeed, according to one tradition, when he had to defend himself against an accusation of his sons that he was senile. He read his play before the tribunal, thus proving his competence and superiority, and was acquitted. But this strife between the generations was no rarity even in ancient Greece, and Sophocles in the cursing of his sons by Oedipus has described the general course of this conflict—in the father who will not be replaced by his son, and in the son who will not be the father's successor.

This interpretation of the Oedipus tragedy first explains why the hero insists upon the discovery, why he had, so to say, set himself the task (like an analyst) of proving that he has slain his father and married his mother. He needs this motivation—not the deed itself—to overthrow an undesirable patriarchal cultural pattern. He is not a son who wants to replace a father, but the man who will not accept the rôle of father. Thus the hero, so to say, accuses himself of Oedipus' crime in order thereby to gain the latter's immortality in being reborn to the mother. This understanding of the legend, however, is not to be obtained from its psychoanalytic interpretation (in Freud's meaning), but only from a reading of its sociological significance. To the extent that our present-day child is still an Oedipus, he is only *an* Oedipus in the meaning of our interpretation of the hero—that is, the child who does not want to be only a child. But the fact that Freud, in order to understand this childish reaction, had to go back to the Oedipus saga shows that it was not explicable from

[5] See Jocasta's justification in Sophocles that many men in their dreams cohabit with the mother; she could almost recall here the old mythical hero Oedipus whom her husband, the king of Thebes, would like to imitate.

[6] In this sense is to be understood J. Burckhardt's famous quotation: "Corresponding to the Oedipus saga, every Greek had an Oedipus fiber which was capable of being directly touched and vibrated."

a purely psychological viewpoint. Freud—like the hero of the drama itself—recalled opportunely this old myth, which he *now* interprets as bespeaking the son's wish, whereas formerly it had signified exactly the opposite, namely, the conflict of the individual ego with the racial ego, that is, a resistance against the Oedipus complex. Through centuries of the dominance of the father-principle and the family organization, there exists in the individual a desire for it, which perhaps may already be latent in the child; but it has nothing to do with the old Oedipus myth, which represents the opposite, namely, a resistance against the foundation and continuance of the family organization. In this sense, also, the Oedipus complex of the present-day child, no matter in what form it manifests itself, may ultimately be a protest of the individual ego against every kind of collective family rôle (son, daughter, etc.). When, therefore, analysts emphasize the biological strength of the Oedipus wish in the present-day child, this seems to me only therapeutically justifiable as a strengthening of the patient's individual ego. But this is not their intention, for the patient is simultaneously led on to overcome this attitude conceived of as "primitive" by the patriarchal bias of the Freudian theory.

It would seem then that the incest motive originally served as an attempt to achieve one's own immortality sexually in the transitional period from a collective belief in the soul to belief in immortality through children. The father-principle was not yet fully accepted by man; he was only the father of the son begotten of the mother, thus he was father of himself, who wanted to continue to exist in the son. Incest as such was not a primitive form of sexual life or marriage, moreover it was not at all valid as an institution, but was only a favor granted to exceptional individuals who had made themselves immortal in their work (heroes). At the stage when a sexual ideology is enforced on man and has its social materialization in a family organization, we see the rebelling father enviously grasping back at the successful Oedipus of the ancient myth, in order himself to become such *an* Oedipus, an effort that at this level of cultural development naturally can no longer succeed and hence must end tragically. For a collective ideology has already given place to a family organization that finds immortality in children, and the individual ego can no longer free itself from this racial fetter. Finally, in a present-day man whose victorious individualism has precipitated the downfall of the father's rule and of the family organization, we find the same motive interpreted as a wish for the father rôle, a motive that originally gave expression to the horror of it. Thus the Freudian theory does not prove to be a psychological *explanation* of the Oedipus theme, which it pretends to be, but only a new *interpretation* of it applied to present-day man and his present *collective* ideology. The poet-dramatist is the successor of the hero, in that he narrates the heroic deed as a recollection of the "good old times"; and the psychologist proves to be the poet's successor in that he interprets it anew for us today.

But these three stages of heroic, poetic, and psychological presentation correspond not only to the historical stages of development but also to the personal. Thus a young poet is likely to be heroic, the aging writer more psychological; the one represents the attitude of the independent ego, the other acknowledges a necessary adjustment and submission to law. So, for example, the young Schiller wrote the revolutionary *Robbers* and the aging poet *Wilhelm Tell,* who no longer opposes every kind of dominance, but only the arrogance of tyranny. Likewise the Oedipus complex in the average individual will also have one significance in childhood and another in puberty or in maturity, and for the artist another import than for the neurotic. Besides, one must still separate the incest wish as such from the father-ideology, for the relation between the two is not so simple as it seems from the psychological view of the son—namely, that he will kill his father in order to possess his mother. The incest desire is a symbol of personal immortality to which the ego clings in order to escape the compulsion of a mere racial immortality through sex. Simultaneously the individual, swayed by the old belief in the soul, defends himself against an acceptance of the new father rôle. So actually the incest with the mother and the slaying of the father are not at all individual expressions of biological tendencies, but typify the individual's racial conflicts. The hero does not kill *his father* but *the father* as representative of the new sexual ideology; he does not marry his mother, but he makes the woman into *the mother* of his children, whom he thus accepts. Hence the two aspects of the Oedipus complex express the same resistance of the individual against the new family concept; the mother relationship expresses it from the standpoint of the racial sexual ego, the father relationship from the standpoint of the individual self.

But the Oedipus complex also has a different meaning according to whether it is simply considered from the standpoint of the individual or from the standpoint of the son or from that of the father. As an individual, one does not want to put himself in the father's place and to become the father, that is, the husband of the mother. As son, one may desire it, but only to deny with it the rôle of the son; that is to say, if one must have a racial function then at least it is best to have that of the father. Finally, with the complete acceptance of the father rôle, the man will naturally love the son more (and not according to the Oedipus scheme, the daughter) because he sees in him his direct successor and heir. If the father prefers the daughter, it shows less willingness to accept the rôle of father, as particularly shown in the incest motive between father and daughter.[7] For this represents on the father's part a similar desire to be reborn now in the daughter, instead of in the mother. The biological Oedipus tendency is thus complemented by a psychical one of the ego which feels attracted to the child of the same sex and not to that of the opposite sex. The child reacts to this double-sided family constellation also in ambivalent, conflicting ways. The son takes refuge in the mother not only from fear *of* the father but just as much from a fear of too great a love *from* the father, he develops a "mother fixation" in order not to be made com-

[7] See *Das Inzestmotiv,* Chapter xi, and its supplement, *Seelenglaube und Psychologie,* pp. 54 ff.

pletely into the son by the father and not to be engulfed as an individual. For the same reason the girl often leans to the father in order to withdraw from the mother's influence, for whom she is only daughter, that is, a continuation of the ego. That means the child is forced through ego motives to protect his individuality against parental egoism, and hence is pushed into another collective dependency, namely, the biological. The parents fight openly or tacitly for the child's soul, whether in the biological sense (opposite sex) or in the egoistic sense (the same sex), and the child uses the parents correspondingly, and plays them one against the other, in order to save his own individuality.

At any rate, we see that the purely egoistic attitude of the child does not only aim at the disintegration of the family, in that the child eliminates the rival and wants to replace him with himself, but the already mentioned anti-Oedipean tendency is operative to keep the parents together, because this guarantees to the child a protection against the all-devouring claim of *one* of the parents. So the child appears as a representative of the family ideology when it needs it for protection. The same tendency we already see, however, in the ancient Oedipus saga if we understand its ethnological significance. Oedipus acquires his "complex" outside the family since he is exposed directly after his birth; rather he founds his own family on the basis of the Oedipus complex, that is, after the completed deed. But this is not an expression of an eternal human longing, it reflects only a definite historical transition of the family organization from the father's rebellion to his acceptance of marriage. Oedipus, in contrast to his father, acknowledges his sons, he wants to be the father of a family, but the old Adam springs up toward the end of his life and urges him to seek his own immortality as once the mythical hero Oedipus had sought it in incest with the mother and had found in it his heroic destiny. The Oedipus of the poet, being sacrificed to a family concept, finally finds consolation in his daughters after he has cast out his wife and cursed his sons, a destiny that is similarly repeated in Shakespeare and other great men, who, so to say, need no sons in order to be immortal and so, in age, turn to the daughter who symbolizes for them a less hazardous youth.

Index

OTTO RANK was long an international figure in the world of psychology. He was born in Vienna in 1884 and received his Ph.D. from the University of Vienna. He began to study psychoanalysis in 1905, first exploring its theoretical bases and then becoming an active practitioner. From 1912 to 1924 he edited two of the leading European psychoanalytic journals, and from 1919 to 1924 was Director of the International Psychoanalytic Institute of Vienna, which he had founded. He also lived for many years in Paris and New York. Dr. Rank died in 1939.

THE TEXT of this book was set on the Linotype in Caledonia, a face that belongs to the family of printing types called "modern face" by printers—a term used to mark the change in style of type-letters that occurred about 1800. Caledonia borders on the general design of Scotch Modern, but is more freely drawn than that letter.

VINTAGE HISTORY—WORLD

V-286 ARIES, PHILIPPE *Centuries of Childhood*
V-59 BEAUFRE, GEN. ANDRÉ *NATO and Europe*
V-44 BRINTON, CRANE *The Anatomy of Revolution*
V-250 BURCKHARDT, C. J. *Richelieu: His Rise to Power*
V-393 BURCKHARDT, JACOB *The Age of Constantine the Great*
V-391 CARR, E. H. *What Is History?*
V-67 CURTIUS, ERNST R. *The Civilization of France*
V-746 DEUTSCHER, ISAAC *The Prophet Armed*
V-747 DEUTSCHER, ISAAC *The Prophet Unarmed*
V-748 DEUTSCHER, ISAAC *The Prophet Outcast*
V-471 DUVEAU, GEORGES *1848: The Making of a Revolution*
V-707 FISCHER, LOUIS *Soviets in World Affairs*
V-475 GAY, PETER *The Enlightenment: The Rise of Modern Paganism*
V-277 GAY, PETER *Voltaire's Politics*
V-114 HAUSER, ARNOLD *The Social History of Art* through V-117 (Four Volumes)
V-201 HUGHES, H. STUART *Consciousness and Society*
V-50 KELLY, AMY *Eleanor of Aquitaine and the Four Kings*
V-728 KLYUCHEVSKY, V. *Peter the Great*
V-246 KNOWLES, DAVID *Evolution of Medieval Thought*
V-83 KRONENBERGER, LOUIS *Kings and Desperate Men*
V-287 LA SOUCHÈRE, ÉLÉNA DE *An Explanation of Spain*
V-43 LEFEBVRE, GEORGES *The Coming of the French Revolution*
V-364 LEFEBVRE, GEORGES *The Directory*
V-343 LEFEBVRE, GEORGES *The Thermidorians*
V-474 LIFTON, ROBERT J. *Revolutionary Immortality: Mao Tse-Tung and the Chinese Cultural Revolution*
V-92 MATTINGLY, GARRETT *Catherine of Aragon*
V-703 MOSELY, PHILIP E. *The Kremlin and World Politics:* Studies in Soviet Policy and Action
V-733 PARES, SIR BERNARD *The Fall of the Russian Monarchy*
V-285 PARKES, HENRY B. *Gods and Men*
V-719 REED, JOHN *Ten Days That Shook the World*
V-176 SCHAPIRO, LEONARD *Government and Politics of the Soviet Union* (Revised Edition)
V-375 SCHURMANN & SCHELL (eds.) *The China Reader: Imperial China,* I
V-376 SCHURMANN & SCHELL (eds.) *The China Reader: Republican China,* II
V-377 SCHURMANN & SCHELL (eds.) *The China Reader: Communist China,* III
V-312 TANNENBAUM, FRANK *Ten Keys to Latin America*
V-322 THOMPSON, E. P. *The Making of the English Working Class*
V-749 TROTSKY, LEON *Basic Writings of Trotsky*
V-724 WALLACE, SIR D. M. *Russia:* On the Eve of War and Revolution
V-206 WALLERSTEIN, IMMANUEL *Africa: The Politics of Independence*
V-729 WEIDLÉ, W. *Russia:* Absent and Present
V-122 WILENSKI, R. H. *Modern French Painters,* Volume I (1863-1903)

V-284 LEWIS, OSCAR *Village Life in Northern India*
V-384 LINDESMITH, ALFRED *The Addict and The Law*
V-76 LINTON, RALPH *The Tree of Culture*
V-407 MACK, RAYMOND *Our Children's Burden: Studies of Desegregation in Ten American Communities*
V-209 MARCUSE, HERBERT *Eros and Civilization*
V-437 NIETZSCHE, FRIEDRICH *The Will to Power*
V-462 PIAGET, JEAN *Six Psychological Studies*
V-258 PIEL, GERARD *Science in the Cause of Man*
V-70 RANK, OTTO *The Myth of the Birth of the Hero* and Other Essays
V-99 REDLICH, FRITZ, M.D. and BINGHAM, JUNE *The Inside Story:* Psychiatry and Everyday Life
V-395 ROKEACH, MILTON *The Three Christs of Ypsilanti*
V-301 ROSS, NANCY WILSON (ed.) *The World of Zen*
V-464 SARTRE, JEAN-PAUL *Search for a Method*
V-289 THOMAS, ELIZABETH MARSHALL *The Harmless People*
V-310 THORP, EDWARD O. *Beat the Dealer*, Revised
V-109 THRUELSEN & KOBLER (eds.) *Adventures of the Mind, I*
V-68 *Adventures of the Mind, II*
V-239 *Adventures of the Mind, III*
V-299 WATTS, ALAN W. *The Joyous Cosmology:* Adventures in the Chemistry of Consciousness
V-466 WATTS, ALAN W. *The Wisdom of Insecurity*